Scientific Information
in Wartime

Scientific Information in Wartime

The Allied-German Rivalry, 1939–1945

Pamela Spence Richards

Contributions in Military Studies, Number 151

GREENWOOD PRESS
Westport, Connecticut • London

Library of Congress Cataloging-in-Publication Data

Richards, Pamela Spence.
    Scientific information in wartime : the Allied-German rivalry,
  1939–1945 / Pamela Spence Richards.
       p.   cm.—(Contributions in military studies, ISSN 0883–6884
  ; no. 151)
    Includes bibliographical references and index.
    ISBN 0–313–29062–8 (alk. paper)
    1. World War, 1939–1945—Science. 2. World War, 1939–1945—
  Military intelligence. I. Title. II. Series.
  D810.S2R53 1994
  940.54′8—dc20   93–25050

British Library Cataloguing in Publication Data is available.

Library of Congress Catalog Card Number: 93–25050
ISBN: 0–313–29062–8
ISSN: 0883–6884

First published in 1994

Greenwood Press, 88 Post Road West, Westport, CT 06881
An imprint of Greenwood Publishing Group, Inc.

Printed in the United States of America

The paper used in this book complies with the
Permanent Paper Standard issued by the National
Information Standards Organization (Z39.48–1984).

10 9 8 7 6 5 4 3 2 1

Copyright Acknowledgment

The author and publisher gratefully acknowledge permission to reprint material from the following source.

From "Die technischwissenschaftlichen Bibliotheken während des Nationalsozialismus," in *Bibliotheken während des Nationalsozialismus* (Teil I) 1990, © 1989 by Herzog August Bibliothek Wolfenbüttel. Used by permission of Hannover University Library and the Technical Information Library (TIB).

Contents

Preface

The present volume is the result of work done over more than a decade in the United States, Germany, France, the United Kingdom and the Netherlands. Many of the participants in the events it describes are still alive and have been generous with their time and advice; others who helped me in my research died before the manuscript could be published. I have been fortunate in one respect: Even though my research focuses on a period of bloody German-American rivalry, I encountered no reluctance on the part of German colleagues of whatever generation to discuss the past or to make pertinent documents available. On the contrary, as the reader will see, German sources provide the backbone of this book. As an American born in 1941, I am grateful that people whose lives have been more disrupted than my own by world events have been so willing to share with me their experiences. I have profited from the fact that my story, although set in a terrible world, is largely one of successes, both Allied and German; for both information supply systems I describe in my book were well-designed, smoothly run, and effective in getting scientists the information they needed. So it is understandable that their participants have some interest in having their story properly told, with credit given to the individuals whose personal sacrifice, dedication and courage made their systems function so well.

My own investigation began in the United States. One of the first people I approached was Frederick Kilgour, whose wartime work is so central to this book and whose encouragement and friendship have been important to its completion. Thomas Fleming, wartime head of the Joint Committee on Importation, kindly passed on to me the Committee's records. Edward A. Chapman also sent me valuable files from his years with the United States Office of Alien Property Custodian.

It would be impossible to list all the individuals who helped me in Germany. One of the earliest was the late Dr. Gisela von Busse, who gave freely of her time to recall her long career at the Prussian State Library. Helmut Drubba of Hannover has assisted me through the years in a variety of ways. I am particularly grateful for his monitoring of the German scholarly press for me. Dr. Michael Knoche has been invaluable for his knowledge of publishing under National Socialism, and Dr. Dieter Schmidmaier for his help in securing historical materials from the former German Democratic Republic. Professor Paul Kaegbein has eased my entry into German library historical circles. I am grateful also to Springer Verlag for access to its archives in Heidelberg.

In the United Kingdom, Andrea Polden of the British Library put me in contact with numerous colleagues active during the war. To her and these many retired British librarians who made themselves so accessible, I am much beholden. From Professor R. V. Jones of Aberdeen I acquired much of what I know about wartime British scientific intelligence; I value equally his books, his letters and his conversation. In the Netherlands the Martinus Nijhoff Company generously opened their archives to me. Others involved in the Dutch book trade during the occupation, including W. A. Swets and Mrs. J. M. Weisbach-Junk, made places in their busy schedules for interviews. And in France, Professor Jean Wyart provided valuable information about scientific publishing in occupied Paris.

My ability to interview these individuals was due to support from a number of agencies, including the Rutgers Research Council, the National Endowment for the Humanities, the American Philosophical Society, Beta Phi Mu, the Association of College and Research Libraries and the Martinus Nijhoff Foundation. The School of Communication, Information and Library Studies at Rutgers University gave me sabbaticals for research and technical assistance in the production of the manuscript.

Emotional support, methodological advice and an invaluable critical eye were provided throughout the years by my husband, Wim Smit, who patiently read through draft after draft. To him, above all, I give my thanks.

Introduction

The Second World War has a special place in the history of scientific and technical communication. At its outbreak, the war threatened to cut off scientific contacts between Germany and the Western Allies as radically as had the First World War. The old personal channels of exchange, such as conferences, visiting professorships and research internships, were all closed in September 1939, and the book trade broke down shortly thereafter. But in 1939 the world of science was much more internationalized than in 1914, and the scientists of the hostile nations were more dependent on the continued flow of foreign information to their laboratories. The government leaders themselves knew that the new war was going to be the most technological ever fought and that the sciences could make the difference for victory. The risks posed by ignorance of the progress of enemy science and technology were too great for the opponents to run.

The governments' attitudes stemmed from the altered relationship between science and military technology by 1939: The weaponry of previous wars had tended to be the result of fairly mature science and technology rather than of newer, evolving areas of technology or derivations from fundamental science itself. World War II was novel in three important respects: First, its military technology was involved with an area of science still at the level of fundamental science, namely atomic physics. Even before the outbreak of war, some scientists on each side had recognized atomic power's potential for weaponry, and, at different points in the war, both German and Allied journals published news of important discoveries in this area. Second, the war's weaponry was linked to several areas of rapidly developing technology based on known but incompletely elaborated scientific principles, notably electronics, rocketry, and jet turbines; and third, the scale on which outstanding scientists and technicians were mobilized was unique and resulted in a historically unprecedented productivity.[1] Consequently, when the war broke out in 1939 and threatened to end personal communication between scientists in the warring camps, both sides set up emergency systems to ensure the import of the enemy's most important scientific and technical publications. These scientific intelligence networks were designed to supply information quietly to the countries' own research teams. They required close cooperation between the scientific and intelligence establishments and depended on new techniques of information gathering, reproduction and circulation that had been developed only in the 1930s.

The parties on each side that were involved in this effort were pretty much the same: governmental and military agencies, scholarly organizations, scientific institutions in academe, industrial and research libraries, and the members of a new profession called "documentation," which concerned itself with the retrieval and delivery of specialized information.[2] The contributions of these parties and their relative importance differ, however, in very interesting ways when we compare their functioning in Germany and the Western Allied countries. These differences are not only the consequences of the war situation. In part they reflect peculiarities in the patterns of organization of higher education, industry, culture, political institutions and library systems that are rooted in the pre-World War I period. Two powerful factors absent among the Western Allies were the totalitarian organization of the German state after March 1933 and its racist hostility to foreign science. The National Socialist government had for ideological reasons begun well before the outbreak of the war to control the flow of foreign scientific and technical publications into Germany. By 1939 Nazi policies had severely curtailed the functioning of the research library system and had damaged the credibilty and content of Germany's distinguished scientific journals.

The primary purpose of this book is to reconstruct the wartime organizations set up by the various governments to ensure, in the midst of the collapse of other forms of international scientific communication, the continued supply of enemy scientific and technical publications. A secondary purpose of the book is to show how the wartime relations among government scientific intelligence agencies, professional documentalists, and the scientific world influenced the development of the postwar government scientific information establishments in the United States, England and Germany.

In the first chapter I will examine the forces that shaped the growth of international scientific communication networks in the twentieth century and the role played by the scientists and institutions of the different nations in those networks. We will review the growth of the ideal of scientific internationalism and examine how this idea was affected by World War I. Consideration will be given to the impact of the Nobel and Rockefeller Foundations in encouraging scientific internationalism as well as to the growth of international scientific publishing and the international exchange of students and professors. We will pay special attention to the international world of atomic physics, which is interesting to us not simply because of its terrible potential in weapons development, but also because wartime knowledge of enemy atomic weapons was largely a product of analyzing foreign scientific journals. No prototypes fell into enemy hands for dissassembly and examination.

Because our study focuses on wartime government support for finding, importing and circulating foreign scientific literature, we must examine the extent to which the authorities of the various countries recognized the importance to domestic research of foreign science. We must also look at techniques available in Germany, the United States and Great Britain for acquiring and circulating enemy literature. All three countries continued to use some channels of the traditional book trade in neutral countries but supplemented imports with the help of new technologies recently developed by publishers, librarians and documentalists. So we must reconstruct the birth and development of each country's documentation movement during the 1930s as the prelude to wartime and postwar developments.

The central section of the book, dealing with the war period, begins with a description of the physical barriers posed by the war to each nation's access to foreign scientific publications. This is a subject of great complexity in the case of the Third Reich, whose area of control expanded and contracted dramatically between 1940 and 1945. The major focus of the wartime section is the setting up by the warring parties of the networks to ensure the supply of enemy scientific literature. This section will focus on how the networks functioned, where their agents worked, what literature they sought, how they obtained it, how they got it into their countries, and how and by whom it was further processed and circulated. In some cases evidence can be given about what effect the publications had on the actual fighting of the war. Because of the advanced scientific research taking place in a number of the countries Germany occupied, a special section in Chapter 5 evaluates the contribution of the occupied countries to the Reich's scientific information resources. A section in Chapter 4 deals with the roundup of German scientific documents on German territory by the United States and Great Britain following the invasion of the Reich in 1945.

One result of these wartime activities was that they became crucial to scientific enterprise after the war in the countries where they were organized. The book's final section, therefore, is a survey of the influence these supply networks had on shaping German and Western Allied governments' postwar scientific information priorities. Here an interesting contrast arose between the United States on the one hand and Germany and England on the other. The United States had started the war with limited government support for collecting scientific and technological information. The war resulted in an immense proliferation of federal scientific information agencies, many of which became permanent. The governments of Great Britain and Germany, on the other hand, had been actively supporting the gathering of foreign literature in all scientific and technical fields since World War I; in their cases the focus is on the many ways World War II transformed their traditional ways of doing things.

NOTES

1. Rostow, W. W., *The United States in the World Arena* (New York: Harper, 1960), p. 59.

2. The word "documentation" to describe information organization, retrieval and processing has been largely replaced in Great Britain and the United States by the term "information science."

1

The Internationalization of Science and Scientific Information in the Twentieth Century

During World War II enormous energy would be expended by the Allied and German governments to keep their own scientists abreast of enemy science. The political readiness to make this commitment was a direct result of two facts: first, each was convinced that victory belonged to the side with the greater scientific preeminence; and second, at the war's outbreak, each side knew the scope and value of the other's work. In order to understand this state of affairs, we must take a look at the world of science in 1939 and review the networks that had evolved by that time to carry news of scientific and technical breakthroughs around the globe. Special attention is given to the international networks of atomic physics because of the peculiar role that branch of science would play during World War II in the feverish quest on both sides for enemy scientific and technical information.

This quest was characterized to a great extent by intelligence derived from the traditional printed scientific literature: It is a fact, for example, that the published description in German physics journals of Otto Hahn and his associates' splitting of the uranium atom in 1938 was a determining factor in the Allies' desperate rush to complete their own atomic project and in their decision to allocate such huge manpower resources to collecting German science literature during the war. At the end of the war, members of the Atomic Scientists of Chicago were quoted as saying that "if Hitler had prevented the publication in 1939 of the first papers on atomic fission, Germany might have remained for a certain time in exclusive possession of a fundamental secret of atomic power."[1] Since Hitler's government had not restricted publication of the Hahn papers, it was hoped that it might be equally lax in other cases, even after the war broke out.

But the exploiting of the enemy's scientific publications depended on more than the enemy's willingness to publish research results: It depended also on the existence of international channels for the communication of those results, and on the rival country's access to them. Finally, and equally importantly, it depended on the rival's ability to analyze the results thoroughly. This meant that the country had to have scientists good enough to understand what they were reading. So the rival country's own position in the scientific universe was a key factor in determining its success in monitoring the research of the enemy.

So, in this first chapter, I will briefly describe the international scientific infrastructure as it existed before World War II; its common purpose; its media, awards systems and facilitating organizations; and international trends in its documentation; and I will attempt to give a general picture of the world of international physics at that time—its centers of activity and chief personnel—since the war that lay ahead would be a "physicists' war."[2]

SCIENTIFIC INTERNATIONALISM BEFORE 1914

Since the scientific revolution of the seventeenth century a tension has existed between the proprietary, exclusionist view of scientific knowledge and the idea that science should serve all of mankind indiscriminately. Throughout the period of the rise of nation states there were utopian voices calling for the sharing of all knowledge rather than its defensive hoarding by one country. Already in 1627 Francis Bacon described in his *New Atlantis* how science would be the source for *all* humanity's future riches and marvels. The eighteenth century increased the emphasis on the universal human potential of science, Condorçet even foreseeing science's ultimate victory over death. Despite the hightide of nationalism in the nineteenth century, the same basic universalistic ideas underlay the work of two of the period's great social engineers, August Comte and Herbert Spencer, both of whom saw science as the force through which mankind as a whole would achieve higher standards of social organization and morality. The realization of many of the idealists' dreams about internationalism in science was made possible in the nineteenth century by improvements in the techniques by which scientific knowledge was communicated. Regular and fast international steam transport by the last quarter of the nineteenth century put current research in the hands of scientists worldwide. Really important news was conveyed across the Atlantic by cable after 1865, and by wireless radio after 1901. Steamship travel made possible the phenomenon of the international exhibition, with its accompanying competitions, international juries and specialized subconventions. Continuing a "technology fair" tradition begun with the London Exhibition of 1851, the Paris Exposition of 1878 was the first to emphasize the organization of simultaneous international scholarly and scientific congresses. This type of periodical ritual continued into the new century: the Universal Exposition of

Paris in 1900 had 50 million visitors and witnessed 127 different international scholarly congresses held simultaneously.[3]

Even greater encouragement for international scientific contact came from the new educational exchanges that were set up at the turn of the twentieth century: As a result of formal agreements between the administrations of Columbia and Harvard Universities and the Prussian Ministry of Culture, some thirty Americans and Germans served between 1905 and 1914 as visiting professors on American and Prussian faculties.[4]

The impetus for much of the conference activity and other scholarly and scientific travel was provided by international associations that sprang up in the last decades of the nineteenth century. The first half of the nineteenth century had seen the founding of national organizations of scientists such as the pioneer Deutsche Naturforschers Versammlung (1822), the model for the (British) Association for the Advancement of Science (1831) and the American organization of the same name (1848). By the turn of the century most of the major scientific disciplines had national organizations in the more developed European countries and in the United States, and there was considerable international organization, often concentrated on specific tasks that needed international cooperation. Among such ventures were the Permanent Committee for the Bibliographic Repertory of the Mathematical Sciences, founded in 1889, the Concilium Bibliographicum set up in Zurich in 1892 to organize the literature of zoology on an international basis, and the International Chemical Union, founded in 1910 to publish the tables of chemical constants.

More general in nature was the International Association of Academies founded in 1889 jointly by the Royal Society of London, the National Academy in Washington and a number of the most prestigious continental academies. By 1914 this organization had 22 members, but its activities were not impressive since the most dynamic scientific communication was now taking place not in the national academies but in the specialized scientific societies. In an attempt to establish a central coordinating body for the various burgeoning international organizations, institutes and congresses, a Union of International Associations was set up in Brussels in 1911, but this proved to be largely a paper enterprise.[5]

What little effective international coordination for the sciences in general that existed before World War I was probably that provided by the Royal Society of London, which served in many ways as an international scientific clearinghouse, with corresponding members all over the world. While certainly the Royal Society drew much of its strength from its position at the heart of a vast and powerful imperial network, its *Catalogue of Scientific Papers* (1800-1900) and *International Catalogue of Scientific Literature* (1901-16) were truly global in scope, not limited to the production of British subjects.

The professionalization in the sciences behind the rise in organizational life, national and international, was also responsible for the enormous growth in scientific periodical publishing before World War I.   International mail improvements resulting from the Universal Postal Union (1875) allowed journals and reviews published for the scientists and their narrowing professional interests to reach larger, less regional readerships. These specialized journals had very limited audiences domestically, but because of growing markets in foreign countries with little or no indigenous scientific publishing, they tended very quickly to become internationally oriented, with international contributors and even editors early in their publishing history. The scientific journals of some countries, such as Germany, tended to be published by commercial publishers in collaboration with scientific associations; in others, such as the United States, they were brought out chiefly by the scientific societies themselves. Before World War I, the Germans dominated international science publishing: In 1909, for example, 45 percent of all the articles indexed by the young American review *Chemical Abstracts* had been published in German journals.[6]   The Germans' own long-established review journals, such as *Chemisches Zentralblatt* (1834) and *Botanisches Centralblatt* (1880), served as the main guides to the literature of their respective disciplines.

Research libraries had trouble organizing the enormous growth of published knowledge. By the turn of the century the pressures of coping with the new output had forced the professionalization of librarianship. The American Library Association was founded in 1876, the Library Association in Great Britain in 1877, and the Association of German Librarians (Verein deutscher Bibliothekare) in 1900. In the profession's early years its leaders concentrated on standardizing the organization and description of books and documents so as to increase their accessibility for users. In 1876 the American librarian Melvil Dewey of Amherst College announced his Decimal Classification for the ordering of materials according to subject, a system that enjoyed great popularity in the new libraries being founded in Great Britain and the United States. Prussia, which unlike England and America had a ministry of culture administering library affairs, became in 1899 the first state to mandate a uniform set of cataloging instructions to be used in its scholarly and scientific libraries (eventually the "Prussian Instructions" were adopted outside Prussia's borders as the basis for all future German cataloging practices).[7] This made possible the first national union catalog—an alphabetical author list of all books printed before 1898 that were held by eleven major Prussian research libraries.

Melvil Dewey's ideas about classification were seen by some of his followers as a means to order not just library materials but all of the records upon which knowledge is stored. Some of these enthusiasts, who called themselves "bibliographers," argued with an almost messianic zeal that the adoption of standardized classification schemes could be the key which would open the door to the universal accessibility of knowledge. And if, as the positivists were preaching at this time, knowledge could save the world, then "bibliography" was actually the key to human salvation. So it was logical that before the First World War a number of the personalities important in bibliography became active in the international peace movement—with the socialists, Esperantists, pacifists and others who thought they had found prescriptions for global harmony. One such individual was Andrew Carnegie, funder of the Peace Palace in the Hague in 1903 and of the Carnegie Endowment for International Peace in 1910. Carnegie was an ardent supporter of Dewey and of the international dissemination of knowledge in general, giving in the course of his life over $400 million dollars for the building and furnishing of libraries all over the world, most of which would use some form of Dewey's system.[8]

Less well known are the activities of the Belgians Paul Otlet and Henri La Fontaine, founders of the International Institute of Bibliography in Brussels in 1895. In the eyes of these men—developers of a Dewey-based classification system they called the Universal Decimal Classification (UDC)—standardized worldwide bibliography was the cornerstone of an international peace constantly endangered by man's ignorance. As their contribution, the Institute of Bibliography began work on a Universal Bibliographic Repertory, planned as a subject list—arranged on cards by UDC—of all the world's published knowledge, in all fields. By 1914 the Repertory had over 11 million cards. La Fontaine, a socialist senator in the Belgian parliament, found a philanthropic sponsor for the Institute in Ernest Solvay, the industrialist and inventor who served as president of the institute from 1907 to 1914. In 1913 La Fontaine's activities and research in support of world peace won him the Nobel Peace Prize, of which he invested the monetary award in the Institute.[9]

The establishment of the Nobel Prizes themselves was an important step in the internationalization of the scientific community. The prizes created an internationally accepted peer review system that transcended the different national systems of awards. Upon the death in 1896 of Alfred Nobel, the Swedish inventor of dynamite, his will had provided 31 million Swedish crowns for the awarding of large annual cash prizes for achievements in physics, chemistry, physiology or medicine, literature and peace. The three science awards—the first two selected by the Royal Swedish Academy of Sciences and the third by the Royal Caroline Medico-Surgical Institute—carried enough money to make their recipients wealthy,[10] and became after their initiation in 1901 the ultimate credentialing system in their fields. More than any other institution in the pre-World War world, the Nobel Foundation, based in a neutral country outside the major power alignments, symbolized the spirit of internationalism in science. In the first fourteen years of the awards, Germans dominated the list of science laureates, representing 14 of the 48 awardees; they were followed by France with 11, England with 5, and Russia, the Netherlands and the United States with two winners apiece.

WORLD WAR I AND THE INTERWAR YEARS

The terrible drama of World War I, with its new weaponry—tanks, Zeppelins, submarines, Big Berthas and especially poison gas—heightened public awareness of the importance of science. In the first years of the war the military was oblivious to the importance of their own scientific resources: Cambridge physicist J. D. Bernal recalled a colleague who offered to organize a meteorological service for the army only to be told that British soldiers fought in all weathers.[11] In June 1915 the science fiction novelist and prophet of science H .G. Wells wrote an angry letter to the London *Times* complaining of the government's lack of attention to scientific matters in the prosecution of the war. All this was suddenly changed by the introduction of poison gas by the Germans on the Western Front in 1915. Long before World War II had become the "physicists' war," the "chemists' war" of 1914-18 had created a new relationship between science and the military.[12]

In 1920, in his phenomenally influential *Outline of History*, Wells argued that "race suicide" was the fate awaiting any nation that failed to master nature through technology. He had already indicated the type of technological mastery of nature that was possible in his description of an "atomic bomb" in his 1914 novel *The World Set Free*. Now science was no longer simply a means to improve man's lot: it could save a race from extinction or cause its annihilation. It followed logically that access to the world's production of scientific information was a cornerstone of national survival. The war had demonstrated to the Allies the consequences of failure to organize their national scientific assets. The Germans, with inferior natural resources, had nonetheless taken the technical initiative throughout much of the conflict. Both the major applications of chemistry that occurred at this time—the Haber process of fixing nitrogen for explosives, and the manufacture of poison gas—originated in German laboratories. After the war, English analysts were convinced that it was the Germans' advanced technology that allowed them to hold out for so long against the rest of the world, losing only one man killed to two among the Allies, and bringing down six airplanes for every one they lost.[13]

This was the background for the sudden surge of government and private support for the development of information processing agencies and technologies in a number of European countries after World War I. In England—almost as economically crushed by World War I as Germany—the government established the Department of Scientific and Industrial Research (1916), with its subsystem of documentation agencies for the different industrial sectors. Likewise, in 1920 the Soviet Union established the Buro inostrannoi nauki i tekhnologii (Bureau of Foreign Science and Technology) under the Supreme Council of National Economy.[14] And in Germany, devastated by ruinous war reparations and the devaluation of its currency, the Reichszentrale für Berichterstattung (National

Center for Scientific Information) was established in 1920 by the Ministry of the Interior. The duties of the Center were to organize the rapid circulation of foreign scientific publications and to provide a reprographic service to copy articles for scientists whose university libraries could no longer afford to subscribe to the originals.

For some scientists and statesmen among the former Allies, it was not enough to rally government and private sponsorship of science and scientific information at home: For almost a decade following the end of hostilities in 1918 this group led a campaign to prevent Germany from regaining its dominant prewar position in these areas. This was a continuation of the wartime campaign of belittling German scientific achievement typified by a 1915 editorial in *Nature* by Sir William Ramsay, one of the most distinguished chemists of his time. Ramsay claimed then that "the restriction of the Teutons will relieve the world from a deluge of mediocrity. Much of their previous reputation has been due to Hebrews resident amongst them."[15] The boycotters of German science consisted primarily of French, English and Belgian scientists, but included also the American George Ellery Hale of the United States' National Research Council. These men sought to use the Treaty of Versailles to limit Germany's scientific and technical capacity by, among other actions, prohibiting German participation in international scientific organizations and projects: They claimed that article 282 of the treaty (which annulled all prewar agreements with Germany) made international collaboration with German scientific organizations and their members illegal for signees of the Treaty, and they set up their own International Research Council in 1918 as a forum for a new "German-free" postwar international science.

The reshaping of the world scientific information order was the highest priority of the International Research Council. During the organization's founding assembly there was proposed the establishment of an International Union of Bibliography and Documentation, and a report was heard from the Federation of Natural Science Societies about measures proposed to replace the leading German reviewing journals by Allied publications. The report concluded that this could best be done by establishing an Interallied Office of Scientific Documentation and by establishing review bulletins in botany, zoology, anatomy, biology and physiology (all areas in which German reviews were traditionally dominant). It was proposed that the International Research Council's affiliated academies would transmit to the new Office all the articles appearing in their countries, and that the Office would in turn send to the individual academies a certain number of articles for analysis.[16]

Neither the International Research Council nor its proposed bibliographic projects produced any long-term results. The Council did manage to reduce Allied and neutral scientific collaboration with Germany significantly in the early 1920s, preventing Germans and Austrians from participating in two-thirds of the international scholarly conferences held   from 1920 to 1924.[17]   But its raison d'être faded with Germany's acceptance into the League of Nations in 1926 and it ultimately dissolved itself in 1931 and was reconstituted under a new name.[18] Its bibliographic projects had to be abandoned, ironically enough because of the intransigence of Allied review publishers.   Certain Allied publishers (chief among them the American Chemical Society's *Chemical Abstracts*) had established healthy market positions after the war which they did not want to give up to a central agency such as the proposed Interallied Office of Scientific Documentation, which had no commercial experience.[19]

Side by side with the fluorescence of scientific nationalism during and right after World War I, there persisted throughout the 1920s and 1930s the belief among many scientists that the fair *international* distribution of knowledge was a necessary precondition for world peace. The forum of expression for much of this idealism was the League of Nations, which in 1922, on the initiative of Henri La Fontaine, set up a Committee on Intellectual Cooperation.   The Committee mobilized some of the most prominent intellectual leaders of the international scholarly world, although Soviet scientists were not invited to join until 1934 and Germans were excluded until 1926 (the exception was Albert Einstein, whose credentials as a pacifist and internationalist were such that he was never included in the anti-German boycott, although he was a German citizen and worked in Berlin).[20]   The Committee was chaired by France's leading philosopher, Henri Bergson, and its other members were Madame Marie Curie-Sklowdowka, Gilbert Murray, the Oxford classicist, and Einstein. At the Committee's very first meeting in August 1922, it established a Sub-Committee on Bibliography. As it reported to the League Council:

> The international organisation for scientific documentation, particularly bibliography, is essential for all intellectual cooperation; scientific relations are very intimately connected with this question. For this reason the world of science unanimously desires that such an organisation may be established as soon as possible.   The Committee gives this priority over scientific research and interuniversity relations.[21]

But such were the complexities of specialized scientific bibliography that virtually nothing was accomplished by the new Sub-committee. Perhaps the diversity of interests among the members of the Committee on Intellectual Cooperation impeded its projects from progress in any one area. In any case, its only really successful bibliographic venture was its general catalog of translations, the quarterly *Index Translationum*, begun in 1932, which listed works translated into and out of the major European languages. Based on information on translations in the national bibliograpies of Great Britain, France,

Germany, Italy, Spain and the United States, the *Index* also included translations to and from the Russian after 1933. The last issue of the *Index* under the League of Nations imprint was that of January 1940. In the late 1940s the project was relaunched under the auspices of the United Nations Educational, Scientific and Cultural Organization (UNESCO).

Much more important to international scientific information than the League of Nations during the interwar period was the support of two American charitable trusts, the Carnegie and Rockefeller foundations. The Carnegie Corporation had been established with an endowment of $135 million in 1911 by steel magnate Andrew Carnegie "to promote the advancement and diffusion of knowledge and understanding among the people of the United States and the British dominions and colonies." Carnegie Corporation grants, and those of its sister organization, the Carnegie United Kingdom Trust, resulted in the construction of 2,509 public libraries and 108 college libraries in the English-speaking world. A large number of these libraries, public and college, had substantial science collections. Their construction meant that, in the English-speaking world anyway, access was much more widely available than before to international science, if mainly through the medium of popular works. In the late 1920s, after the death of Carnegie, the Corporation began contributing directly to academic institutions for the endowment of science.[22]

The Rockefeller Foundation tended in its early years to concentrate more specifically on the subjects of science and technology than did the Carnegie fund. Endowed with $189 million in 1913 by John D. Rockefeller "to promote the well-being of mankind throughout the world," the Rockefeller Foundation was largely supportive of public health and medicine. Rockefeller-financed National Research Council Fellowships sent many young Americans abroad to study during the 1920s, but the Foundation's funding was in no way restricted to the United States. The Foundation did not join in the western boycott of German science. Early in the 1920s, at the height of the Germany's scientific isolation and during the darkest days of Germany's postwar inflation, the Rockefeller Foundation began to subsidize the foreign journals collections of a number of important German research institutions. Nor did the Foundation join in the general Western ostracism of Soviet science: In 1930 physicist Lev Landau studied in Zurich on a Rockefeller Fellowship.[23] With German-educated Max Mason as its president after 1930, the Rockefeller Foundation continued its financial support of German academic science through 1937, even paying for the construction and equipment of whole institutes and their libraries at Göttingen and Berlin. These subsidies persisted despite increasing criticism at home of assistance to a racist regime.[24]

THE WORLD OF PHYSICS IN THE 1920s AND 1930s

The Rockefeller Foundation's support of German science stemmed naturally from its mission to support research at its most advanced. Despite all of the hardships of defeat and humiliation, Germany was, by the early 1930s, once again a major scientific center. But the topography of physics had changed somewhat as a result of World War I, with some of the attention once reserved for Germany shifting across the Atlantic. Moreover, the greater speed with which scientific news traveled in the post-World War I world—due both to communications technology and to the increased mobility of the scientists themselves—meant that none of the breakthroughs of the 1920s and 1930s remained exclusively national, but was converted almost instantly into the intellectual property of the international physics community. A dramatic example of this came in the late 1920s, when the *New York Tribune* arranged for the transatlantic cable transmission of the unified theory of electromagnetic and gravitational fields announced by Einstein. The full text of the cabled paper, including its mathematical formulae, was reproduced in photofacsimile on the front pages of both the *Tribune* and the *New York Post*.[25]

The First World War had totally severed relations between the centers of physics in Germany and Austria and those outside—the radium laboratory of Mme. Curie in Paris and the Cavendish at Cambridge among the most important—but by the late 1920s communication both between all these centers and with new sites of physics activity in the United States and Denmark exceeded prewar conditions. The availability of Rockefeller Foundation funds for fellowships and visiting professorships also played an important role in the new level of international activity, but the most important stimulating factor was the revolution in physics started by the introduction of quantum theory just before the war, an innovation which in 1911 Henri Poincaré claimed would cause "the greatest and most radical revolution in natural philosophy since the time of Newton."[26] This revolution had started shortly after the turn of the century, when Max Planck became puzzled by the behavior of tiny energy units he called "quants," and concluded that energy exchanges at the particle level take place in a catastrophic fashion. This conclusion riveted the attention of following generations of physicists on atomic behavior. Much later Robert J. Oppenheimer would look back on the 1920s, when he was a student at Göttingen, as the "heroic time" in physics. While some young Americans—Oppenheimer included—also contributed, the revolution was mainly accomplished on the European mainland by two groups of physicists, one of which took the "radical path" to quantum mechanics exemplified by Niels Bohr in Copenhagen and Max Born at Göttingen, the other of which accepted the more conservative approach of Einstein at the Max Planck Institute in Berlin.[27]

Werner Heisenberg, who reinterpreted the basic concepts of mechanics as applied to atomic particles and received the Nobel Prize at age thirty-one in 1933, was in Born's group. The members of the two schools met often for debates at a variety of places—professional society congresses, invited conferences, visiting lectures—within an ever-widening geographic circle.

While many American students still attended German universities to finish their physics education in the 1920s and 1930s, it became increasingly likely in the 1930s that the great German professors would come to them. America had gotten a late start in organizing physics: *Physical Review* was only founded in 1893 and the American Physical Society established in 1899. By the 1920s, however, a number of large universities has distinguished physics faculties. Daniel Kevles has shown how during the 1920s and 1930s the twenty leading American universities whose physics faculty members produced 75 percent of the papers in *The Physical Review* became magnets for European physicists. With money lavishly available, these large schools, in particularly the California Institute of Technology in Pasadena, had by 1932 hosted over twenty of the great Europeans, including six present or future Nobel Laureates.[28]

Inevitably, important research began to be done on American soil, and by the early thirties the eminent Europeans who came to America came not only to teach but to learn.[29] In 1932 three Nobel Prize-winning discoveries in physics took place in the United States: At Columbia Harold Urey discovered deuterium, an isotope of hydrogen; at Caltech Carl Anderson established the existence of the positron, the positively charged counterpart of the electron; and at the University of California at Berkeley E. O. Lawrence achieved one million electron volts in his new cyclotron, which whirled charged particles to tremenendous speeds.[30]   Thus the United States had attained a rough parity in physics with the other leading scientific nations even before events in Europe brought about the migration of refugee scientists.[31] When in 1932 Albert Einstein permanently settled at the Institute for Advanced Study in Princeton, New Jersey, French physicist Paul Langevin commented that the United States would now become the "center of the natural sciences".[32]   Four years later, after the flight from Hitler to America of scores of European physicists, *Newsweek* claimed that "the United States leads the world in physics."[33]

British physicists finally shed the intense prewar veneration of German science that had caused them to model the Imperial College of Science and Technology, opened in 1907, on the Technical University of Berlin.[34] More and more they looked to the United States for scientific innovation: In 1916-17 numerous articles had appeared in *Nature* on American physics.[35] The tendency of young English physicists to earn their doctorates at German universities had also been lessened by the introduction of the doctorate at English universities in 1919.[36] Besides, English physics was entering a glory period of its own, and the Cavendish Laboratory at Cambridge, run by New Zealander Ernest

Rutherford—whose own research into atomic elements and radioactivity had won him the Nobel Prize in 1908—attracted a large international contingent, including the brilliant Russian Pyotr Kapitsa. German physics students were now going to English universities—for example, the son of Carl Bosch, Nobel Laureate in chemistry, was a student of physicist F. A. Lindemann (later Lord Cherwell) at Oxford in 1937.[37]

While the chief centers of physics research were in Germany and the Anglo-Saxon world, Paris retained considerable lustre as the site of the work of the Curies. Marie Curie and her husband Pierre had made their Radium Institute one of the earliest loci for research into radioactivity, for which Madame Curie had been awarded Nobel Prizes both in physics (with her husband in 1903) and chemistry (alone, in 1911). Later her daughter Irène and her husband Frédéric Joliot continued the Curies' research in radioactive atoms and were awarded the Nobel Prize for chemistry in 1935. Between 1933 and 1940 the Curies' laboratories, and their experiments bombarding the atomic nuclei of a variety of elements with neutrons, attracted some of Central Europe's most outstanding refugee physicists.

Copenhagen had joined the ranks of international physics centers by 1930. Entirely because of the intellectual energies of Niels Bohr, who had received the Nobel prize in 1922 for his investigations of atomic structure and radiation, the annual meetings Bohr began to organize in Cophenhagen in the 1920s grew over the next decade to be the single most important opportunity for dialogue in atomic physics. Bohr had been deeply involved in the revolution in quantum physics centered in Germany, but it was a sign of scientific as well as political developments that the lingua franca used in the Copenhagen conferences, initially German, changed in the course of the 1930s to English.[38]

Among the countries which were sites of advanced physics research, the Soviet Union was an anomaly.   Ostracized politically until the mid-1930s, disadvantaged by language, distance, lack of funds and a government convinced of the threat of "capitalist encirclement," Soviet physicists participated less than their Western colleagues in the international exchanges of the period. And yet advanced physics was being pursued in the Soviet Union, and its results were not unknown to the rest of the world. English physicist J. D. Bernal, after all, listed the Soviet Union in 1939 as in the immediate second tier of physics research, with France, following Germany and the Anglo-Saxon world.[39] From the early 1930s Abram F. Ioffe's Physico-Technical Institute in Leningrad served as the country's main center for atomic research, with young I. V. Kurchatov, the future "father of the Soviet atomic bomb," heading the Nuclear Physics Laboratory there after 1938. Other centers were the Radium Institute in Leningrad, the Lebedev Physical Institute and the Institute of Physical Problems in Moscow, and in Khar'kov the Physico-Technical Institute. In these institutes Soviet physicists worked in well-equipped laboratories that were actually more advanced than those in Western and Central Europe at the time.[40]

The Soviet cyclotron at the Radium Institute in Leningrad was the first particle accelerator in Europe. Designed by a team headed by Kurchatov, it was operative in 1937.[41]

Despite their relative physical isolation, the personnel involved in Soviet atomic research before World War II were among the most highly qualified in the world: Pyotr Kapitsa, Lev Landau, Pavel Cherenko, Igor Tamm and Nikolai Semenov all would eventually receive Nobel Prizes for physics research they did in the 1930s. During this period the work of at least some of them was known outside Russia: Landau had been a Rockefeller Fellow in Zurich and Kapitsa had spent more than a decade at Cambridge working with Rutherford before 1934 (other members of the top Russian physics team who had spent time in Cambridge were Kyrill Sinel'nikov and Yulii Khariton). Visits to the Soviet Union from foreign visitors were not frequent, but France's Joliot-Curie lectured in Leningrad in 1932[42] and in 1934 an international Mendeleev Conference in Moscow was attended by a large number of foreign scientists, including Otto Hahn and Lise Meitner.[43] In the 1930s Soviet physicists were regular contributors to the best German- and English-language physics journals: Between 1 January 1938 and 15 June 1940, for example, the American *Physical Review* published seven letters to the editor (described as "brief reports of important discoveries in physics") from researchers in Moscow, Leningrad and Tomsk, as well as a full article by a team in Khar'kov. So Soviet physics, despite the enormous obstacles it faced, stubbornly remained part of the advanced research network.

A new urgency entered the dialogue between atomic physicists in the late 1930s, when it became clear that the fission of certain types of atoms would release a new type of almost unimaginably great energy. In 1938 Otto Hahn and his associate Fritz Strassmann at the Max Planck Institute in Berlin had split the uranium atom by bombarding it with neutrons, causing a tumult in the world of physics. In December 1938 refugee scientists Lise Meitner and her nephew Otto Frish concluded from Hahn's experiments that heavy atoms—unstable atoms with extra neutrons—could be split in two halves, news which Niels Bohr took with him on a trip to New York the next month. With John Wheeler of Princeton, Bohr then demonstrated that nuclei of the heavy uranium atom U-235 (as opposed to those of the common uranium isotope U-238) were indeed fissile. By March 1939 most physicists accepted that this rare uranium isotope could be disintegrated and emit neutrons, which, if accumulated in large enough quantities, could start a chain reaction. With enough uranium-235, there was the chance of a devastating explosion.

Almost immediately scientists began speculating about channeling the new energy source for practical use. In the Soviet Union, a team under Kurchatov reported at a conference in April 1939 that enough neutrons were emitted per fissioned uranium nucleus for the continuous reproduction of nuclear energy.[44]

And in June 1939 Siegfried Flugge suggested in the journal *Die Naturwissenschaften* that the atomic energy released by fission might be exploited practically if cadmium were used as a "brake" to prevent the chain reaction from getting out of hand.[45]

Between January and June 1939 more than 50 research articles on the fission of the uranium atom were published in England, Germany and the United States.[46] In his memoirs, English physicist C. P. Snow recalled the frenzy with which the news spread: "By the summer of 1939 it was known all over the scientific world. Publication was open. The German physicists read the Bohr-Wheeler paper and the rest of the literature with, of course, as much realization as the Americans and English. So did Lev Landau in the Soviet Union, who ranked with Kapitsa as the leading Russian physicist. As Snow wrote later, "All the scientific knowledge was there and waiting. If it could ever be applied, that would be a matter of engineering..."[47]

During the war that began in 1939 physicists on each side of the conflict lived in fear of enemy progress in this "matter of engineering." This fear gave a special urgency to general concerns about enemy weaponry innovations and was a driving force in the wartime development of scientific intelligence gathering techniques. Over the course of the war, members of this new intelligence community found that the great bulk of their most useful information was derived from "open," or publicly available, sources.[48] But scientific publication had undergone its own revolution in the 1930s, and its new formats would present both challenges and opportunities to Allied and Axis agents.

MICROFILM AND INTERNATIONAL DOCUMENTATION IN THE 1930s

The revolution in physics, as well as accelerated activity in industrial applications of chemistry during the 1920s and 1930s, produced an explosion of publications in science and technology that posed new problems in organization and storage. Scientists and bibliographers desperately sought practical solutions in new mechanical techniques and experimented with the various methods of photographic reprography developed since the beginning of the twentieth century. After microfilm came into use in banks in 1928, it began to dominate professional discussions of how best to store and spread scholarly and scientific knowledge, and its partisans grew in number and vociferousness. In fact, the passion of the debate in the 1930s about microfilm's potential for curing the world's ills equaled that concerning "universal" bibliography in the years preceding World War I.

Microphotography's potential uses for information storage had been recognized since the technology's earliest develoment in the midnineteenth century, and in 1854 its use for producing library catalogs had first been recommended.[49]   In 1906 Paul Otlet and an engineer collaborator, Robert Goldschmidt, had proposed a prototype microfiche card in a monograph entitled *Sur une forme nouvelle du livre: le livre microphotographique.*[50] It was not, however until Eastman Kodak's introduction in 1928 of its Recordak camera to microfilm bank checks that scholarly and scientific microreprography became practical. The United States was the main source of innovations in this field in the 1930s. In 1934 a new microfilm camera had been designed by a naval doctor to photograph medical publications for use at sea. Named for its inventor, Lieutenant Rupert Draeger, the Draeger camera made possible for the first time the efficient, high-speed microfilming of library materials, and was installed in that year in the United States Department of Agriculture Library (now the National Library of Agriculture), starting the world's first library service offering microfilm in lieu of the interlibrary loan of publications.[51]

Interest in microfilm mushroomed among those working in scholarly and scientific information in the 1930s. In 1931 Otlet's International Institute of Bibliography changed its name to the more inclusive International Institute of Documentation. (The organization's letterhead gave a definition of the newly adopted term, documentation, as "the assembling, classification and distribution of documents of all kinds in all areas of human activity.") This change of name indicated, among other things, the organization's interest in nonbook forms of information, including those produced by reprography.[52] Depressed world economic conditions delayed the spread of the expensive cameras and reading machines on which microfilming depended, but great ingenuity was shown in altering Recordaks and German Leika still cameras for library use.

A climax of international interest in microfilm was reached at the International Exposition and the World Congress of Universal Documentation held in Paris in August 1937. The exposition, held at the Trocadero, was intended "to unite nations in peace and to celebrate the progress of Art and Science." It included two exhibits of microfilm—one of the equipment used at the Bibliothèque Nationale (including an American-designed camera), and a much more elaborate stand set up by the University of Chicago and paid for by the Rockefeller Foundation and the American Chemical Society. The University of Chicago exhibit included an entire microfilm laboratory, complete with darkroom, and used Rupert Draeger's camera and Recordak and Optigraph reading machines. Draeger's camera, which received the exposition's gold medal, reduced over 200,000 pages to microfilm in full view of amazed passers-by.[53]

Simultaneous with the exposition an international scholarly congress for documentalists had been organized at the Maison de Chimie by Jean Gérard, president of l'Union française des organismes de documentation, and sponsored by the League of Nation's Committee for Intellectual Cooperation. Twenty-eight governments, forty-five countries and about forty institutions were officially represented at the congress.

The delegates' excitement about microfilm, stimulated by the exhibitions, was increased by the remarks of H. G. Wells, a member of the congress' organizing committee, who had been asked to speak on microfilm's connection to his concept of the "World Brain." One of Wells' pet themes in the 1930s was how the general failure to coordinate and utilize knowledge during the decade's series of economic, political and military crises was threatening world stability. In 1936 he had told a meeting of the Royal Institution in London that "few of us now fail to appreciate the stupendous ignorance, the almost total lack of grasp of social and economic realities, the short views, the shallowness of mind, that characterized the treaty-making of 1919 and 1920."[54]   The consequences of man's living, as Wells claimed he did, "in a world of unused and misapplied knowledge and skill,"[55] had been made dramatically clear to filmgoers in the English-speaking world in 1936 when the movie version of Wells' 1933 novel *The Shape of Things to Come* had been released (as *Things to Come*). The movie depicted a massive Second World War reducing mankind to scattered groups of near-savages. Wells' proposed solution to the threats posed by "unused and misapplied knowledge and skill" lay in the evocation of what he took to calling the "World Brain," a universal organization and classification of knowledge and ideas.

In his talk at the Congress on 20 August 1937, Wells told the group of 460 documentalists gathered in the Maison de Chimie that they were the wave of the future: According to Wells, "it is dawning on us, we lay observers, that this world of documentation and bibliography is in fact nothing less than the beginning of a world brain—which (when it is fully developed) will constitute a memory and perception of current reality for the entire human race."[56] Wells went on to say that what particularly excited him was being shown by the proponents of microfilm at the Congress that the World Brain "need not have any single local habitation because the continually increasing facilities of photography render reduplication of our indices and records continually easier. In these days of destruction, violence and general insecurity, it is comforting to think that the brain of mankind, the race brain, can exist in numerous replicas throughout the world."[57]

So according to H. G. Wells, the members of the new profession of documentation, armed with the new technology of microfilm, were crucial to the survival of civilization. Wells did not make it quite clear whether their skills would actually ward off world catastrophe or would be used by superbeings to recreate civilization after its destruction. The weight of his words in Paris seemed to emphasize the latter contingency: "The world is a Phoenix," he said. "It perishes in flames and even as it dies it is born again. This synthesis of knowledge is the necessary beginning to the new world."[58]   Likewise, in *Things to Come*, he had shown how a benign dictatorship of scientists and engineers, personified by airmen, had built from the rubble of global war a society of unprecedented freedom and beauty.

By the time H. G. Wells spoke in Paris, his ideas had attracted the attention of a number of scientists hoping to influence government policy about the use of scientific knowledge. This group included J. D. Bernal, a Cambridge physicist active in organizations opposed to the use of science for war ends. Bernal was a subscriber to the goals of the International Peace Campaign that had met in Brussels in 1936 and whose scientific subcommission had resolved that "war is fatal to science, not only by breaking up its fundamentally international character, but even more by destroying its ultimate purpose of benefitting the human race."[59]

In his influential book *The Social Function of Science*, published in 1939, Bernal applauded Wells' idea of a world "brain" or encyclopedia.[60] Bernal saw it not so much as a tool for race survival as a means of securing a social peace threatened by fascism: the world encyclopedia was needed because "the combined assault on science and humanism by forces of barbarism has against it, as yet, no general and coherent statement on the part of those who believe in democracy and the need for the people of the world to take over active control of production and administration for their own safety and welfare."[61]

The Social Function of Science laid out a very specific plan for packaging and distributing scientific knowledge to empower people to participate in their own governance. Declaring the printing press to be "the principal barrier to adequate scientific publishing and bibliography,"[62] Bernal advocated the direct reproduction of typewritten text by photography at centralized publication offices, where the refereeing and further distribution would take place. Bernal's plan was greatly influenced by the American information science pioneer Watson Davis, microfilm enthusiast and cofounder of the American Documentation Institute in 1937 (see Chapter 2). In the appendix of *The Social Function of Science* Bernal included in its entirety Davis' plan for a Scientific Information Institute (and by so doing gave the plan publicity far outside the narrow documentation circles in which it was already known). The essentials of the plan were (1) the centralization of scientific publishing and bibliography, with the resulting economy of operation and improvement of service; (2) the substitution of photographic duplication for printing, coupled with the development of reduced-size duplication; and (3) the use of a scheme of numerical indexing and automatic finding and sorting devices for filing and selecting the bibliographies and articles. An important component of Davis' plan was its incorporation of most of the existing media of scientific publishing. It would be a monopoly in the same sense that the post office was a monopoly, operated for public benefit, without profit. Davis maintained that "if it is not practically all-inclusive, it will fail."[63]

But despite plans for social betterment and international cooperation laid by scientists and documentalists in the late 1930s, Europe was preparing for war. Even during the World Documentation Congress in Paris in 1937 gas masks had been displayed at the exposition and public instruction given on how to deal with gas bomb attacks.[64] Just two years later the countries that had sent the three largest delegations to the Documentation Congress—France, Germany and Great Britain—would be involved in a war in which the application of science at its most advanced levels would provide the decisive weaponry. In all the advanced Western countries eventually involved in the conflict, the leading documentalists, aided by the scientists they served, convinced their governments that their skills as transmittors of strategic scientific information were critical to victory.

On both sides of the conflict documentalists would be involved in building massive government-supported programs to import and circulate the journals in which enemy scientists reported their discoveries. And on both sides the journals targeted for import covered all of the subjects interesting to nations waging war in the 1940s: acoustics, aviation, bacteriology, electrotechnology, fuel chemistry, high-frequency technology, medicine, rubber and synthetics, to name only a few.

While this account will report on the acquisition of enemy knowledge in many fields, it will devote special attention to the quest for information on atomic science. This is interesting not just because of the frenzy of interest in the subject on the eve of the war and of the awesomeness of the power anticipated in it. Another factor, already mentioned in the Introduction, makes atomic research uniquely interesting to this study: Unlike other weapons developed in the course of World War II, such as airborne radar and rockets, the atomic bomb was not used until the very end of the conflict and no example of it ever fell into the hands of the enemy for subjection to the techniques of "reverse engineering." The only carriers of the most advanced knowledge in this new field were either individuals, their laboratory equipment or their published research results.

All three would be targets of the scientific intelligence staffs of all the warring powers. There exist scores of books on the clandestine methods used or attempted to extract atomic and other secrets from researchers and convey them to rival powers.[65] But Sherman Kent, OSS veteran and author of the classic postwar analysis *Strategic Intelligence for American World Policy* (1949), stresses the greater general importance of *published sources* for foreign intelligence. He quotes colleagues who maintain that "90% of what you must know" can be obtained from such sources, among which Kent includes scientific and technical literature.[66] This will be the focus of our study: how and under what circumstances the analysis of scientific and technical literature went on; what difference it made, especially in atomic physics; and finally, what postwar impact it had on government attitudes towards the collection of foreign scientific and technical literature.

NOTES

1. David L. Hill, Eugene Rabinowitch, and John A. Simpson, Jr., "The Atomic Scientists Speak Up: Nuclear Physicists Say There Is No Secrecy in Atom Bomb and No Defense Against It," *Life*, no. 18 (29 October 1945):45.

2. Daniel J.Kevles, *The Physicists* (New York: Knopf, 1978), p. 320.

3. Boyd Rayward, *Universe of Information* (Moscow: International Federation of Documentation, 1975), p. 75. See also John E. Findling, *Historical Dictionary of World's Fairs and Exhibitions, 1851-1988* (New York: Greenwood Press, 1990).

4. Brigitte Schroeder-Gudehus, *Les Scientifiques et la Paix* (Montreal: Presses de l'Université de Montreal, 1978), p. 51.

5. Schroeder-Gudehus, *Les Scientifiques et la Paix*, p. 25.

6. "Sources of Journal Literature Abstracted in *Chemical Abstracts*", in *Chemical Abstracts Services Statistical Summary 1907-1984* (Columbus OH: Chemical Abstracts Service, 1987), p. 2.

7. Ernst Mehl and Kurt Hannermann, *Deutsche Bibliotheksgeschichte* (Berlin: Eric Schmidt, 1951), p. 364.

8. See Joseph Wall, *Andrew Carnegie* (Oxford: Oxford University Press, 1980.

9. Rayward, *Universe of Information*, p. 196.

10. The average value of the prize grew from $30,000 in 1901 to $800,000 in 1993.

11. J.D. Bernal, *The Social Function of Science* (London: Routledge and Kegan Paul, 1939), p. 171.

12. Schroeder-Gudehus, *Les Scientifiques et la Paix*, p. 71.

13. J.D. Bernal, *The Social Function of Science*, pp. 172, 199.

14. T. F. Karatuny, "Technical Libraries in the USSR," in Francies Simon (ed.), *Libraries in the USSR* (Hamden CT: Linnet, 1971), p. 55.

15. Sir William Ramsay, in *Nature* 94 (1915): 138. Quoted in Bernal, *The Social Function of Science*, p. 182.

16. Schroeder-Gudehus, *Les Scientifiques et la Paix*, p. 139.

17. Schroeder-Gudehus, *Les scientifiques et la Paix*, p. 133.

18. Germany never joined the International Research Council, although it was finally invited to do so in the late 1920s, nor did it join the successor organization, the International Council of Scientific Unions, until after World War II. See Schroeder-Gudehus, *Les Scientifiques et la Paix*, p. 298.

19. Schroeder-Gudehus, *Les Scientifiques et la Paix*, p. 140.

20. Schroeder-Gudehus, *Les Scientifiques et la Paix*, p. 259.

21. Texts of the Committee's deliberations and the various motions placed before it are given in E. C. Richardson, *Some Aspects of International Library Co-operation* (Yardley, PA: F. S. Cook, 1928), pp. 68-79. Quotation is from this source. Quoted in Rayward, *Universe of Information*, p. 257.

22. Kevles, *The Physicists*, p. 190.

23. Rudolf Peierls, *Bird of Passage: Recollections of a Physicist* (Princeton: Princeton University Press, 1985), p. 49.

24. Christie Macrakis, "Wissenschaftsförderung durch die Rockefeller Stiftung im Dritten Reich," *Geschichte und Gesellschaft* 12 (1986):350.

25. Kevles, *The Physicists*, p. 175.

26. Kevles, *The Physicists*, p. 163.

27. Kevles, *The Physicists*, p. 163.

28. Kevles, *The Physicists*, p. 197.

29. Roger L. Geiger, *To Advance Knowledge: The Growth of American Research Universities 1900-1940* (New York: Oxford University Press, 1986), p. 233.

30. Geiger, *To Advance Knowledge*, p. 239.

31. Geiger, *To Advance Knowledge*, p. 233.

32. Kevles, *The Physicists*, p. 221.

33. Quoted in Kevles, *The Physicists*, p. 282. According to Kevles, *Newsweek*'s claim was justified.

34. Peter Alter, *The Reluctant Patron: Science and the State in Britain 1850-1920*, trans. Angela Davies (Oxford: Berg, 1987), p.56.

35. Alter, *The Reluctant Patron*, p. 200.

36. R.V. Jones, interview with the author, 14 August 1990.

37. Idem.

38. Hendrik Casimir, *Haphazard Reality: A Half Century of Science* (New York: Harper and Row, 1983), p. 194.

39. J. D. Bernal, *The Social Function of Science*, p. 194.

40. Arnold Kramish, *Atomic Energy in the Soviet Union* (Stanford CA: Stanford University Press, 1959), pp. 15-19.

41. Zhores A. Medvedev, *Soviet Science* (Oxford: Oxford University Press, 1979), p. 262.

42. Kramish, *Atomic Energy in the Soviet Union*, p. 16.

43. Otto Hahn, *My Life: The Autobiography of a Scientist* (New York: Herder and Herder, 1970), p. 146.

44. Kramish, *Atomic Energy in the Soviet Union*, p. 22.

45. Maurice Goldsmith, *Frédéric Joliot-Curie* (London: Lawrence and Wishart, 1976), p.71.

46. Goldsmith, *Frédéric Joliot-Curie* , p. 71.

47. C.P. Snow, *The Physicists* (Boston: Little, Brown, 1981), p. 102.

48. Sherman Kent, *Strategic Intelligence for American World Policy* (Princeton: Princeton University Press, 1949), p. 215.

49. Frederick Luther, "The Earliest Experiments in Microphotography," *Isis* 41 (December 1950), pp. 277, 279.

50. Robert Goldschmidt and Paul Otlet, *Sur une forme nouvelle du livre: le livre microphotographique*, Publication 81 (Brussels: International Institute of Bibliography, 1906).

51. Peter Hirtle, "Atherton Seidell and the Photoduplication of Library Material," *Journal of the American Society for Information Science* 40(1989):427.

52. Helmut Arntz, "International Federation of Documentation," *Encyclopedia of Library and Information Science* (New York: Marcel Dekker, 1974), vol. 12, p. 382.

53. Boyd Rayward, "The International Exposition and the World Documentation Congress, Paris 1937," *Library Quarterly* 53 (1983): 254-68.

54. H. G. Wells, "World Encyclopaedia: Lecture Delivered at the Royal Institution of Great Britain, November 20, 1936," in H. G. Wells, *World Brain* (Garden City, NY: Doubleday, Doran, 1938), p. 6.

55. Ibid., p. 10.

56. H. G. Wells, "Speech to the Congrès Mondial de la Documentation Universelle, Paris, August 20 1937," in Wells, *World Brain*, p. 91.

57. Idem. Fascination with microfilm was not limited to scholarly and esoteric circles. As a symbol of the latest in modern technology, microfilm was placed in a time capsule buried at the New York World's Fair in 1938, to be opened in the year 6939.

58. Ibid., p. 92.

59. J. D. Bernal, *The Social Function of Science*, appendix 9, p. 459.

60. Soviet scholars consider Bernal's book the most influential science policy document of the era. See P. A. Rachkov, *Naukovedenie* (Moscow, 1974), p. 12, and Gennady Gurgenizde, "Problems of the Science of Science," *Social Sciences* (1974):74. Cited in Linda L. Lubrano, *Soviet Sociology of Science* (Columbus, OH: American Association for the Advancement of Slavic Studies, 1976), p. 5.

61. Bernal, *The Social Function of Science*, p. 307.

62. Bernal, *The Social Function of Science*, p. 453.

63. Bernal, *The Social Function of Science*, appendix 8, p. 449.

64. "Not So Pretty or Pleasant in One Exhibit in Paris," *Science News Letter* 32 (October 1937), p. 232.

65. Some examples are Samuel Goudsmit's *ALSOS* (1947), David Irving's *The German Atomic Bomb* (1967), and David Kahn's *Hitler's Spies* (1978).

66. Kent, *Strategic Intelligence for American World Policy*, p. 215.

2

National Government Support for Scientific Information in Great Britain and the United States before World War II

GREAT BRITAIN

Over the first four decades of the twentieth century a number of organizations established in Great Britain that made it the international leader in the acquisition of the documents of foreign science by the outbreak of the Second World War.[1] They provided the basis on which the government could build the information system that became a hub of Allied collaboration between 1941 and 1945. For a full understanding of how it worked, a brief overview of its birth, development and relationship to the government is necessary.

All the elements of scientific documentation—systematic collection of scientific information, its organization and circulation—were present in Great Britain by the 1920s, but responsibility for them was dispersed among scientific institutions, national government agencies, and industry. The oldest of these components, the Royal Society, had grown, with the help of subsidies from the Crown, to be a magnet for information about scientific activities throughout the world, with observations flowing in from its many foreign correspondents. Through its *Philosophical Transactions* (from 1665) and its *Proceedings* (from 1832), the Royal Society maintained two of the most important scientific organs of the eighteenth and nineteenth centuries. As scientific publishing expanded throughout the world, the Royal Society pioneered in bibliographical coverage through its *Catalogue of Scientific Papers 1800-1900* and *International Catalogue of Scientific Literature* (1901-16).

Problems encountered in publishing these catalogs were the origin of the Royal Society's twentieth century concern with improving the techniques of scientific documentation. After the abandonment of the *International Catalogue of Scientific Literature* during the First World War, the Royal Society played a central role in the decision of the Conjoint Board of Scientific Societies to publish a *World List of Scientific Periodicals*. The first edition (1925-27) gave the location in 150 libraries—twenty-one in the United Kingdom—of 25,000 titles published from 1900 to 1920. This and three subsequent editions were basic bibliographical tools until the 1950s.[2] The position of Great Britain at the center of a worldwide empire accelerated the British government's participation in the work of international documentation. In 1887, the Board of Trade established "as a lasting emblem of the unity and loyalty of the Empire"[3] the Imperial Institute in South Kensington. While its main purpose was to win public support for the empire, the Institute pioneered in government-supported documentation by furnishing the information necessary for the better production and marketing of the plant and animal products of British territories overseas. This work was later extended by the Imperial Agricultural Bureaux. Each bureau was situated at an experimental research station or institute specializing in one subject, and functioned as a center for information about its subject; the bureaux also served as abstracting bodies, with each publishing a journal composed of abstracts of current scientific information on its subject.

The most important step taken by the British government in international scientific documentation was the creation of the Department of Scientific and Industrial Research in 1916. Great Britain's entry into the war had brought into relief the country's dependence on imports from Germany, a dependence that had been hammered at in the press since the appearance in 1896 of Ernest E. Williams' polemic, *Made in Germany*. Calls for the establishment of a British equivalent of the famous technological university Berlin-Charlottenburg were partially responsible for the establishment of the Imperial College of Science and Technology in 1907. But by 1914 Great Britain still produced less than one-quarter of the dyestuffs needed by its textile industry, and it was also dependent on Germany for magnetos, drugs and the tungsten needed by steelmakers. In 1915 the president of the Board of Education, Arthur Henderson, argued in a White Paper for the establishment of a Department of Scientific and Industrial Research:

> It is well known that many of our industries have since the outbreak of the war suffered through our inability to produce at home certain articles and materials required in trade processes, the manufacture of which has become localised abroad, and particularly in Germany, because science there has been more thoroughly and effectively applied to the solution of scientific problems bearing on trade and industry and to the elaboration of economical and improved processes of manufacture. The present scheme is designed to establish a permanent organisation for the promotion of industrial and scientific research.[4]

The British government had, of course, sponsored research before the founding of the Department of Scientific and Industrial Research. Besides supporting the Imperial Institute of Science and Technology the government had sponsored research for its own use, first through such institutions as the Royal Observatory and the Royal Mint. After 1899 the government sponsored research for industrial use through the National Physical Laboratory at Teddington. In addition, at the height of the panic about the loss of German imports in 1915, the government had begun giving 10,000 pounds a year for research to the new British Dyes Limited Company it had helped to set up to secure Great Britain's supply of synthetic dyes.[5] But the establishment of the Department of Scientific and Industrial Research, besides supporting basic research, also provided for documentation on all technologies important to the British economy, in time of peace as well as in time of war. The department was attached to the highest level of the government, reporting directly to the Lord President of the Privy Council—a demonstration of the importance the national authorities attached to science and its documentation.

The department's scientific documentation activities were located in the research institutes which it controlled and in the industrial research associations which it helped to support. In 1919 there were only two institutes—the National Physical Laboratory and the Fuel Research Station in East Greenwhich—but by 1936 these had proliferated to twenty-four. Each institute concentrated on one subject (e.g., food or fuel) and was responsible for issuing periodical abstracts of the literature in its fields throughout the world. Departmental grants to the industrial research associations were contingent upon evidence that the associations engaged in both research *and* documentation. There were ultimately over 30 such industrial research associations, each primarily supported by its own industry; each maintained a library and acted as an information bureau for its members, issuing abstracts of papers in current periodicals in its own fields of interest.[6]

Several further measures were taken to consolidate the survey of research under the authority of the department and to expedite its documentation during this early period. Certain fields of research transcended the boundaries of particular industries, and, to deal with these, "coordinating boards" were established in 1919 and 1920 in chemistry, engineering and physics. A radio board existed already; a fabric coordinating board was added later.

In 1920, the department was charged with the coordination of all military as well as civilian research. By this time there was considerable scientific research taking place at military institutions: At Woolwich the Army had a Military College of Science with a physics department of some standing; the Navy had from 1924 on a Department of Scientific Research and Experiment with a research laboratory adjoining the National Physical Laboratory at Teddington; and in the same year the Department of the Air set up a Directorate of Scientific Research. The Department of Scientific and Industrial Research's new responsibility for military scientific information meant that information on weapons, aeronautics and electronics development was supposed to be collected by the appropriate coordinating board. The coordination of military information was never as efficient as intended, perhaps because of the services' continued prejudice against science as middle class and "ungentlemanly."[7] It probably helped somewhat to allay military suspiciousnes that a former military pilot, Oxford chemist Henry Tizard, served from 1920 to 1929 as the assistant secretary of the department and as the individual responsible for conduct of the various coordinating boards.[8] Tizard (later Sir Henry), a man of extraordinary insight and organizational ability, gained renown a decade later for leading Britain's development of defensive radar.

Some of the impetus for the military work overseen by the coordinating boards was still provided by fear of the Germans—as when in 1921 War Office reports were received that the Germans had developed powerful electromagnetic waves capable of killing people and detonating explosives. The main work of the boards, however, was coordinating research projects of specific interest to one of the services.[9] The most strategically important results came not from the services, however, but from the Radio Research Board, which in 1924 began experiments that in the short term resulted in improved radio reception but led a decade later to the practical application of radar.[10]

Tizard's interest in assuring British scientists' access to published research led to his participation in an organization created to aid the specialized libraries being set up to support the Department of Scientific and Industrial Research's documentation activities. The early history of documentation as a professional practice in Great Britain is largely coterminous with that of the Association of Special Libraries and Information Bureaux (Aslib). The idea that there are certain fundamental principles underlying the classification, indexing and abstracting of specialized information had been accepted by more progressive European and American scientific librarians since the foundation of the International Institute of Bibliography in Brussels in 1895 (see Chapter 1). The Department of Scientific and Industrial Research itself devoted some attention to documentation at a conference of its research associations convened in 1919. The first meeting in the United Kingdom focusing exclusively on scientific and technical information was the conference in 1926 of the Association of Special Libraries and Information Bureaux. (The association itself had held its first congress in 1924.) Many of the organizers of the conference in 1926 were librarians at industrial information bureaus and research associations which had been created by the Department of Scientific and Industrial Research.

In the course of the 1920s, the association became a national center for documentation. Its inaugural conference of September 1924 at High Leigh in Hertfordshire was attended by only 84 persons, but by 1925, the organization had aroused enough international attention to attract to its second conference at Balliol College, Oxford, the grand old man of documentation himself, Paul Otlet, as well as F. Donker Duyvis from the Hague, who was Otlet's successor as chief lobbyist for documentation on an international scale. From its inception, the association attempted to promote maximal exploitation of Great Britain's existing resources in scientific information. To this end it began publication in 1928 of the serial *Aslib Directory: A Guide to Sources of Specialized Information in Great Britain and Ireland.* After the *Directory* appeared, the association started encouraging cooperation among British libraries in the same field. A number of these libraries were helped to form union catalogs of their combined holdings which would assist them in requesting the loan of copies from one another.

The full utilization of foreign scientific journals already in British libraries was a special objective of the association because of the high cost of such publications. The *World List of Periodicals* helped to locate foreign journals, but many remained inaccessible because of the inability of their potential users to read the languages in which they were published. When Henry Tizard became president of the organization in 1930, he called a conference of British indexing and abstracting agencies—government, industrial and those of scholarly societies—to discuss language barriers between scientists of different countries. A survey at this conference indicated that Russian and Japanese scientific literature, as well as that in Hungarian, Polish and Czech, was widely ignored. [11]

Subsequent proposals by the council of the association, in 1930 and 1939, to establish a panel of expert translators under the auspices of the association were apparently without result.[12] Progress was made, however, in publicizing the holdings of rare and expensive foreign science materials. From 1935 onward, the association focused on microfilm as a means of increasing the circulation of publications held in the country only in single copies. The twelfth annual conference discussed microphotographic technology, and in 1937, the headquarters of the association established a clearinghouse for information on microfilming. In no other country—not even the United States, where microfilm technology was more advanced than in England—did librarians and documentalists so early have access to an organization solely devoted to techniques for acquiring and circulating general scientific and technical information.

As the documentation activities of the Association of Special Libraries and Information Bureaux grew in scope, so did its need to find an appropriate institutional base. This was provided to a limited extent by the Science Museum Library in South Kensington, which at that time subscribed to more scientific periodicals than any library in the United Kingdom. The library itself had been founded in 1857 to serve the staff of the new Natural History Museum. After the British Museum transferred to it the responsibility for acquiring and storing the literature of the natural sciences, it developed into the greatest repository of world scientific knowledge in Great Britain. The Patent Office had a larger collection in 1900, but it was subordinated to the Board of Trade and was narrowly confined to service as a reference library for the Patent Office; thus its accessibility was limited. The Science Museum Library, which after 1913 also served the Imperial College of Science and Technology, was administered by the Board of Education, which stimulated its cooperation with other scientific libraries.

The position of the Science Museum Library as, in effect, the national science library, came about as a result of the failure of various schemes in the 1920s for the loan of scientific publications between libraries. It also owed much to the imagination of the library's director from 1925 to 1935, Dr. S. C. Bradford. Bradford was a chemist by training and a documentalist by avocation. He had followed the ideas of Otlet and La Fontaine since the turn of the century and was a champion of their extension of the Dewey Decimal Classification, the Universal Decimal Classification. Bradford studied the statistics of journals usage and became convinced that only by developing his institution into a national central lending library in science and technology could the growing British demand for scientific literature be met.[13] In 1927, he began to lend publications from the Science Library by post to universities, industrial research organizations, and the research institutions of the Department of Scientific and Industrial Research. This postal service was a great success: by 1936, the number of books sent on loan through the post exceeded the use of books by readers in the library.[14]

Despite the central position of the Science Museum Library, it never became a full-fledged documentation center. Bradford's successor, J. Lancaster Jones, director from 1935 to 1945, played an active role in the Association of Special Libraries and Information Bureaux and was a proponent of microfilm technology. However, his institution had neither the staff nor the funds to perform the tasks of indexing, abstracting and translation that, besides acquisition and dissemination, are the duties of a documentation center. In terms of service, the Science Museum Library was outstripped by the Technische Hochschule in Berlin, where an "Informationsstelle" had been reviewing, translating and photostatting international scientific and technological journals in response to postal requests since 1931 (see Chapter 3); but the Informationsstelle could not compete in the number of journals collected. By 1939 the Science Museum Library had the largest collection of scientific periodicals in Europe.[15] It was logical that when war came and threatened foreign journal subscriptions, the library should take a leading role, with the Association of Special Libraries and Information Bureaux, in devising means to ensure these publications' continued acquisition by British libraries.

Much of Great Britain's preparedness in documentation was a result of her fear of technological slippage. This fear was grounded in the experiences of World War I and exacerbated by the breakthroughs being made by German physics in the interwar period. Great Britain was fortunate in having a man of the calibre and energy of Henry Tizard, who was able, even after assuming responsibility in the late 1930s for forging a national defense system based on radar, to support the creation of a wartime "technology watch" on the Germans.

In the atmosphere of increasing international political danger, the warning voice of H. G. Wells also helped to create a productive tension at the highest levels in Great Britain. Sir William Stephenson, the "man called Intrepid" who fathered Anglo-American collaboration in intelligence activities, later credited Wells' influence on his own work, in particular the novelist's "passionate belief that in the science fiction wars to come, our first line of defense would be information, rapidly conveyed."[16] It was precisely this awareness among both documentalists *and* the founders of Allied intelligence that would be responsible for the timely design and activation of the emergency information network that would serve the Allies so successfully during the coming World War.

THE UNITED STATES

The position of the United States in the world of scientific documentation in the late 1930s was connected to the level of the country's general scientific activity. As was the case in Great Britain, government support for both science and its documentation in the United States resulted from fear of superior foreign achievement. In the United States, however, the country's late entrance into the international world of science, coupled with its federated system of governance, retarded sustained central government support before World War II. By the late 1930s, the United States had moved into the ranks of the major centers of science and scientific documentation. The country had mushroomed in size and resources during the nineteenth century and escaped lightly from its brief involvement in the First World War. Recovery from the worst effects of the worldwide economic crises of 1929 was already under way when the wave of refugees from Europe began to enrich its universities' scientific faculties, its research institutions and its journal literature in the mid-1930s. Nobel prizes in the sciences became less rare for Americans: Only two Nobel Prizes were awarded to American scientists before 1920, but from 1930 to 1940 they captured eight. Likewise, in some areas of documentation, the Americans were nosing out the formidable Germans: The American Chemical Society's *Chemical Abstracts* (1907-) had by 1939 overtaken *Chemisches Zentralblatt* as the most important record of chemical research.

But only a very limited amount of the American scientific activity that was winning international recognition by the 1930s resulted from support by the federal government in Washington. Throughout most of the nineteenth century, Congress, mirroring strong local interests, acted as a check on federal spending for science or technology. As was the case with Great Britain, the stimulus for government support, when it came, was external. In the United States, from the midnineteenth century on, the history of federal support for science consisted largely of reactions to the threat or reality of war. The military trauma that raised federal consciousness about the importance of support for science came earlier than Great Britain's: The Civil War was the watershed: From that time, at the outbreak of each new conflict, or threat of one, the federal government set up a new central scientific body with the responsibility of coordinating research and resources, and new legislation was passed to support the collection and circulation of scientific and technical information in certain fields.

The Civil War, which removed the decentralist Southern states from Congress as a voting bloc, also marked the beginning of sustained peacetime federal involvement with technical information. Outside the Army engineering school at West Point and the library of domestic and foreign patents begun in the reorganized Office of the Commissioner of Patents in 1836, no consensus had been achieved on federal obligations or rights to support scientific collections. (The brief and accidental career of the Smithsonian Institution as a national scientific library in the early 1850s ended when its collections and international exchange agreements were turned over to the Library of Congress in 1866, and it survived solely as a museum administration.) An attempt was made to provide the government with access to scientific expertise by the founding of the National Academy as an advisory board in 1863. But in the United States it was not the advisory Academy but rather two mission-oriented government agencies that emerged as the major catalysts for government-sponsored research and documentation.

The Department of Agriculture was split off from the Patent Office in 1862. It differed from other federal departments in that almost from the beginning it supported a central library and a coordinating information system. In 1868, its library was founded; by 1872 it comprised 8,000 volumes. By encouraging a national and international network of "plant explorers" to send in interesting publications, and through the acquisition of wider responsibilities such as meteorology, forestry and drug administration, the library had by the outbreak of World War I grown to be one of the greatest agricultural libraries of the world, with a collection of 122,000 books and periodicals. Distribution of agricultural knowledge was furthered by the publication of the library's first printed catalog in 1880, followed in 1902 by an agreement with the Library of Congress to cooperate in the printing and distribution of catalog cards for new titles in agricultural fields. A cradle of American documentation technology, the agriculture library began in 1911 to use photocopies instead of sending original periodical issues on interlibrary loan.[17]

The library of the Department of Agriculture was only one part of the nationwide network of agricultural information created during and immediately after the Civil War. The act of Congress establishing the Department of Agriculture in 1862 gave as its mission "to acquire and diffuse among the people of the United States useful information on subjects connected with agriculture in the most general and comprehensive sense of the word," and its library and the published library bulletins of the 1890s are evidence of that mission. Other agencies were also founded around this time with similar goals: The Land Grant College Act of 1862 sponsored by Representative Justin C. Morill of Vermont, provided for the founding, with federal resources, of colleges in every state for the direct instruction of the laboring classes, with the sciences, rather than the classics, dominating the curriculum. A nation at war was concerned—as France would be after 1870—with the quality of its technology and with the technical literacy of its population. While few of these new land-grant colleges had real research programs before the turn of the century, they all had libraries which served as diffusion points for materials from the national library of agriculture as well as for engineering literature—in fact, the Morill Act can be seen as the most important piece of federal legislation in support of technical information before World War II.

The Civil War period also gave birth to another mission-oriented government agency for technical information—that of the Surgeon General of the Army, from which the National Library of Medicine would emerge almost a century later. The carnage of the Civil War had increased interest in information on the medical phenomena being witnessed in the field. By 1865 the budget of the Army Medical Department was $20 million a year, and when a young medical officer named John Shaw Billings took over its small library in 1868, he was able to channel some left-over funds into increasing the collection. By the early 1870s Billings had won acceptance for the idea that the Surgeon General's library would be a national, not just a military, information resource. Accordingly, he established a reference service staffed with copyists, abstractors and translators ready to answer any reasonable request. Books and periodicals were lent to medical societies or to individuals outside Washington on receipt of deposit.

Billings also instituted a system for acquiring foreign publications. By enlisting the aid of American consuls abroad, establishing exchange agreements with foreign medical societies, and directing his agents to subscribe to the best British, French, German, Swiss, Austrian and other foreign journals, Billings built his library—a collection of 124,000 titles in its own new building by his retirement in 1895—into the world's most complete medical collection. By the first years of the twentieth century, almost half of the library's acquisition budget was being spent on European publications.[18]

Even more important than his library was Billings' contribution to the field of medical documentation. Frustrated by the fact that the articles listed in the Royal Society's *Catalogue of Scientific Papers* were arranged by author, Billings started his own subject index of medical articles in 1874. In 1879 the publication began of his *Index Medicus*, a monthly classified list of the current medical literature of the world, based on the holdings of the Army Medical Library. A country still below European standards in most of its scientific research, the United States by the outbreak of World War I was, through the genius and energy of one man, the world's leader in medical documentation—a field whose strategic importance would dramatically increase with the introduction of chemical warfare.[19]

Compared to those in the fields of medical and agricultural information, federal government contributions to the documentation of other specialties were modest before World War I. The most important of these contributions lay in the efforts to centralize publication done by the federal government itself. Printing for the government, which had been done on commission by private printers since the founding of the republic, was put in the hands of the newly created Government Printing Office in 1861. During the following decades, the rash of federal legislation regulating industry of the Progressive Era placed more and more information in the hands of the federal government, and federal government publications, especially industrial statistics from the Department of Commerce, grew accordingly in volume. The federal government began in 1890 to print a *Monthly Catalog* of it publications, arranged by title. Purchase of the original documents listed in the *Monthly Catalog* was simply a matter of placing an order with the Superintendant of Documents in Washington. The *Monthly Catalog*, providing a continuous overview of the ever-widening world of government-collected data, quickly became the most important single acquisitions tool in specialized libraries of all varieties.

For the rest, progress in the documentation of pure and applied science in the United States before World War I resulted from professional societies' activities rather than from direct government aid. The *Engineering Index*, a monthly survey of the world's engineering literature, was started by the Association of Engineering Societies in 1884 and prospered from the country's sustained expansion. The large Engineering Societies Library in New York City grew into a true documentation center for its field, using the new technology of photostating for duplicating bibliographies and supplying translations for a fee. The American chemical industry, dwarfed by European—especially German—competition, managed to launch its own index in 1907, when the American Chemical Society started *Chemical Abstracts* as an English-language survey of the world's chemical literature in direct competition with *Chemisches Zentralblatt*, dating from 1834.

WORLD WAR I AND ITS AFTERMATH

Although World War I heightened perception of science's importance to national defense and created concern about the United States' dependence on foreign science and technology, it did not result in permanently increased federal support for scientific and technical information. In April 1917 America had an inadequate supply of optical glass (for range-finders and gunsights), its army had no gas shells or gas masks and its airplanes had neither machine guns nor flight instruments for combat.[20] Partially because of the United States' short involvement in the war, most of the new institutions that were set up to confront these inadequacies never became fully-budgeted parts of the federal establishment and failed to achieve the permanency of, for example, England's Department of Scientific and Industrial Research (1916).

The first efforts to confront the breakdown in the flow of foreign scientific publications into the United States originated not in the government but among the publications' most direct consumers: scientists, scholars and librarians. As early as November 1916 the American Library Association appointed a Committee on Importations to negotiate the problem of getting German-produced literature through the British blockade. Working through the United States Department of State, the Committee succeeded in the summer of 1917 in convincing the British Foreign Office to release a book shipment detained in Rotterdam. And in January 1918 the Committee secured for the American Library Association a State Department license under the terms of the Trading with the Enemy Act, which permitted the regular import of library materials. For the rest of 1918 the Committee acted as a clearinghouse for American research libraries, ordering German scholarly and scientific publications through neutral booksellers in Berne, Rotterdam and other cities.[21]

Of the federal agencies finally created to deal with the information emergency, the most important as a prototype for future federal technical information systems was the National Research Council's Research Information Service. The National Research Council, the first attempt in the history of the United States government to involve scientists directly in the nation's defense, had been formed by President Woodrow Wilson in 1916 as an appendage of the National Academy of Sciences. It had become apparent to Wilson that the Academy, dating from the Civil War, was too moribund to serve as a central science organization of a government threatened by a highly technological war.[22]

The mandate of the National Research Council, whose membership was drawn from universities, industry and the government, was to stimulate and coordinate research, both foreign and domestic, for war aims, and "to gather and collate scientific and technical information at home and abroad, in cooperation with government and other agencies, and to render such information available to duly accredited persons."[23]

To carry out this mission a Research Information Service was established early in 1918 with a central committee made up of the chief of military inteligence, the director of naval intelligence and a representative of the National Research Council. Following the precedent established by the Surgeon

General's Library and the Department of Agriculture, the Research Information Service set up its own overseas information supply system: In February 1918 two scientists were sent as scientific attachés to the American embassies in London and Paris to open branch offices of the information service in those cities; later a similar arrangement was made for Rome. Astronomer George Ellery Hale, the Director of the Mount Wilson Observatory, hoped at the time that the information service might "be considered as the pioneer corps of the Council, surveying the progress of research in various parts of the world, selecting and reporting on the many activities of interest and importance ... and disseminating it to scientists and technical men and to institutions which can use it to advantage."[24]   But the Research Information Service did not long survive the war, and the scientific attachés in foreign cities came home. Like its mother agency, the National Research Council, it was supported by a hodge-podge of emergency funding which lapsed once the crisis had past; the Council's original grants from the Carnegie and Rockefeller foundations were replaced by irregular funds derived from commissioning Research Council scientists to the military for specific programs. During the interwar years the Council lost most of its importance, though it remained a government agency and its executive secretary, Vernon Kellog, was interested in scientific bibliography. In the early 1920s he undertook to salvage the floundering *Concilium Bibliographicum*, the classified catalog of zoological literature published in Zurich, and was responsible for securing the *Concilium* a temporary reprieve in the form of a three-year Rockefeller Foundation grant. In 1923 he sponsored a conference at the National Research Council on the indexing and abstracting of scientific information; twelve years later, in the depths of the Depression, the National Research Council called another conference on the same topic.[25]

Improved scientific documentation was also one of the motives behind the leading role played by the National Research Council in the founding of the International Research Council, the organization intended to put an end to German scientific dominance in the postWorld War I world (see Chapter 1). Even though the United States rejected the League of Nations itself, the Department of State paid the dues of the National Research Council as its representative to the International Research Council throughout the 1920s. But as we have seen, none of the International Research Council's grandiose bibliographic and documentation projects was ever realized due to the objections of established American review publishers. In actual practice, the contribution of the National Research Council to improving American scientific and technical information during this period was very limited. Its most positive function in this regard was probably its role as a funding conduit through which the Rockefeller Foundation sent promising young American scientists to Europe to study on National Research Council fellowships.

BETWEEN THE WARS

The interwar years were in general a period of decreased government involvement in technical information, although there were exceptions in some specific areas. In the 1920s, for example, there was a brief flurry of interest in supporting science and technology in the Department of Commerce. Commerce Secretary Herbert Hoover, a mining engineer and one of the few men in the government with an active appreciation of science, tried unsuccessfully to start a national science foundation with private funds from industry. Only the Department of the Army, already involved with technical information through its Army Medical Library and the many hydrographic and topographic reports it published through the Government Printing Office, expanded its activities, launching a Technical News Service in 1929 for its air force.

In general, funds from private philanthropy had to provide the support for documentation which in Great Britain, and to a certain extent in Germany, was provided by the government. The importance of Rockefeller and Carnegie foundation funding in sustaining the National Research Council has already been mentioned. In 1926 a group of biologists tried to end American dependence on German botanical and zoological abstracting journals by founding *Biological Abstracts*. The Rockefeller Foundation switched its support from the Swiss-based *Concilium Bibliographicum* (for zoology) and absorbed the new American abstract's costs for the first ten years, ensuring *Biological Abstract*'s ultimate survival into a highly profitable enterprise.[26] In 1926 the Rockefeller Foundation also gave $25,000 toward the expansion at the Library of Congress of the national union card catalog describing the holdings of America's research libraries. In the same year, the Carnegie Corporation of New York gave the University of Chicago an endowment for a new school for library administration which would become a cradle for documentation research in the late 1930s.

Other philanthropies also contributed. Gifts from the estate of E. W. Scripps, the newspaper publisher, supported research done throughout the 1920s and 1930s in improving methods of delivering scientific information to users. In 1921 Scripps endowed a Science Service to help popularize science by making scientific news available to newspapers and wire services. The Service's staff, based at the National Academy of Sciences in Washington, also produced books and magazine articles of their own and after 1926 ran a series of radio programs on science topics of public interest. The Service was so successful that in the mid-1930s it laid the groundwork for expanding into Great Britain, establishing a London office and an organizing committee which included H. G. Wells.

After Watson Davis became Science Service's chief in the late 1920s, the Service also began to focus on improving methods of delivering scientific literature to research scientists, since Davis was convinced that such improvements were a precondition for strong science. In 1935 Davis established a Documentation Division within Science Service to concentrate exclusively on bibliography and the delivery of copies of documents to users. Interestingly, the funding for Davis' new Division inside the Science Service came from a source outside the Scripps empire, because the Division's mission was not considered by all the members of the Service's executive committee as being within its intended scope. The donor agency for documentation activities at Science Service was the American Chemical Foundation, endowed for the support of chemical research and education with funds it received through the mid-1930s from German patents seized during the First World War. The $15,000 made available to Watson Davis in 1935 by the Chemical Foundation permitted his Documentation Division to support research in new photoduplication technologies, language problems in scientific publication and bibliography, classification problems in science, and mechanisms for automatic retrieval of information. In particular Davis was able to support further work on the microfilm camera developed by Navy lieutenant Draeger, with the result that it, rather than Kodak's model, was chosen for the Paris Exposition of 1937.

By the 1930s the foundations provided virtually the only support for scientific information, because the Great Depression was, predictably, a time of dramatic cuts in public spending in general. Government revenues plummeted, and public interest in science declined: It has been suggested by scholars of the period that science itself was seen by some as one of the culprits behind the overproduction of the 1920s that led to the Depression.[27] To make problems worse for American libraries, the devaluation of the dollar by 40 percent in 1933-34 devastated subscriptions to foreign periodicals: At the Army medical library, for instance, the subscription list was cut from 2,041 in 1932-33 to 1600 in 1933-34.[28]

The long spell of austerity forced scientific and technical librarians to look for cheap alternative methods for collecting, storing and disseminating information. Interest centered on microfilm, which had been in use since the late 1920s and which dominated thinking about documentation by the mid-1930s. An initial problem was posed by American copyright law, which, strictly construed, made illegal the copying of even a few pages for scholarly use. A meeting in March 1935 between a joint committee of librarians and the Copyright Committee of the National Association of Book Publishers worked out a compromise known as the "Gentlemen's Agreement," allowing single copies for research use.[29]

By the time the Gentlemen's Agreement had been worked out, several of the federal government's technical libraries had become centers of innovation in the use of microfilm for the reproduction and circulation of expensive scientific and technical publications. At the library of the Department of Agriculture in 1934

Atherton Seidell and Watson Davis of Science Service began a copy service called "Bibliofilm" using microfilm. Bibliofilm proved such a success as a substitute for interlibrary loan that by 1937, after Bibliofilm was bought by Science Service, cameras were installed in the National Bureau of Standards Library, the United States Geological Survey Library and the Army Medical Library.

At a time when most libraries did not have microfilm equipment, Bibliofilm provided a much-needed service. Inevitably, as exposure to the new technology spread among librarians, many of them became interested in setting up their own microfilm laboratories. This interest was reflected in the programs of the various library associations: In 1936 the American Library Association held its first symposium on microphotography at its annual conference in Richmond, Virginia, and the following year there was a demonstration of microfilm at the Medical Library Association's annual conference. The need for a central facility for microfilm technology dwindled as the capabilities of individual libraries grew, and in 1941 the Bibliofilm service was dissolved.

By the spring of 1937 interest in microfilm was high enough to convince Watson Davis and his associates to found a separate organization, which they called the American Documentation Institute, specifically to focus on the development of microfilm as an aid to learning. Its start-up costs were defrayed by some money left over from the $20,000 grant to the Documentation Division of Science Service from the American Chemical Foundation; in 1938 it received $7,500 from the Carnegie Corporation and in 1938 $1,000 from the Rockefeller Foundation. Here certainly, the records concerning funding for scientific information support the conclusion of the historian of education Roger Geiger that "when the interwar period is viewed as a whole, the foundations appear as the most dynamic element in the research system."[30]

While the American Documentation Institute received no financial support from the federal government, the majority of the people involved in its founding came from various government bureaus and all of its ex officio members were government officials: the Librarian of Congress, the Secretary of Agriculture, the Commissioner of Education from the Office of Education, the Chairman of the Central Statistical Board and the Surgeons General of the Army, the Navy, and the United States Public Health Service.[31] Institutional members of the Documentation Institute were professional and scientific societies, foundations, and government agencies. During the Institute's first years, when it had taken over the running of Bibliofilm from Science Service, it was involved in the development of microfilm readers, cameras and services and the fostering of negotiations on the photoduplication of copyrighted materials.[32]

A number of the people involved in the Institute's founding were delegates to the World Congress of Universal Documentation in Paris in August 1937. When the United States government had accepted the invitation of France to participate in the congress, the Department of State had appointed the American delegation.   Watson Davis was a member of the organizing group of the congress and was head of the American delegation, which included among its nine members three representatives of government agencies—the Library of Congress, the Department of Agriculture and the Office of Education.[33]   The American exhibit at the International Exposition going on simultaneously with the documentation congress consisted of a complete microfilm laboratory.   A cooperative venture involving the American Library Association and the University of Chicago (with funding from the Rockefeller and American Chemical foundations), the laboratory exhibit won the Grand Prix, the exhibition's highest award (see Chapter 1).

Within a year of the Documentation Congress, enthusiasm for the new technology in the United States led to the founding of a journal specifically devoted to the use of microfilm in documentation: With $5,000 from the Carnegie Corporation, the American Library Association's Committee on Photographic Reproduction launched the *Journal of Documentary Reproduction* in 1938. Its first editor was Vernon Tate, head of a state-of-the-art microfilm laboratory at the National Archives.   Aiming specifically at librarians who wanted to know how to use the technology for bibliographic purposes, the journal also discussed technical issues in microphotography and reviewed the pertinent literature.   It continued under the auspices of the American Library Association until the war forced its cessation in 1943 (after the war its production was taken over by the Documentation Institute).[34]

In the United States, the growth of microfilm technology and its intensive application to documentation were born of the Depression and the need to reproduce expensive originals for multiple access.   Except for a brief period during World War I, the United States government had not shown any interest in general scientific documentation, limiting its involvement to mission-oriented agencies like the Department of Agriculture and the Surgeon General's medical library.   During the Depression, however, hard-pressed government libraries provided the sites for developing some pioneering documentation techniques. These new techniques were not originally seen specifically as conduits to foreign literature, but they would prove crucial in keeping American scientists supplied with foreign literature during World War II. They also laid the basis for a combined Anglo-American scientific intelligence effort that would affect the shape of postwar British and American government attitudes toward the relation between scientific information and national defense.

NOTES

1. A close rival was Germany, which had long held a commanding position in certain fields of scientific documentation, e.g., chemical information.

2. Bernard Houghton, *Out of the Dinosaurs: The Evolution of the National Lending Library for Science and Technology* (London: Clive Bingley, 1972), p. 21.

3. These words were spoken by Queen Victoria at the Institute's opening ceremony. Quoted in Peter Alter, *The Reluctant Patron: Science and the State in Britain 1850-1920*, trans. Angela Davies (Oxford: Berg, 1987), p. 64. The Imperial Institute was renamed the Commonwealth Institute in 1958 and moved to its present site in Holland Park in 1962.

4. Sir Harry Melville, *The Department of Scientific and Industrial Research* (London: George Allen and Unwin, 1962), p. 23.

5. Alter, *The Reluctant Patron*, p. 186.

6. E.M.R. Ditmas, "Special Libraries," *Royal Society Empire Scientific Conference 1946* (London: Royal Society, 1948), p. 707.

7. R. V. Jones, chief of British air intelligence during World War II, has reminded the author that this attitude was not exclusively British. He cites David Pritchard's *The Radar War: Germany's Pioneering Achievement 1904-45* (Patrick Stephens Ltd., 1989), where a description is given of a working class German flyer who is grounded early in the war by his aristocratic commanding officer after the flyer shot down five enemy planes with the help of airborne radar. The commanding officer considered the flyer's reliance on technology "unsportsmanlike" (p. 69). Jones, letter to the author, 5 May 1992.

8. Ronald W. Clark, *Tizard* (London: Methuen, 1965), p. 57.

9. These projects included investigating the use of selenium cells in detecting X-rays and problems of aircraft silencing and metal fatigue and determining whether alcohol could be extracted from artichokes. Clark, *Tizard*, pp. 62-64.

10. Idem.

11. R. S. Hutton, "The Documentation of Scientific Information among Scientists," *Royal Society Empire Scientific Conference 1946* (London: Royal Society, 1948), p. 691.

12. "Aslib Panel of Expert Translators," *Aslib Information, III* (March 1930), p. 2; and "Proposed Cooperative Translation Scheme," *Aslib Information, XXIX* (March 1939), p. 2.

13. Houghton, *Out of the Dinosaurs*, pp. 10-15. The National Central Library, set up in 1916 by the Carnegie United Kingdom Trust and supported by the central government after 1930, shared its stocks with a number of British libraries but was very weak in the sciences. It was eventually absorbed by the

National Lending Library for Science and Technology. See also D. T. Richnell, "The British Library and the Universities," in Keith Barr and Maurice Line (eds.), *Essays on Information and Libraries* (London: Clive Bingley, 1975), p. 133.

14. For Bradford's influence on documentation, see E.M.R. Ditmas, "Dr. S.C. Bradford," *Journal of Documentation* 4 (December 1948), pp. 169-74.

15. D. J. Urquhart, *The Principles of Librarianship* (Metuchen, NJ: Scarecrow, 1981), p. 28.

16. William Stevenson, *The Man Called Intrepid* (New York: Harcourt Brace Jovanovitch, 1962), p. 16.

17. For coverage of the early years of federal support for agricultural information, see A. Hunter Dupree, *Science in the Federal Government: A History of Policies and Activities to 1940* (Cambridge, MA.: Harvard University Press, 1957), chapter 8.

18. For the early years of the Army Medical Library, especially Billings' administration, see Wyndham Davis Miles, *A History of the National Library of Medicine* (Bethesda, MD: U.S. Department of Health and Human Services, 1982), chapters 1-10.

19. Unquestionably as a result of Billings' stimulus, the librarians of medical schools and teaching hospitals were the first special-interest group in the nation's newly organized profession of librarianship to split off from the mother body of the American Library Association. In 1898 these librarians formed the Medical Library Association.

20. Daniel J. Kevles, *The Physicists* (New York: Alfred J. Knopf, 1978) p. 118.

21. Arthur P. Young, "The American Library Association and World War I" (University of Illinois, Urbana-Champaign: Unpublished Ph.D. thesis, 1976), p. 30.

22. The National Academy published little, its *Proceedings* appearing only irregularly. As federal agencies acquired their own science bureaus, the Academy became increasingly superfluous and in 1915 the Carnegie Corporation refused it a grant partially on the grounds that it failed to advise the government. Kevles, *The Physicists*, pp. 43 and 111.

23. Dupree, *Science in the Federal Government*, p. 328.

24. Dupree, *Science in the Federal Government*, p. 313.

25. National Research Council, "Conference on Abstracting and Documentation of Scientific Literature" (1935), 48 pp. Quoted in Irene Farkas-Conn, *From Documentation to Information Science* (New York: Greenwood Press, 1990), p. 38.

26. William Cambell Steere, *Biological Abstracts/BIOSIS: The Evolution of a Major Scientific Information Service* (New York: Plenum, 1976), p. 67.

27. Dupree, *Science in the Federal Government*, p. 340, and Kevles, *The Physicists*, p. 237.

28. Miles, *A History of the National Library of Medicine*, p. 261.

29. Adhered to until the 1976 revision of the United States copyright law, the Gentlemen's Agreement permitted making only one copy at a time for scholarly purposes. It did not allow large-scale or even limited multiple copying of copyrighted materials. "The Gentlemen's Agreement and the Problem of Copyright," *Journal of Documentary Reproduction* 2 (January 1939), pp. 29-36.

30. Roger L. Geiger, *To Advance Knowledge: The Growth of American Research Universitites 1900-1940* (New York: Oxford University Press, 1986), p. 100.

31. Farkas-Conn, *From Documentation to Information Science*, p. 58.

32. The American Documentation Institute was renamed the American Society for Information Science in 1968 to reflect the organization's interest in all aspects of the information-transfer process. See Claire K. Schultz and Paul L. Garwig, "History of the American Documentation Institute: A Sketch," *American Documentation* (April 1969), pp. 152-160.

33. Other American delegates included representatives from the University of Chicago, the Carnegie Endowment for International Peace, the University of Michigan, and the Free Public Library of Monclair, New Jersey. See Boyd Rayward, "The International Exposition and the World Documentation Congress, Paris 1937."

34. See Pamela Spence Richards, "Information Science in Wartime: Pioneer Documentation Activities in World War II," *Journal of the American Society for Information Science* 39 (September 1988), pp. 301-306. In 1950 the American Documentation Institute assumed responsibility for the journal's republication as *American Documentation* until 1968, when its title was changed to *Journal of the American Society for Information Science*, reflecting the new name of the documentation institute.

3

National Government Support for Scientific Information in Germany before World War II

In pre-World War I Germany, with its confederate constitution, scientific and educational affairs had remained the province of the individual states; the imperial government in Berlin had consequently hardly faced the problem of scientific information. This changed somewhat under the Weimar Republic after 1919. Weimar continued in principle the federalized cultural administration of pre-World War I Germany. In practice, however, the economic crisis and foreign hostility to German science in the early 1920s forced the central government to extend some help to the scientific information activities of the beleaguered German professional organizations and commercial scientific presses. But massive government support and the imposition of government information control do not begin until the establishment of totalitarian government in Germany in 1933. For our purposes it is useful to divide the account into chronological sections, beginning with some background information about the old German Empire.

GERMANY BEFORE 1933

The information system on which German scientific preeminence was based before 1914 consisted of a mixture of private and public elements. Privately owned, massive review journals, such as the *Chemisches Zentralblatt,* and powerful commercial publishing houses, such as that of Julius Springer (founded in 1842), were sustained by a publicly and privately supported research library system unrivaled in the world.

In the course of the nineteenth and early twentieth centuries, the various German states had developed a decentralized research library network in which the task of collecting current scientific and technical information was split between two broad groups. On the one hand, making available research publications mainly in the pure sciences, were public institutions such as the two huge state libraries at Munich and Berlin and the libraries of the universities.

These facilities were funded by the states in which they were located and were open to the general public as well as to the universities' students and faculty. The largest of these libraries reported their new acquisitions to the Royal Library in Berlin, which subsequently announced them in its *Berliner Titeldrucke* (1892-).

The publications of the applied sciences, on the other hand, were collected mainly by Germany's burgeoning industrial research libraries, which received no government support. Some of these libraries were founded and developed by trade or technical associations, such as the Coal Mining Association's huge Bergbau-Bibliothek (Mining Library) in Essen, founded in 1880, and the library of the Verein Deutscher Eisenhüttenleute (German Steel Association) in Düsseldorf, founded in 1905. Others were maintained by single corporations, such as the immense libraries of the Bayer and Krupp organizations, founded in 1897 and 1873, respectively. These proprietary libraries had highly selective acquisition policies and served only the members of their own firms.[1]

Lying somewhere in between these two broad groups of libraries, but initially not so important as they, were the libraries of Germany's public technological universities, the so-called Technische Hochschulen. Mostly founded in the course of the nineteenth century near the seats of industry, the technological universities addressed themselves purely to training in the applied sciences. They did not gain equal status with the general universities until 1899, when they received the right to grant doctorates.[2]

Despite Germany's triumphs in the pure and applied sciences before World War I, no one in Germany, especially in the applied sciences, felt that this system of information delivery was adequate. The lack of technical publications in the general state and university libraries was loudly lamented, as was the narrowness of scope of the technological university libraries. The professional associations were dissatisfied with the textbook-oriented, restricted collections of the latter and called for a government-supported national central library of science and technology. Basic to many of the demands for reform was the sense that the establishment of technological colleges near the seats of industry rather than as faculties of the general universities had driven a wedge between the applied sciences, pure sciences and liberal arts that could have unhealthy consequences.[3] The Weimar period, following what the English prime minister Lloyd George called an "engineer's war,"[4] would see greater attention given the problem of scientific and technical information delivery and the role of the technological universities in the process.

The reputation of German science abroad had been dealt a heavy blow in October 1914, when 93 German professors, including such luminaries as Wilhelm Röntgen and Max Planck, issued a manifesto denying all German guilt for the war and, among other things, justifying the German burning of the library of Louvain University. In retaliation, the Royal Society of London removed all Germans and Austrians from its list of foreign members; the French Academy of Sciences dropped the signers of the manifesto.[5] The British naval blockade of 1915-1918 further isolated German scientists and caused critical gaps in their collections of foreign publications.

The most devastating effect of the war on Germany was economic. The reparations imposed on Germany by the Treaty of Versailles produced an inflationary spiral that so devalued the German mark that the purchase of foreign publications continued to be difficult right through November 1923, when a new mark, exchangeable for one trillion of the old marks, was introduced. Of approximately 6,000 foreign journals held by publicly funded German libraries in 1914, for example, only 1,700 were still being subscribed to in 1921.[6] In that year the Prussian State Library was able to renew its subscription to only 150 of the 2,300 scientific periodicals it had received in 1914.[7] A glimpse of the personal consequences these shortages caused German scientists is given by physicist Rudolph Peierls, who recalled in his memoirs that until shortly before he matriculated at the University of Berlin in 1925 an organization of student volunteers had worked in shifts in the university library *hand-copying* essential foreign books which the library could not afford to buy.[8]

The boycott of German science by the Allied and neutral scientists participating in the activities of the International Research Council complicated Germany's resumption of its prewar scientific relations with other countries. Brigitte Schroeder-Gudehus, author of the most thorough study of German scholarly relations during this period, has calculated that of the approximately 195 scientific congresses which took place between 1920 and 1924, 129 (or about two-thirds) were without the participation of either German or Austrian scientists.[9] Even the use of the German language by colleagues (such as Dutch and Scandinavian scientists) for whom German had been the international scientific language was forbidden at these congresses. The boycott extended even to articles of German authorship: Max Planck, as secretary of the physics-mathematical section of the Prussian Academy, wrote in a report on the situation in 1919:

> The most effective means used against the "domination" of German science is the exclusion of Germany from the international bibliographies, in which German scientific works are supposedly disproportionately represented. The establishment of international reviewing organs which are intended to drive out the German review journals, which "through collaboration and cooptation, have monopolized the entire scientific production of the world", has been especially effective.[10]

The boycott caused German scientists to look with greater interest on collaboration with Soviet scientists, who were also shunned internationally at this time, for like the scientists of the defeated Central Powers, Russian scientists had not been invited to join the International Research Council. German scientific relations with Russia dated back to the eighteenth century, leading in the nineteenth century to condemnation of the St. Petersburg Academy by Russian nationalists as a "German institution."[11] These relations reached a high point from 1922 to 1926. During this period a number of Russian scholars gave seminars at German universities: Mathematician P. S. Alexandroff, for example, went to Göttingen every year from 1923 to 1930, and from 1926 on gave regular lectures at the Mathematisches Institut, where a contemporary called his ideas "very important, very influential."[12] When in 1925 the Soviet Academy at Leningrad celebrated the two hundredth anniversary of its founding, the Verband der deutschen Hochschulen (Association of German Higher Education) lent major assistance in the preparations. German scientists of the highest rank attached importance to these exchanges: In 1923 a group including Albert Einstein, Max Planck and Adolf von Harnack, president of the Kaiser Wilhelm Gesellschaft, formed a committee specifically to promote contacts between German and Soviet scholars.[13]

The collaboration extended to the book trade: Profiting from over a century of experience in the East, German scientific and technical publishers exploited the Soviet push for technological development by bringing out special Russian-language editions of German journals. In the 1920s Ost Europa Verlag in Berlin published both *Germanskaia Tekhnika* (German Technology) and *Vostochno-evropeiskii Zemledelets* (East European Agronomist).[14] The Soviet government, in fact, established its own agency in Berlin to collect, translate and publish in Russian selected German scientific works. The Soviets' Biuro inoctrannoi nauki i tekhnologii (Bureau of Foreign Science and Technology) was active from 1921 to 1928 in importing into the Soviet Union a steady stream of current German works, including those of Einstein.[15] For much of the 1920s and 1930s, the German scientific information network was the chief route through which news of Western science was channeled to Eastern Europe and the Soviet Union.

However profitable the relations with the Soviet Union may have been for Germany, it was clearly in the interests of German science to resume normal relations with researchers in the more scientifically advanced countries of the West. A major feature of the isolation of German scientists during the immediate post-World War I period was their lack of access to English, French and American scientific journals. In 1920 two quasi-governmental agencies were established in Germany to deal with this problem. The better known, the Notgemeinschaft der deutschen Wissenschaft (Emergency Association of German Science)—which survives today as the Deutsche Forschungsgemeinschaft

(German Research Society)—set up an office in the Prussian State Library from which it tried to coordinate the foreign purchases of German scientific and scholarly libraries and help them avoid costly duplication. It also supplemented the librarians' budgets with its own funds. A national system for interlibrary loan launched in 1924 further reduced the need for foreign purchases.

Less well known are the efforts of the Reichszentrale für wissenschaftliche Berichterstattung, the national office for scientific documentation. Founded in 1920, the Reichszentrale was supported by the minister of the interior and administered by the Prussian Academy of Sciences, where it was housed. Its director was Karl Kerkhof, a fanatic scientific nationalist and the author of a book called *The War Against German Science* published in 1922. Kerkhof remained convinced of the persistence of a worldwide conspiracy against German science well into the 1930s and he devoted his life both to identifying cases of offense and, more usefully, to building new channels of access to foreign science for Germany's scientists.[16] The Reichszentrale, through pioneering use of photocopying technology, quickly became a clearinghouse for foreign scientific periodical literature. Kerkhof encouraged the publishers of Germany's great reviewing journals, which regularly received copies of foreign journals, to lend those journals to the Reichszentrale for photocopying for interested German scientists.[17] The activity of Kerkhof's photocopying unit, ultimately housed at the Technische Hochschule of Berlin in Charlottenburg, grew dramatically: In 1923 it supplied 6,440 copies and in 1938 174,000.[18]

Aid from foreign countries also helped fill the gaps in library holdings created by the war of 1914-1918. The Scandinavian countries donated their entire output of scientific publications, which had been stockpiled during the blockade when they could not be delivered to Germany. Switzerland sent gifts, and the American Library Association collected and sent duplicates from American libraries.[19] In assistance for German science libraries by far the most important foreign agency was the Rockefeller Foundation. Early in the 1920s the Foundation, working closely with the Notgemeinschaft der deutschen Wissenschaft, began to support German scientific institutions, generally by taking over the costs of their periodicals and specialized literature.[20]

A direct result of the British blockade and the postwar boycott was the ignorance of scientists outside Germany of research going on at German institutions. As Germany's exclusion from international science continued into the mid-1920s, a number of steps were taken in Germany to make German scientific accomplishments known to foreign scientists. The Deutsche Akademische Austauschdienst (German Academic Exchange Service), for example, was founded in 1925 specifically to encourage international connections for German academics. In the same year the indefatigable Karl Kerkhof launched a periodical called *Forschungen und Fortschritte* (Research and Advances) to publicize German science abroad, especially in neutral countries. Appearing fortnightly, *Forschungen und Fortschritte* contained articles on the latest German scientific discoveries, institutional news, and reports of congresses. Though written for a lay audience, it published articles by men of the stature of Max Planck, Max von Laue and Johannes Stark. It began to appear monthly in Spanish in April 1927 (as *Investigacion y Progreso*, but did not appear in either English or French at this time, as Kerkhof believed such translations would have supported "the not unsuccessful attempts of the English and French to advance their own tongues as the languages of science at the expense of German."[21] Kerkhof's efforts were supplemented by the foreign activities of Germany's private scientific publishers, notably Springer Verlag. In order to get into international circulation the work done by German mathematicians during the British blockade, Springer began to publish the *Mathematische Zeitschrift* in January 1918, nine months before the war ended.

Germany's scientific isolation came to an end after 1926, when German joined the League of Nations. The prestige of German science had not been substantially affected by either the war or the boycott, and it continued after 1918 undiminished: from 1918 to 1921, for example, Germans were awarded five Nobel Prizes in chemistry and physics. Einstein, the most famous scientist in the world, was a German citizen, after all; and when he received the Nobel Prize for his theories of relativity in 1922, it was the German ambassador to Sweden who accepted the award at the official ceremony for Einstein, who happened to be in the Orient at the time.[22] After Germany joined the League of Nations, German academics were more frequently invited to other countries. And when new institutions were planned abroad, such as the secularized Istanbul University or the Institute of Advanced Study in Princeton, New Jersey, their creators sought to appoint German scientists to senior posts. In 1932 Abraham Flexner, first director of the Institute of Advanced Study, appointed John von Neumann and Albert Einstein from Berlin.[23] Around this time the Rockefeller Foundation stepped up its support of German science, deciding in 1930 to provide funds for the building and equipment of a completely new physics institute at the University of Berlin.[24]

By the end of the 1920s, the reacceptance of German science was accompanied by the return of German scientific publishing to its prewar status. The publishers had to cope with persistent financial problems and with the growing rivalry of the United States in some disciplines, notably chemistry. But a survey conducted in 1932 by the German ministry of foreign affairs on the standing of German publications abroad showed that, although interest in German belles lettres had declined because fewer foreigners could read German, the high status of German science made the use of German scientific publications so essential to foreign scientists that the latter continued to learn at

least to read the language.[25] So German scientific publishing was kept in the
forefront by the excellence of German scientific research.

Two growing markets outside the west contributed to the financial health of
German scientific publishing. The Soviet Union was one of these markets. In
1925 Karl Kerkhof boasted, "The Reichszentrale has been successful since 1922
in securing the Russian market for German review journals, despite the great
efforts of the Allies to drive out German literature there as well."[26] Some
rather unscientific confirmation of Kerkhof's claim was provided by
mathematician Max Dehn. In 1940, when Dehn was in flight from the Nazis
across the Soviet Union, he inspected a library in Vladivostok during a train stop
and found that in the entire library there was but one shelf of mathematical
books—the "Yellow Series" ("Die Gelbe Reihe") published by Springer Verlag
and edited by Richard Courant since its inception after World War I.[27] The
only other important non-Western market was Japan, which was second only to
the United States as a purchaser of German scientific literature. In Japan the
fields of the natural sciences, medicine, mathematics, and law were dominated
by Japanese who had studied in Germany (one Japanese medical school still
maintained German-language lectures into the 1930s), and in the 1930s the
Rothacker firm in Tokyo was the most important book dealership in the
country.[28]

Some reports claim that by 1932 the sales of the firm of Springer were
greater than the combined total of all the other scientific publishers in the
world.[29] Certainly Springer in the early 1930s dwarfed other scientific
publishers throughout the world; and its success can be seen as evidence that by
the end of the Weimar period the sustained quality of German science had
repaired whatever damage had been done to its reputation by the defeat of 1918.
By the late 1930s, German science and its personnel in Germany were being
shunned again for political reasons. By this time, however, both the German
state and German industry had sufficiently strengthened the foreign scientific
information supply network set up during the 1920s to prevent a recurrence of
the isolation from Allied research that Germany had experienced from 1915 to
1918.

GERMANY 1933-1939

The scientific information policies formulated by the Nazis were full of
contradictions and affected some intellectual areas more than others. One
principle, however, ran throughout, namely, the need to purge German cultural
life—including science—of the influence of Jews and "Jewish thought." The
Law for the Reconstruction of the Civil Service of April 1, 1933, mandated the
dismissal of communists and leftists as well, but was mainly aimed at Jews,

who, although constituting less than 1 percent of the total German population, were said to have held 12 percent of the professorships.[30] All appointments in German schools and universities fell under the laws of the civil service, as did jobs of librarians in university and public libraries.

The law ultimately caused the loss to Germany of some 15 percent of its teachers and researchers, including 20 Nobel laureates forced from their university positions, of whom all but one ultimately left Germany.[31] The Civil Service Law of 1933 slowed German advances in those fields of the pure sciences such as physics and mathematics where Germany had owed much of her preeminence to Jews. By the end of that year, 26 percent of Germany's academic physicists, 20 percent of its mathematicians and 13 percent of its chemists had left their posts. [32] In physics alone, some of Germany's most internationally renowned researchers, including Albert Einstein, Max Born, Hans Bethe, Rudolph Peierls, Otto Frisch, Eduard Teller, Leo Szilard, Eugen Wigner, Victor Weisskopf and Lise Meitner, were ultimately forced to emigrate because of their racial origins.

The United States was the major beneficiary of the dismissals. Here the Emergency Committee in Aid of Displaced Foreign Scholars, a group of American academics under the chairmanship of the director of the Institute of International Education, was the main agency aiding relocation of the refugee scientists. The committee's principal financial support derived from the Rockefeller Foundation, which gave it $1,411,000 between 1933 and 1945.[33] British universities also found places for outstanding refugees. A group of British academics, who formed the Society for the Protection of Science and Learning, found appointments for scores of refugees throughout the British Empire, including India. The Society, of which Lord Rutherford served as president, was supported partly through the donation by the teachers at the London School of Economics of 3 percent of their annual salaries.[34] Of the group of refugee scientists who settled in Great Britain, 30 were by 1951 members of the Royal Society.[35] A number of Latin American countries, including Panama, Colombia, Venezuela, Chile and Peru, provided employment, with Ecuador alone offering 12 academic positions. Places were also found in Persia, Egypt, Iraq, Syria and the Scandinavian countries.[36]

The non-Western country affected most dramatically by the wholesale expulsion of German scholarship in the 1930s was Turkey, where the universities of Istanbul and Ankara stood ready to appoint refugee German academics. Such appointments were arranged through the Notgemeinschaft deutscher Wissenschaftler im Ausland (Emergency Association of German Scientists Abroad), a group organized in Zurich by dismissed German academics. Under the chairmanship of Philipp Schwartz, a pathologist formerly at the university of Frankfurt, the Notgemeinschaft initiated contact with the Turkish authorities through German and Swiss friends. By 1939 over 100 German academics had been placed in positions in Turkey.[37] Classes at Ankara and Istanbul were taught with the help of a translator, although the contracts signed by the Germans stipulated that they would do everything in their power to teach in Turkish after their third year in Turkey.[38]

The Soviet Union also took in some of the refugee scientists. F. Demuth, Schwartz's successor as chairman of the Notgemeinschaft, recalled in 1951 that the society had sent the Soviet Union a number of young physicists and biologists who continued their scientific work there until the signing of the German-Soviet nonaggression pact and the outbreak of the war in 1939. But he added that "of the 100 physicists who were sent to Russia from our lists, many were expelled and many more are missing. This weighs greatly on our conscience, but the situation was such that one could not be choosy when offers came in."[39] (The expulsions to which Demuth referred were the delivering up to the Nazis of scientists—and others—who had fled from them to the ostensible safety of the Soviet Union.)

Although the dispersion helped to spread the high standards of German science abroad, the scientific institutions in German declined markedly in their international reputation and those scientists who remained in Germany were likewise tarnished. In certain fields the dismissals and resignations in the mid-1930s removed Germany from consideration as a country whose scholarly production could be taken seriously in that area of research. Dutch physicist Hendrik Casimir recalled that "before the end of 1933 the University of Göttingen, the cradle of matrix mechanics and of much modern mathematics, had been reduced to insignificance. Berlin, without Einstein and Schrödinger and without younger stars like Wigner, von Neumann, Szilard and Fritz Landau, was losing much of its already slightly tarnished glory."[40] Other scientific disciplines were removed from the mainstream not so much by the loss of the scientists themselves as by radically altered emphases—genetics, for example, was reduced more or less to the study of race. And the disciplines in which new chairs and institutes were created, such as "the science of race" (Rassenkunde), inheritance (Vererbungslehre) and folklore, were of little interest to foreign scientists.

The altered quality of German scientific research was apparent to domestic observers as well. Within one year of the civil service laws, research at the universities had deteriorated so visibly that German industry was weighing the possibility of training doctoral candidates itself rather than run the risk of diminished competitiveness.[41] Industry's fears were certainly not groundless: Modern historians of German technology, pointing to the dependence of technology on physics and the other pure sciences, cite the civil service law as one of the causes of the radical downturn in the number of German patents granted after 1932—from 26,201 in 1932 to 16,525 in 1939.[42]

SCIENTIFIC PUBLISHING

National Socialist policies concerning scientific publishing were characterized by vacillation and inconsistent enforcement. The desire of the propaganda ministry to purge scientific journals of foreign and Jewish elements had to be balanced against the important role that the journals were seen as playing in maintaining the prestige of German science abroad and—most important—in drawing needed foreign currency into the Reich.

Early in the Nazi regime the authorities made clear, through the granting of large subsidies, the importance they attached to the continued strong sales overseas of German books and periodicals. In the early 1930s the price of German scientific periodicals had risen dramatically: the increasing size of the issues and the devaluation of the dollar in 1933 combined to make many German journals too expensive for the American library market. In the course of 1934 the committee on periodicals of the American Library Association considered countermeasures such as collective buying or even a boycott. After an anguished correspondence between Ferdinand Springer and Charles Harvey Brown, chairman of the association's periodicals committee, about growing American resistance to the high prices, Springer convinced the ministries of propaganda, education and finance of the threat to Germany's scientific prestige in foreign countries. Representatives of these ministries met with Brown in May 1935, and in late June the ministry of propaganda announced that as of August of that year the price of German books and periodicals would be reduced by 25 percent.[43] According to the law that took effect on 9 September 1935, and remained in force till 1945, government funds would be used to compensate the publishers for the reduced price. The administration of the subsidy was placed in the hands of the Wirtschaftsstelle des deutschen Buchhandels (Economic Office of the German Book Trade), a division of the Reichsschriftumskammer (Reich Chamber of Literature). The ministry of finance made 10 million marks available to the German publishing industry for that year to subsidize the sales of German journals abroad.[44] Export figures for the following year show an immediate rise in foreign subscriptions to the subsidized journals.[45]

At the same time, however, that the authorities were spending millions of marks to support the foreign sales of journals, they were pursuing policies which resulted in the loss of much of the prestige of German journals abroad. The emigration of German-Jewish scientists following their expulsion from the German civil service usually meant their resignation from their editorial positions. Though both Richard Courant and Max Born continued to act as editors for Springer for a few years after their emigration, after 1938 any Jewish contribution to or collaboration with a German journal was impossible. In 1938, for example, Ferdinand Springer—himself half-Jewish—was forced to ask the managing editor of *Zentralblatt für Mathematik*, then in Denmark, to remove from the masthead the name of Tullio Levi-Civita, who had recently lost his chair at the university of Rome as a result of Italian racial legislation.[46]

The restrictions went far beyond purging editorial boards. There was no legal basis for the ban on "Jewish literature" in the scientific press until the decree of 15 April 1940 ("Amtliche Bekanntmachung der Reichsschriftumskammer Nr. 70")[47]; nonetheless, from 1936 on, restrictive guidelines were issued by party officials responsible for particular areas of scientific activity. On 25 July 1936, for example, the Reichsleitung für Volksgesundheit (the Reich Office of Public Health) sent out a circular requesting that books by Jewish emigrants not be reviewed at all in the German medical press, and that review of books by other Jews avoid enthusiastic praise.[48] To assist editors in their vigilance, lists of foreign scientists whom the Nazis had (sometimes quite erroneously) determined to be Jews were circulated to editors by party officials.

The foreign scientific press was regarded with suspicion as a possible vehicle for "Jewish science." In 1938 the medical profession was told in a circular by the Reichsärzteführer (Reich Physician-in-chief) that "German doctors should only subscribe to foreign journals if these have Aryan publishers and editors."[49] The circular added that the physician-in-chief's office was in the process of establishing which foreign publishing companies were controlled by Jews. The ban on subscriptions would not, however, apply to companies led by those of racially mixed ancestry. Despite all of the party's admonitions, however, important Jewish works continued to be reviewed well into the war by some German scientific journals with international audiences. For example, volume 102 (1942) of the *Zentralblatt für die gesamte Neurologie und Psychiatrie* contains reviews of works by Maurice Pincus, J.L. Abramson, Nathan Einhorn, Theodore Abel, David Cohn and Benjamin Friedman.[50]

Ultimately, all contributions from authors who were not German were suspect. In 1935 Philipp Stöhr, professor of anatomy and dean of the medical faculty at the university of Bonn, wrote a series of angry letters to university officials, medical editors and the Börsenverein der deutschen Buchhändler expressing his outrage about the number of foreign authors found in German scholarly journals: "It is a very serious matter when German journals, which are important vehicles for the transmission of German culture, derive their intellectual content from abroad, especially from Russia."[51]

Stöhr's demand for restrictions against foreign authors was rejected by many colleagues: Professor Curt Elze of the university of Rostock wrote to Springer in protest: "We must do everything we can to unite "gesamt-deutsche [German, Austrian, Dutch, Flemish, Scandinavian and German-speaking Czech—*author*] authors in our journals, otherwise they will go elsewhere, as is already unfortunately the case with Scandinavian scientists. If non-Germans want to publish in our pages, we should welcome it."[52] The president of the

Börsenverein der deutschen Buchhändler wrote to the minister of education in the same vein: "50 to 70 percent of the production of German scholarly journals is exported. If we reject foreigners as contributors, we will lose them to other cultures not only as subscribers to our journals but also as contributors to our economy (chemistry, optics, etc.)."[53]

There were in fact no laws passed in Germany during the 1930s prohibiting the inclusion of articles of foreign authorship in German journals, and the extent to which editors of German scientific journals continued to publish such contributions varied widely. In the highly respected *Zeitschrift für physikalische Chemie*, papers by non-German authors declined from 61 percent in 1927 to 33 percent in 1937,[54] but the foreign contributions in other journals varied little if at all during the prewar Nazi years. Such was the case with the *Archiv für experimentelle Zellforschung besonders Gewerbezüchtung* (85 percent foreign in 1932, 85 percent in 1938) and *Foux's Archiv für Entwicklungsmechanik* (55 percent foreign in 1932 and 59 percent in 1938).[55]

But while the foreign presence remained strong in many German scientific journals throughout the prewar years, the contributions from Great Britain, the United States and the Soviet Union seemed to vanish almost entirely by the late 1930s, with articles from other countries, notably India, filling the void. In 1933 the highly esteemed *Die Naturwissenschaften* had included among its 133 main articles 2 by British and 3 by American scientists; in the 1939 issues there was none from either of these countries. Similarly, in 1934 the *Zeitschrift für Physik* published among its total 179 articles 5 from Great Britain and 2 from the United States but of the 206 articles it published in 1938 none was from Great Britain and only one was from the United States. The disappearance of Soviet contributions was even more dramatic: In 1934 the *Zeitschrift für Physik* contained nine articles of Soviet authorship and in 1938 none. The same journal published six articles from India in 1934 and eleven in 1938. In sum, while a number of German journals continued to publish foreign scientific articles at the end of the 1930s, they were no longer vehicles for the work produced by the important scientific centers outside Germany. And certainly Germany was no longer a conduit of Western science either to or from the Soviet Union.

However diminished the role of the German scientific journals, it is clear from the shelves of British and American libraries that international interest in German scientific publications remained strong in 1939. The United States Department of Commerce reported that of the $1.5 million spent by American institutions and bookstores on foreign books and journals in 1939, more than half was spent on German publications.[56] Moreover, when war conditions threatened to sever the supply of German scientific journals to Great Britain and the United States, the governments of both countries, as we will see, set up elaborate and expensive procedures to import these journals.

RESEARCH LIBRARIES

National Socialist rule undermined the function of the publicly supported research libraries upon which German science and scientific publishing had depended. Party control and regulation of these institutions was brought about by the centralization of their administration. The official end of Germany's cultural fragmentation and the elevation of Bernhard Rust to Reich minister of science, education and popular culture in 1933 shifted the focus of all research librarians to Berlin. From now on research library heads were no longer to be apppointed by the local states' cultural ministries, but by Rust. The longstanding but unofficial leadership position of Prussia in library affairs was taken over by the Reich, and the previously voluntary cooperation of some of the other states was now made mandatory. An example of this coordination was the fate of the old Prussian Advisory Council for Library Affairs, founded in 1907, upon which served the most eminent librarians of the day, including Hugo Andres Krüss, director of the Prussian State Library (formerly the Royal Library), as well as Georg Leyh of Tübingen. Aware of the need for greater research library coordination, the Council was in the midst of an ambitious library survey when it was nationalized in 1936 and found itself reporting to Rust's Ministry. As its participants sensed that they were being used as tools by the party to force library centralization, the survey lost its momentum and its results were never published.[57]

By no means all centralization measures were this unsuccessful, however. The transfer of the library agencies of the Notgemeinschaft der deutschen Wissenschaft to the Prussian State Library, with its huge bibliographic resources, was later conceded by at least one of the affected parties to be fairly logical.[58] The Notgemeinschaft's national exchange center (Tauschstelle), established in 1926 to encourage the national and international exchange of books, was in 1934 moved into the Prussian State Library, as was its Beschaffungsamt der deutschen Bibliotheken (Central Procurement Office for German Libraries), a clearinghouse for scholarly foreign acquisitions, run by Gisela von Busse. Real improvements were instituted in international library loans, an area in which German libraries had been exploited (it was claimed that in 1934 foreign countries borrowed fifteen times as many books from German libraries as from those of France and England combined, while frequently the books called for were available within the country of the requesting foreign library). After 1937 all international requests were routed through the Deutsche Zentralstelle für den Internationalen Leihverkehr (Central Clearinghouse for International Loans) at the Prussian State Library, which determined whether or not the requesting country itself held the particular title.[59]

Also moved to the Prussian State Library was the Auskunftbüro der deutschen Bibliotheken (Information Bureau of German Libraries), which, by providing the location of books in German libraries, was the linchpin of the widely admired German national interlibrary loan system.[60] Library education, which was beginning to include some discussion of documentation issues, was also standardized nationally. Whereas formerly state requirements and certification had varied, impeding personal mobility and encouraging discrepancies in practice, the rules pertaining to eligibility, education, and examination of academic and research librarians throughout Germany were standardized by a Ministry decree in 1938.

The most spectacular of the National Socialist state's efforts toward all-German library coordination was its extension of the Prussian union catalog to include (at least theoretically) the holdings of all the Reich's research libraries. The printing of the Prussian union catalog had been begun by Prussia in 1931, and by 1935 eight volumes had appeared, including the holdings of Prussian research libraries, the Bavarian State Library, and the Austrian National Library. In May 1935 the Reich education ministry ordered the expansion of coverage to make it the *Deutscher Gesamtkatalog* (German Union Catalog), this title starting with volume nine, letter "B." Altogether, with the assistance of Rockefeller funding, fourteen volumes were published before war conditions forced the suspension of publication.[61]

Although opposed by some as overambitious, and labeled by Georg Leyh, head of the Tübingen University library, as a "tribute paid by the libraries to the totalitarianisms of the time,"[62] the *Deutscher Gesamtkatalog* was long considered by many German librarians to have been the crowning achievement of the period. Its coverage was supplemented by the German book trade's annual trade list, the *Deutsche Nationalbibliographie*, which was begun in 1931 by the publishers' central library in Leipzig, and which in 1937 began producing printed catalog cards of its new accessions (called *Leipziger Titeldrucke*). Taken together, these catalogs gave Germany on the outbreak of World War II the most complete current record of its book and periodical output of any country in the world.[63]

While the tangible symbols of German librarianship such as the *Gesamtkatalog* were impressive in scope, it was soon apparent at the practical working level of the profession that the net effect of National Socialist library innovations was constrictive, rather than the opposite, and that the elaborate research library network was characterized more by what it kept out than by what it embraced. The first evidence of this constriction was in the area of personnel, with the forced dismissal of Jews and leftists mandated by the Law for the Reconstruction of the Civil Service in April 1933. The exact number of librarians affected is not clear, but it seems likely that several score must have lost their employment as a result (eight academic librarians were dismissed from the Prussian State Library alone.)[64] Although subsequent large-scale purges of librarians never took place under the Nazis, several directors of state libraries (in Stuttgart, Darmstadt, Dresden, Bremen, and Munich) were fired for political reasons between 1933 and 1935, and Heinrich Uhlendahl, head of the Deutsche Bücherei in Leipzig, was arrested briefly and released only after loud protest from the profession and the book trade.[65]

Harassment of dissidents continued, as Rust's Ministry tried to "coordinate" the profession by replacing recalcitrants with librarians who were party members. There must have been, at least initially, more than a few librarians sympathetic to the Nazis: at a librarians' convention in 1938, party member Rudolf Kummer, library consultant to Rust's Ministry, emphasized how important to the Nazi cause the work of some of the audience had been before 1933; these librarians' painstaking research into the genealogies of hundreds of German academics, authors, and publishers, according to Kummer, had been essential to the party's ability to eliminate Jewish elements from German cultural life so swiftly after taking power.[66] Several of the men with the best academic and professional credentials receiving appointments as library directors during this period were Nazis of long standing. Rudolf Buttner, head of the State Library of Bavaria from 1935 to 1945 and co-editor of the academic librarians' central professional journal, *Zentralblatt für Bibliothekswesen*, had been one of the first members of the party,[67] and Joachim Kirchner, director of the library of the University of Munich from 1941 to 1945, had also been a National Socialist before 1933, and was a protégé of party ideologue Alfred Rosenberg.[68] Both men held doctorates and were the authors of numerous scholarly articles.

It was Kirchner, who, at a librarians' convention in Darmstadt in 1933, first stated the importance of reforming the education of academic librarians so as to produce practitioners who applied "folkish attitudes to their perception of scholarship": It would be the task of these future generations of librarians to "direct the acquisitions policies of our research libraries so that they would reflect folkish points of view, buying as little foreign literature as possible, stressing instead valuable works sprung from the German spirit."[69] It went without saying—as Kummer would remark in 1938—that candidates for library training in the National Socialist state must themselves be members of the party or a party organization, a rule that was the more easily applied when admissions criteria to library schools were nationally standardized that same year.[70] The success of National Socialist "coordination" of the profession—at least in certain geographical regions—is indicated by a description in a 1946 survey of an (unnamed) German university library where only one member of its academic library staff received from occupation authorities the status *unbelastet*, or unincriminated by party affiliation.[71]

On the whole, however, Nazification of the library profession was far from complete: the "Thousand-Year Reich" was of too short a duration, and its educational policies pursued too indifferently by leaders distracted by more pressing military matters, to bring this about. Georg Leyh, for example, whom the National Socialists had forced from the presidency of the association of German librarians in 1937 after he publicly impugned the trustworthiness of the party, managed to survive as director of the university library at Tübingen without joining the party. Local attempts to force him out were consistently rejected by the Ministry in Berlin on the grounds of his stature in German librarianship. [72]

Reich-imposed controls on services to readers were complicated in Germany by the scattered pattern of research libraries at universities. The late nineteenth and early twentieth centuries had seen the proliferation and growth in Germany of scores of institute libraries to support the German seminar-oriented university curriculum. These special-subject libraries were funded and administered by their institutes independently of the main libraries of the universities. Acquisitions were controlled by the institutes' professor-directors, and daily administration was usually in the hands of a member of the institute's academic staff rather than of a professional librarian. [73]   Generally, the prestige, political power, and personal character of the institute's director were the strongest factors in determining the reaction of the institute libraries to Reich restrictions on readership and reading materials.

The restriction of the circulation of "undesirable" materials immediately mandated by the party in 1933 was probably more thorough at the central than at the institute library level, if only because of manpower constraints in the institutes. Certainly, conformity to party dictates on censorship was no easy matter, as a querulous 1935 *Zentralblatt* article by Hans Peter Des Coudres made clear. He pointed out that, while the Ministry banned the general circulation of Marxist and pacifist literature, it nonetheless insisted that forbidden materials that fell into a library's assigned collection area continue to be acquired, "since a successful scholarly campaign against bolshevik, Marxist and pacifist poison presupposes an acquaintance with the pertinent literature. "[74] The continued flow of "seditious" material raised the possibility of unreliable librarians themselves being politically influenced by the forbidden materials; to prevent this the Ministry decreed that the servicing of these materials be entrusted only to "the smallest possible circle of trustworthy professionals." Des Coudres offered two suggestions for the solution of the problem of cataloging forbidden materials. Either the catalog cards for "undesirable literature" could indicate that the books did not circulate, or they could be eliminated from the catalog altogether and the works be included only on the shelf list available to the librarians alone. He dismissed a decree of September 1934 ordering the creation of special catalogs for proscribed books as hopelessly time-consuming.

In practice, the identification and withdrawal of "seditious" materials from collections numbering in the millions were erratic. At the library of the University of Munich, for example, an "R" (for *Remota*, meaning that the book was on the shelves but not in the catalog) was stamped on the undesirable books, but frequently their cards remained in the catalog without any indication of the "R"-status. In the catchword catalog, the whole section under "communism" was removed, but numerous works by Jewish authors remained.[75]

The responsibility of librarians for determining who was eligible to read censored literature was regarded by the profession as particularly onerous. Certification of eligibility was given by local political authorities and could vary in format from region to region, yet woe betide a librarian who refused access to a party favorite or gave it to someone whose reliability came into doubt. (When forbidden materials were released for use, they were never permitted to leave the building because of the danger of photoduplication.)[76] Adding to the librarians' insecurity was the difficulty of determining exactly what was forbidden, since the supplements to the government's list of forbidden foreign literature were notoriously slow in appearing. Predictably, ethical considerations of censorship mandates are not found in the library literature of the Third Reich. National Socialist law, in any case, recognized no conflict here. Civil rights were not based on concepts of individual freedom but were defined and limited by the interests of the Volk. Thus the denial of library services to Jews in 1938 was seen as a logical extension of folkish philosophy: any participation of such individuals in German cultural life was dangerous and bound to lead to its degeneration.

In practice, librarians in research libraries implemented the provisions of the eligibility restrictions without much protest. In the Prussian State Library, for example, the distinguished orientalist bibliographer Oswald Cohen, many of whose publications bore the library's imprint, was denied access to the reading room after November 1938. When books were delivered to him at the circulation desk he was forced to read them standing up, despite his advanced years, while young Germans sat at the reading room desks.[77]

The policies of the National Socialists affected the growth of the research libraries' collections as adversely as they did services to their readers. Long before the devastations of the war, the damage to collections became evident. While it is difficult to determine what, if any, losses to research library collections resulted from the book burnings of May 1933,[78] it is certain that under the National Socialists forces were put into play that negatively affected growth patterns in research collections. Economic measures were used to implement policy goals: German research libraries had been living with severe budgetary limitations since 1914, but the Nazis elevated frugality—which, they claimed, "had made the Prussian state great in its time"—to the level of pious national duty.[79] Since the military defense of the Volk was the nation's highest priority, it followed that library collections focusing on science and technology would be favored at the expense of research libraries with general collections. (Typically, when in 1935 the state took over the functions of the Notgemeinschaft der deutschen Wissenschaft, which had previously sought to

develop all areas of research, including the humanities, it installed physicist
Johannes Stark as its president.)[80]

After 1933 there was an absolute decline seen in the quality and quantity of
German titles which librarians could draw upon for acquisitions even if funds
could be found: Joseph Goebbels' Reichsschrifttumskammer (Reich Chamber of
Literature), part of the Reichskulturkammer (Reich Cultural Chamber), had the
power after September 1933 to censor books before publication and to force
"undesirable" periodicals out of production by cutting their paper rations.
Moreover, bibliographers were cut off from "undesirable" German titles that
appeared outside Germany by the fact that the German national bibliography
published by the Deutsche Bücherei (which became state-owned in 1940) simply
did not list these materials. In fact, between 1933 and 1938 the only regular
view librarians had of the extensive overseas German press production was
through the accessions lists submitted to the Prussian State Library's *Berliner
Titeldrucke* by the Austrian State Library, although after the annexation of
Austria in 1938 even these accessions were controlled by the National Socialists.
From 1939 to 1944 the Deutsche Bücherei did send out to research libraries,
as an unofficial monthly supplement to the *Deutsche Nationalbibliographie*, a list
of forbidden books accessioned by the Deutsche Bücherei, but these titles were
not available to individual libraries and the lists themselves were not for public
consumption. Ultimately they included 5,485 titles.[81]

By the late 1930s it was increasingly difficult for German scholars and
scientists to keep in touch with foreign research, especially if they were based
at a university rather than at a Technische Hochschule or at a governmental
defense research institution. The policy of frugality limited all German
expenditures abroad that were not directly connected with military preparedness.
At the Darmstadt librarians' convention in 1933, Joachim Kirchner had enjoined
his colleagues to buy as few foreign imprints as possible.[82] Since the contents
of most of these publications were considered worthless by orthodox National
Socialists, and their purchase undermined the Volk's ability to fulfill its
"military destiny," it was not long before all foreign acquisitions were looked
upon with disfavor if not suspicion.

Libraries specializing in science and technology, whose contribution to
national defense was clear, were naturally favored at the expense of general
university libraries. Restriction of foreign acquisitions by university libraries
conformed with both government economic policy and ideology. Not only was
scarce foreign currency saved through the cancellation of foreign subscriptions,
but public access to foreign ideas was limited. In 1936 Josef Goebbels obtained
the power to prohibit the import of foreign publications, and from 1937 on all
orders for foreign publications placed by research libraries supported from the
public treasury had to be approved by a special unit of the Gestapo, operating
first at headquarters in Berlin, then in Cologne.[83] They were approved only

if the Gestapo were convinced that the publications were vital to national defense; if so, they would grant the foreign credits necessary for their purchase. These regulations were applied at the highest levels. Gisela von Busse, who directed the much-reduced foreign publications acquisitions unit for Germany's scholarly libraries run by the Notgemeinschaft der deutschen Wissenschaft, had personally to visit the Gestapo headquarters on the Albrechtsstrasse in Berlin to argue for the release of foreign credits for subscriptions.[84] While individual library directors were sometimes able to arrange for ad hoc methods of acquisition through exchange, foreign travel, or the good offices of friendly foreign librarians,[85] the years after 1933 represented a period of decline in foreign holdings for university libraries: Georg Leyh, director of the library of the University of Tübingen throughout the Nazi era, recalled that by 1945 foreign publications had attained the rarity of manuscripts.[86]

SCIENTIFIC AND TECHNICAL DOCUMENTATION

While general research libraries languished in Germany under the Nazis, a quite different scenario was unfolding for the Reich's scientific and technical libraries, both publicly and privately funded. Just as general research libraries were being most sharply restricted, the Reich's scientific and technical libraries were entering a period of unprecedented growth. To understand why the National Socialists, who were contemptuous of foreign science and technology on ideological grounds, could, in certain contexts, come to make it such a high priority, it is necessary first to examine the position of business in the Third Reich, for it was in this sector that the pressure for improvement in foreign information supply came. Historians of Nazism disagree about the extent to which big business was responsible for Hitler's rise to power, but there is a consensus that once the Third Reich was founded, the influence of industry on the government was infinitely greater than it had been during the Weimar Republic.[87] Evidence of the National Socialists' close ties to big business abounds: a few illustrations are the routine forwarding of the minutes of Hitler's secret cabinet meetings (Geheimer Kabinettsrat) to Krupp headquarters in Essen,[88] government subsidizing of I. G. Farben's synthetics industry through the establishment of high tariffs on imported natural products,[89] and, most dramatically use of prisoners from the SS's concentration camps as slave labor in private industry.[90]

Party ideologues may have been slow to recognize the importance of foreign science, but Germany's industries, fearing that the global economic crisis of 1929 would usher in a new period of isolation, had already taken steps to ensure its flow into the country. Pioneering in this area was the giant I. G. Farben cartel, which had been formed in 1916 out of six of Germany's largest chemical concerns, including Bayer and Hoechst, and whose general director, Carl Bosch, was a co-winner of the Nobel Prize for chemistry in 1931. In that year I.G. Farben had set up an organization named Chemnyco in New York City whose main purpose was to gather American scientific and technical publications and reports and dispatch them to Farben's Statistical Department in Berlin. The official purpose of Chemnyco was the handling of Farben's patent arrangements with firms in the United States, but in reality it operated as a scientific and technical intelligence-gathering unit, costing the mother company $84,000 per year. Chemnyco's subscription list ot American publications was sixteen single-spaced pages long; its journals alone cost $4,000 to obtain.[91] In its ten years of existence Chemnyco forwarded to Berlin information on subjects as diverse as synthetic rubber tires, Du Pont's nylon invention, and, later, progress in atomic research.[92] I. G. Farben's vast Statistical Department on Unter den Linden, to which technical reports and publications were sent from Farben subsidiaries the world over, operated during the Third Reich as a sort of giant technical and economic reference library for many agencies of the government, including the German High Command and the Gestapo.[93]

Similarly, Krupp used its American subsidiary in Wilmington, Delaware, Krupp-Nirosta, to expedite the flow of American technological information to its huge library back in Essen,[94] where by 1937 Krupp maintained a collection of 100,000 volumes, 13,500 reports and 750 journal subscriptions.[95] Herbert Tamme, wartime director of the Krupp technological library, was convinced that under the Reich his library was infinitely richer in current foreign information than any of Germany's public research facilities. Part of the abundance of foreign materials in the Krupp library during that period Tamme attributed to the restricted nature of its readership, giving the Gestapo no cause to worry about the "liberalizing" or "defeatist" effect of chance remarks in the British or American journals.[96]

Few German industries had the worldwide information-gathering networks of I. G. Farben or Krupp at their disposal, and pressure was increasingly put on the German government to improve the availability of foreign materials by the libraries of the technological universities. When the National Socialists came to power in 1933, they responded more readily to these pressures than had the Weimar regime. The logical base for expanding such operations was the technological university at Charlottenburg, a suburb of Berlin, which had the largest library of any technological university in Germany. In 1931 the Reichszentrale für wissenschaftliche Berichterstattung had moved its photographic unit from Unter den Linden in central Berlin to Charlottenburg to be able to process more quickly the requests it received for copies of the technical reports routinely deposited with it by technological research institutions throughout Germany. In 1932 the technological university library, under the direction of Albert Predeek, had begun publishing a catalog of foreign technical journals currently held in German libraries (*Verzeichnis der ausländischen Zeitschriften welche in deutschen und einigen nichtdeutschen Bibliotheken laufend gehalten werden*).

With the encouragement of industry and the new National Socialist government, a new Informationsstelle (information center) at the library began in the fall of 1934 to issue and circulate to industry reviews of the world's current periodical literature in certain areas that were not covered by existing means. Unlike other information centers, which announced the possession of titles, Predeek's unit circulated abstracts of their contents as well. By 1935, the information center on the Berliner Strasse in Charlottenburg was subscribing to 1,500 periodicals and was producing more than one hundred reviews every two weeks (or about 2,400 per year) in the areas of electrical engineering, air compression, machine tools, and woodworking machinery. The summary-type reviews, prepared by bibliographer-engineers, appeared more quickly than those in journals, and readers could have photocopies of the originals sent to them within twenty-four hours of their request's receipt. From its inception, this service was international in scope: the originals could be translated into any one of seven languages.[97] The Berlin Information Center must have been very efficient: a grateful British user stated at the International Documentation Conference held at Oxford in 1938 that he had been able to get from Berlin copies of practically any technical paper of any date of publication from any country in the world for fourpence a page plus postage.[98]

Although never formally designated as such, Predeek's unit came to operate as the de facto central technical documentation agency of the Reich, in part because of the role assigned by Nazi policy to the entire Technological University at Berlin-Charlottenburg. After the party's initial neglect of science had been changed by pressure from industry into a drive to harness research to defense production, a Reich research council was set up in 1937 with the encouragement of Hitler, Göring and Army Chief of Staff Wilhelm Keitel to coordinate all research being done in Germany. (Some efforts along this line had already been made in 1934 by centralizing the control of all the universities, previously in the hands of the states, under the Reich minister of science and education.) The research council's first president, General Karl Becker, the first general on active duty ever to have been named to the Prussian Academy of Science, was, besides being chief of the Heereswaffenamt (Army Ordnance), also a professor of ballistics and dean of the new faculty of defense science founded at Berlin-Charlottenburg in 1935.[99]

The Reich research council did not ultimately achieve its goals, but Becker greatly increased the prestige of the Berlin technological university within the party: a new building complex for the new military science faculty was undertaken as part of Albert Speer's grandiose plans for the whole capital, with Hitler himself laying the cornerstone in November 1937. Although never completed (in 1942 the last construction workers were conscripted), the project made of the Berlin technological university the visible symbol of defense research in the Reich. Education Minister Rust even saw in Becker's new faculty the bridge that in the Nazi state would span the long-deplored gap between the applied sciences and the liberal arts, and he announced at the ground-breaking ceremonies that Berlin-Charlottenburg would be the Reich's "universal technological university."[100] In this context, with its strategic importance recognized as party policy, the library flourished, and by 1943 its collection had grown to a quarter of a million volumes and 100,000 dissertations.[101]

The same increasing emphasis on defense-related technology that led to the Nazis' build-up of the complex at Berlin-Charlottenburg provided an impetus to the budding German documentation movement. In fact, the National Socialists' ultimate recognition of the importance of documentation to the winning of the war united efforts that had hitherto come from several different organizations. Work toward improved coordination of technical information communication in Germany had originated in the Deutscher Normenausschuss (German Standards Association), the German member of the International Standards Organization. Active in German industry since its founding in 1917, the German Standards Association had set up a committee on professional library standards (Fachnormenausschuss für Bibliothekswesen) in 1927, under the chairmanship of Hugo Andres Krüss, director of the Prussian State Library.[102]

The 1930s witnessed a quickening of organized documentation activities in Germany as in Great Britain and the United States—and the end of the decade saw increased government involvement in and support for these efforts in Germany. In 1935 the German Standards Association joined Paul Otlet's International Institute for Documentation so that Krüss' committee on professional library standards could represent German interests in the documentation organization. Some idea of the importance given to the committee's activities by the National Socialist government is conveyed by the large, high-level delegation sent to the 1937 World Congress of Documentation in Paris, where Krüss shared the podium with H. G. Wells and gave an address on the "Domination of Knowledge." Present at the Paris conference also were representatives of Goebbels' Reich Chamber of Literature (Reichsschrifttumskammer), the Reich Economic Chamber (Reichswirtschaftskammer), the Reich Ministry of Education (Reichsministerium für Wissenschaft, Erziehung und Volksbildung), the Reich Archives, and the German Chemical Society. Acting on behalf of the highest government cultural and economic authorities, the German delegation extended its country's invitation to the international organization to hold its 1940 meeting in Germany in connection with the 500-year Gutenberg Jubilee (the 1940 conference, cancelled because of the war, was supposed to be held in Frankfurt, Mainz, Berlin and Leipzig during the first two weeks of August).[103]

Within Germany, the activities of the committee on professional library standards were multiplying. In 1937 the German Standards Association bulletin, *DIN Mitteilungen*, announced that "amongst the tasks imposed by the Reich government on German technology and industry, technical literature and documentation play a special role. The authorities make it very clear that everything must be done to achieve the greatest possible improvements through cooperative efforts."[104] In the same year the journal announced that because of the stress laid by member industrial firms on the importance of documentation to their work, "the German Standards Association feels obligated in the future to devote much more space in the *DIN Mitteilungen* to documentation matters."[105] As its responsibilities multiplied, the Committee on Professional Library Standards was broken down into task groups for classification, physical standards for journal production, cooperation between bibliographies and review journals, cooperation between information centers, and photoreprography (not established until 1940).

Fritz Prinzhorn, library director of the technological university of Danzig and one of the key figures in documentaton during the Reich, served as chairman of additional task groups for journal administration and for indexing of foreign and difficult-to-obtain technical journals. The main goal of the latter task group was to be the creation of subject-field union catalogs of technical periodicals. By 1937 Prinzhorn was able to claim that the journals in certain fields, such as electrical engineering and aerodynamics, were already fully indexed, abstracted and circulated, but he urged the establishment of more information centers like that at Berlin-Charlottenburg. In 1940, despite the outbreak of the war in the preceding September, Prinzhorn's indexing task force was able—in cooperation with the German Chemical Society (Deutsche Chemische Gesellschaft)—to publish a union catalog of journals in chemistry and related fields.

In sum, then, Germany entered the war with a well-organized apparatus for the evaluation and circulation of both domestic and foreign scientific and technical literature. This apparatus, unlike that of Great Britain, had not been forged so much out of the fear of falling behind foreign science as from a determination not to relive the isolation of the period of World War I and immediately thereafter. The Germans' scientific information supply system was later strengthened by the National Socialists' recognition of the importance of scientific documentation to military development. Equally important, the German government made no effort to control the publications of German scientists, including the physicists who were in the middle of a series of dramatic discoveries about atomic fission. Even though physicist Paul Hartech had notified the German War Ministry in April 1939 that uranium fission could make possible "an explosion which is many orders of magnitude more effective than the present one,"[106] publication of experimental results of atomic fission remained open. Another German scientist, Siegfried Flügge, even claimed after the war that he had intentionally published an article in the summer of 1939 in *Die Naturwissenschaften* to warn the world that German scientists were working on a chain reaction—a warning that was quickly picked up by the British.[107] So the information system that the Nazis had inherited and then streamlined to aid their own military buildup would also help the rest of the world to develop defenses against German aggression.

NOTES

1. Norbert Fisher, "Die Spezialbibliotheken," in Georg Leyh, ed., *Handbuch der Bibliothekswissenschaft*, 2nd ed. (Wiesbaden: Harrassowitz, 1961), vol. 2, pp. 603-604.

2. Karl-Heinz Ludwig, *Technik und Ingenieure im Dritten Reich* (Düsseldorf: Droste Verlag, 1974), p. 24.

3. Paul Trommsdorff, "Die Bibliotheken der technischen Hochschulen," in Fritz Milkau, ed., *Handbuch der Bibliothekswissenschaft*, 1st ed. (Leipzig: Harrassowitz, 1933), vol. 2, pp. 514-519.

4. Ludwig, *Technik und Ingenieure im Dritten Reich*, p. 32.

5. Daniel J. Kevles, *The Physicists* (New York: Alfred J. Knopf, 1978), p. 141.

6. Georg Leyh, "Die deutschen Bibliotheken von der Aufklärung bis zur Gegenwart," in Leyh, ed., *Handbuch der Bibliothekswissenschaft*, vol. 3, part 2, p. 333.

7. Brigitte Schroeder-Gudehus, *Les Scientifiques et la Paix* (Montreal: Presses de l'Université de Montréal, 1978), p. 236.

8. Rudolf Peierls, *Bird of Passage: Recollections of a Physicist* (Princeton: Princeton University Press, 1985), p. 20.

9. Schroeder-Gudehus, *Les Scientifiques et la Paix*, p. 133.

10. Reinhard Sigmund-Schultze, "Kerkhofs Reichszentrale," *Spektrum* 11 (1988), p. 30.

11. Alexander Vucinich, *Empire of Knowledge: The Academy of Sciences of the USSR 1917-1970* (Berkeley: University of California Press, 1984), p. 43.

12. Constance Reid, *Hilbert-Courant* (New York: Springer, 1986), p. 320.

13. The committee was called the Westphal Committee. See Gerd Voigt, *Otto Hoetzsch 1876-1946: Wissenschaft und Politik im Leben eines deutschen Historikers* (East Berlin, 1978). Quoted in Michael Burleigh, *German Turns Eastward: A Study of Ostforschung in the Third Reich* (Cambridge:

Cambridge University Press, 1988), p. 33. Brigitte Schroeder-Gudehus has pointed out that the anti-Western orientation of many German scientists during the boycott period was a combination of hurt pride and a desire to distance German science from what was seen as the servile, bourgeois, liberal-democratic policies of the Weimar Republic (p. 294).

14. Werner Keller, *East Minus West Equals Zero: Russia's Debt to the Western World 862-1962* (New York: G. P. Putnam, 1962), p. 199.

15. A. I. Mikhailov, A. I. Chernyi, and R. S. Giliarevskii, *Scientific Communications and Informatics* (Arlington, VA: Information Resources Press, 1984), p. 258.

16. Karl Kerkhof, *Der Krieg gegen die deutsche Wissenschaft: Eine Zusammenstellung von Kongressberichten und Zeitungsmeldungen* (Wittenberg, 1922). For Kerkhof's tireless campaign for a counterboycott of Allied science, see Schroeder-Gudehus, *Les Scientifiques et la Paix*, p.253.

17. Reinhard Sigmund- Schultze, "Kerkhofs Reichszentrale," p. 436.

18. Leo Stern, ed., *Die Berliner Akademie in der Zeit des Imperialismus* (Berlin: Akademie Verlag, 1979), p. 390.

19. Ernst Mehl and Kurt Hannermann, *Deutsche Bibliotheksgeschichte* (Berlin: Eric Schmidt, 1951), p. 372.

20. Kristie Macrakis, "The Rockefeller Foundation and German Physics under National Socialism," *Minerva* 27 (Spring 1989), p. 35.

21. Sigmund-Schultze, "Kerkhofs Reichszentrale," p.31.

22. Brigitte Schroeder-Gudehus, *Les Scientifiques et la Paix*, p. 261.

23. Abraham Flexner, *I Remember* (New York: Simon and Schuster, 1940), p. 385.

24. Kristie Macrakis, "The Rockefeller Foundation and German Physics under National Socialism," p. 38.

25. Paul Hövel, "Die Wirtschaftsstelle des deutschen Buchhandels," *Buchhandelsgeschichte* 1 (1984), p. B5.

26. Sigmund-Schultze, "Kerkhofs Reichszentrale," p. 30.

27. Reid, *Hilbert-Courant*, p. 432. Dehn did not specify which library he visited in Vladivostok, but the only postsecondary institution in the city at that time was the small Far Eastern University (Dal'nevostochnyi Universitet), which emphasized technology. See the *Bolshaia Sovetskaia Entsiklopediia* (1st ed.), vol. 11 (1930), p. 555.

28. Hövel, "Die Wirtschaftsstelle des deutschen Buchhandels," p. B12.

29. Tom Bower, *Maxwell: The Outsider* (London: Aurum, 1988), p. 28.

30. Edward Hartshorne, *The German Universities and National Socialism* (London: Allen and Unwin, 1937), p. 163.

31. Alan Beyerchen, *Scientists Under Hitler* (New Haven, CT: Yale University Press, 1977), p. 47.

32. Beyerchen, *Scientists Under Hitler*, 44.

33. Demuth, "Die Notgemeinschaft der deutschen Wissenschaftler im Ausland," *Deutscher Rundschau* (July 1951), p. 613.

34. Idem.

35. Demuth, "Die Notgemeinschaft der deutschen Wissenschaftler im Ausland", p. 615.

36. Ibid., p. 614.

37. Idem.

38. Heinrich Becker, Hans-Joachim Dahms, and Cornelia Wegeler (eds.), *Die Universität Göttingen unter dem Nationalsozialismus* (München: K. G. Saur, 1987), p. 95. For an exhaustive treatment of the German intellectual emigration to Turkey, see   Horst Widmann, *Exil und Bildungshilfe: Die deutschsprachige Emigration in Türkei nach 1933* (Bern: Herbert Lang, 1973).

39. Demuth, "Die Notgemeinschaft der deutschen Wissenschaftler im Ausland," p. 615.

40. Hendrik Casimir, *Haphazard Reality: Half a Century of Science* (New York: Harper and Row, 1983), p. 194.

41. Beyerchen, *Scientists under Hitler*, p. 70.

42. Karl-Heinz Ludwig, *Technik und Ingenieure im Dritten Reich* (Düsseldorf: Droste Verlag, 1974), pp. 211, 227.

43. File B22a, Springer Verlag Archives, Heidelberg.

44. Hövel,"Die Wirtschaftsstelle des deutschen Buchhandels," p. B10.

45. "Jahresbericht 1936/37," *Vertrauliche Mitteilungen der Fachschaft Verlage* 22 (1937), pp. 3-8. Quoted in Michael Knoche, "Wissenschaftliche Zeitschriften in nationalsozialistisichen Deutschland," in Monika Estermann and Michael Knoche, eds., *Von Göschen bis Rowohlt: Zur Geschichte des deutschen Verlagswesen* (Wiesbaden: Harrassowitz, 1990), p. 263.

46. Reid, Hilbert-Courant, p. 432.

47. Published in *Börsenblatt für das deutschen Buchhandel* of 23 March 1940. Scientific authors did not have to belong to the Reichsschriftumskammer and thus did not have to conform to the 1933 editorial laws prohibiting "non-Aryan writings" (*Reichsgesetzblatt 1933*, Part I, p. 713). See Michael Knoche, "Wissenschaftliche Zeitschriften in nationalsozialistischen Deutschland," p. 271.

48. File 1. 18. 3, Springer Verlag Archives, Heidelberg.

49. Idem.

50. Knoche, "Wissenschaftliche Zeitschriften in nationalsozialistischen Deutschland", p. 272f.

51. File 1. 18. 3, Springer Verlag Archives, Heidelberg.

52. Idem.

53. Idem.

54. Thomas Hapke, "Die Zeitschrift für physikalische Chemie, Stöchiometrie und Verwantschaftslehre und ihre Nachfolger". Unpublished thesis, Fachhochschule für Bibliotheks- und Dokumentationswesen, Köln, 1987. Quoted in Knoche, "Wissenschaftliche Zeitschriften in nationalsozialistischen Deutsland", p. 268.

55. Knoche, "Wissenschaftliche Zeitschriften in nationalsozialistischen Deutschland," p. 268.

56. U.S. Office of Alien Property Custodian, "Report to the President on the Periodical Republication Program" (Washington, D.C., 1945), p. 3, mimeographed copy.

57. Marta Dosa, *Libraries in the Political Scene* (Westport CT: Greenwood Press, 1974), p. 75f.

58. Gisela von Busse, interview with the author in Bad Godesberg, Germany, 23 August 1982. See also her *Struktur und Organisation des wissenschaftlichen Bibliothekswesen in der Bundesrepublik Deutschlands* (Wiesbaden: Harrassowitz, 1977), p. 516.

59. Rudolf Kummer, "Das wissenschaftliche Bibliothekswesen im national-sozialistischen Deutschland," *Zentralblatt für Bibliothekswesen* 55 (September/October 1938), p. 409.

60. In 1935 the English expert John H. P. Pafford labeled it the best in the world. See Dosa, *Libraries in the Political Scene*, p. 74.

61. Pamela Spence Richards, "Aryan Librarianship: Academic and Research Libraries under Hitler," *Journal of Library History* (1984): 242.

62. Georg Leyh, *Die deutschen wissenschaftlichen Bibliotheken nach dem Kriege* (Tübingen: J.C.B. Mohr, 1947), p. 27.

63. *Encyclopedia of Library and Information Science* (New York: M. Dekker, 1968-1983), vol. 9, pp. 419-445, s.v. "German Library System of the Present—Federal Republic of Germany," by Hermann Fuchs.

64. Dosa, *Libraries in the Political Scene*, p. 59. An extensive list of dismissed personnel is in Erwin Marks, "1945: Eine Wende in unserem Bibliothekswesen," *Der Bibliothekar* 5 (May 1975), pp. 289-296. See also the appendices of Walter Schochow, *Die Preussische Staatsbibliothek 1918-1945* (Berlin: Preussischer Kulturbesitz, 1989).

65. Erwin Marks, "1945: Eine Wende," p. 292, and Georg Leyh, *Die deutschen wissenschaftlichen Bibliotheken*, p. 469.

66. Kummer, "Das wissensenschaftliche Bibliothekswesen im nationalsozialistischen Deutschland," p. 407.

67. Georg Leyh, "Die deutschen Bibliotheken von der Aufklärung bis zur Gegenwart," *Handbuch der Bibliothekswissenschaft* (Wiesbaden: Harrassowitz, 1957), vol. 3, part 2, p. 378.

68. Ladislaus Buzàs, *Geschichte der Universitätsbibliothek München* (Wiesbaden: Ludwig Reichert, 1972), p. 183.

69. Joachim Kirchner, "Schrifttum und wissenschaftliche Bibliotheken in Nationalsozialistischen Deutschland," *Zentralblatt für Bibliothekswesen* 50 (August/September 1933), p. 524.

70. Kummer, "Das wissenschaftliche Bibliothekswesen", p. 412. But the exclusion of non-Nazis was not total: Antje Bultmann Lemke, later a professor of information studies at Syracuse University, was admitted to the University of Leizpig library school during the war without proof of party membership, largely because it was too burdensome for the authorities in Leipzig to corroborate her statements with party officials in her birthplace, Jena. Interview with the author, Syracuse, New York, 1 June 1982.

71. Leyh, *Die deutschen wissenschaftlichen Bibliotheken*, p. 31.

72. Leyh, *Handbuch der Bibliothekswissenschaft*, p. 469.

73. J. Periam Danton, *Book Selection and Collection: A Comparison of American and German University Libraries* (New York: Columbia University Press, 1963), p. 43.

74. Hans Peter Des Coudres, "Das verbotene Schrifttum und die wissenschaftlichen Bibliotheken," *Zentralblatt für Bibliothekswesen* 52 (September/October 1935), pp. 460 ff.

75. Buzàs, *Geschichte der Universitätsbibliothek München*, p. 179.

76. Des Coudres, "Das verbotene Schrifttum," p. 468f.

77. Walter Schochow, *Die Preussischer Staatsbibliothek 1918-1945* (Berlin: Preussischer Kulturbesitz, 1989), p. 45.

78. Ladislaus Buzàs implies that reports of book burnings in scholarly libraries are exaggerated or wholely fabricated. Buzàs, *Geschichte der Universitätsbibliothek München*, p. 178n.

79. Kirchner, "Schriftum und wissenschaftliche Bibliotheken", p. 523.

80. Mehl and Hannermann, *Deutsche Bibliotheksgeschichte*, p. 374.

81. Heinrich Uhlendahl, "Die Deutsche Nationalbibliographie nach dem Kriege," *Zentralblatt für Bibliothekswesen* 63 (May/June 1949), p. 276. An indication of how rich the diversity of thoses titles was is found in Richard Cazden, *German Exile Literature in America 1933-1950* (Chicago: American Library Association, 1970).

82. Kirchner, "Schrifttum und wissenschaftliche Bibliotheken", p. 521.

83. Georg Leyh, "Die deutschen Bibliotheken von der Aufklärung bis zur Gegenwart," in *Handbuch der Bibliothekswissenschaft*, 2nd. ed. (1957), vol. 3, part 2, p. 471.

84. Interview with Dr. Gisela von Busse, Bad Godesberg, 23 August, 1982.

85. Leyh, "Die deutschen Bibliotheken von der Aufklärung bis zur Gegenwart", p. 471.

86. Leyh, *Die deutschen wissenschaftlichen Bibliotheken*, p. 13.

87. Henry Turner, ed., *Nazism and the Third Reich* (New York: Quadrangle, 1972), chapter 4.

88. William Manchester, *The Arms of Krupp, 1587-1968* (Boston: Little, Brown, 1964), p. 406.

89. Richard Sasuly, *I.G. Farben* (New York: Boni and Gaer, 1947), p. 111.

90. Manchester, *The Arms of Krupp*, p. 492.

91. David Kahn, *Hitler's Spies: German Military Intelligence in World War II* (New York: Macmillan, 1978), p. 87.

92. Sasuly, *I. G. Farben*, p. 277.

93. Joseph DuBois, *The Devils' Chemists* (Boston: Beacon Press, 1952), p.58.

94. Manchester, *The Arms of Krupp*, p. 406.

95. Heinz Gomoll, "Die Werkbücherei der Fried. Krupp A.G. in Essen," *Zentralblatt für Bibliothekswesen* 54 (1937), p. 194.

96. Telephone interview with Herbert Tamme. Fort Lauderdale, Florida, 31 December 1982.

97. Albert Predeek, "Die Informationsstelle für technisches Schriftum in der Bibliothek der Technischen Hochschule Berlin," in *Proceedings of the Fortieth Anniversary Congress, 1935* (Copenhagen: International Institute of Documentation, 1935), preface, pp. 3-5.

98. J. Edwin Holstrom, "Bibliographical Tools from the Point of View of the User," *Transactions of the Fourteenth Conference of the International Federation of Documentation, 1938* (The Hague: International Federation of Documentation, 1938), p. 31.

99. Ludwig, *Technik und Ingenieure im Dritten Reich,*, pp. 217-219.

100. Ibid., p. 221.

101. Norbert Fisher, "Die Spezialbibliotheken," in Georg Leyh, ed., *Handbuch der Bibliothekswissenschaft*, 2nd. ed. (Wiesbaden: Harrassowitz, 1961), vol. 2, p. 601.

102. Mariane Buder, *Das Verhältnis von Dokumentation und Normung von 1927 bis 1945 in nationaler und internationaler Hinsicht* (Berlin: Institut für Normung, 1976), p. 21.

103. *Dokumentation und Arbeitstechnik* (May 1939): 1.

104. *DIN Mitteilungen* 20 (1937): 236.

105. Ibid., p. 365.

106. Robert Chadwell Williams, *Klaus Fuchs, Atom Spy* (Cambridge MA: Harvard University Press, 1987), p. 37.

107. Siegfried Flügge claimed to R. V. Jones after the war that this had been his intention in publishing the article. James Tuck, a physicist and an associate of Jones in British intelligence, saw the article in July 1939 and

recognized its implications.   See R. V. Jones, *Reflections on Intelligence* (London: Heinemann, 1989), p. 242.

4

The Allied Wartime Supply System for Enemy Scientific Information

GREAT BRITAIN 1939-1942

In Chapter 2 we looked at Britain's strong prewar position in scientific documentation. The outbreak of war in 1939 wrought havoc on the flow of scientific information to that country, and by the summer of 1940 German air raids on England were taking their toll on some of its most important scientific libraries. The actual damage done by aerial bombardment was grave, despite the measures for preservation and defense taken by some library administrators. The Science Museum Library, for example, had already evacuated 20,000 volumes to Hampshire by September 1939, and, by the end of the war, had evacuated 60,000 more.[1] All in all, over one million volumes in British libraries were destroyed by air attack during the war. The Science Museum Library and the Patent Office were both spared, but the British Museum Library lost almost a quarter of a million volumes in one night in May 1941,[2] while University College London lost 70,000 volumes. In the provincial cities, which became targets of German air attacks from November 1941, the scientific holdings damaged were chiefly those in public libraries: Coventry Public Library lost 150,000 volumes; public libraries in Exeter and Plymouth were also hard hit.[3] Except for London, the great university libraries were unharmed; the library of the Cambridge Philosophical Society—now the Cambridge Periodicals Library—one of the most important collections of current scientific publications outside London, was not damaged.[4]

The worst problem faced by British scientific libraries between 1939 and 1945 concerned the import of foreign periodicals. German domination of the sea and air routes to England in the first three years of the war severely restricted the import of publications, especially those of enemy countries. Libraries in Great Britain, as elsewhere, got their foreign subscriptions through agreements for exchange with libraries and learned and professional societies abroad, or through the book trade. During the First World War, book dealers in neutral countries such as Switzerland and the Netherlands had prevented channels from closing entirely, and there seemed no reason in 1939 to assume that this would not be the case in the new war.

Soon after the war began, the British government restricted the purchase of enemy goods to holders of special import licenses. The system caused some hardship: The Cambridge Philosophical Society Library, for example, was unable to obtain such a license for months and had to make its large overseas orders through the University Library.[5] Booksellers in neutral countries such as the Netherlands—until May 1940—and Switzerland were still able to order from Germany for English buyers; a Dutch firm could report in the winter of 1939 that "up till now we have had no trouble in dispatching German journals to abroad [sic]."[6] The exchange of journals, involving no transfer of money, continued as well as the circuitous postal routes would permit. However, materials from the Soviet Union, until June 1941 neutral in the war, came only very scantily.

The flow of periodicals was severely disrupted by the German invasion of Denmark, Norway, the Netherlands, Belgium and France in the spring of 1940. British orders for German journals were then shifted, when possible, to book dealers in Sweden, Portugal and Switzerland, although Swiss dealers had trouble exporting after the German occupation of Vichy France in late 1942. The import of American publications, too, became difficult as the sea battle in the Atlantic Ocean grew in ferocity after 1941: A whole shipment of issues of American scholarly and scientific periodicals published in late 1940 and bundled together for distribution to British libraries was lost when the ship carrying it was sunk by torpedo.[7] By April 1941, the [British] Association of Special Libraries and Information Bureaux reported that no copies of French, German or Italian periodicals had reached the United Kingdom after the issues of May 1940, and that technological literature from the Soviet Union was greatly delayed.[8]

While such heavy losses were suffered, demand by the armed forces and industry for scientific and technical information grew more and more urgent. At the Science Museum Library reduced usage was anticipated during the war, and consequently 40 percent of the staff was released, but borrowing from the library in fact increased: the total number of borrowing institutions rose from 450 before the war to over 1,000 by 1945. The library reported that the areas most intensely used for defense activities were physics, chemistry and engineering—all subjects in which German journals were traditionally strong and in which the library had increasing difficulty in keeping current as imports dried up.[9]

Anxiety about the breakdown in the delivery of German scientific publications was great among British scientists and documentalists by 1940. As J. D. Bernal wrote at the time: "It was not so much that German scientists were in the front rank of discovery, but that Germany had taken on the task of the systematization and codification of all science, so that the record of the progress of human knowledge was largely in German hands."[10]   By the summer of 1940 the Association for Special Libraries began to take action to maximize access to the few copies of German journals that had gotten into Britain in the preceding year. In June 1940, it started to issue a series of *War-time Guides* indicating where in Great Britain foreign publications could be found on such subjects as fuel, electrical engineering, telecommunications, agriculture and general engineering.[11] The association's officers were interested in the possibility of using photoduplication to multiply the few available issues of foreign journals, but this posed legal problems because the International Copyright Law and the Patents Emergency Act of 1939 restricted photocopying of imported materials to cases where there was clear evidence of urgent need for the material.[12] To demonstrate this urgent need the Royal Society, with the help of the Rockefeller Foundation, commissioned the Association of Special Libraries and Information Bureaux in June 1941 to survey British specialized libraries and find out how the breakdown of scientific communication was affecting their services; 810 circulars were sent out as a part of the "Aslib Enemy Periodicals Project". Of the 245 libraries that replied, most had not received any German periodicals since May 1940, and all agreed that American journals were an inadequate substitute.[13]

The survey revealed an interesting anomaly, namely that British governmental libraries had much less difficulty than other institutions in acquiring enemy publications. The association also found that it was not hard for booksellers to obtain import licenses or permission from the Treasury to pay agents in neutral countries.   The main problem seemed to be that transportation through Switzerland and Portugal was very slow. The association's report to the Royal Society noted, however, that "these problems are totally absent in a few select cases of powerful bodies such as the Bank of England, which is neither willing to share its supply of periodicals or divulge its source of supply."[14] The case of His Majesty's Stationery Office was particulary interesting: it claimed in its response that it was not using special privileges, such as diplomatic pouches, for delivery. The association nonetheless sensed discrimination:

> Nothing definite can be proved, but in practice the packages of publications ordered by HMSO come through with reasonable regularity, whereas those for other importing agents are subjected to indefinite delay. The result has been to discourage all but the most persistent importers and thus virtually to throttle all supplies except those coming to government libraries.[15]

In August 1941 the results of the survey were sent in a secret memorandum to the scientific advisory committee of the War Cabinet. The following recommendations were made: (1) periodicals should continue to be collected by individual libraries; (2) the association or some other agency should become a clearinghouse for locating scientific and technological publications in the United Kingdom; (3) the association should investigate means by which librarians and booksellers might more swiftly receive German periodicals; and (4) the association should encourage the collection, somewhere in the country, of one copy of each issue on a list of important periodicals.[16]

While this last recommendation seemed to be laying the groundwork for a possible future photocopying project, solutions to the legal obstacles to such a project were slow in coming. In October 1941, yet another memorandum was sent by the association to the War Cabinet's scientific advisory committee. This note contained complaints from the secretary of the association, Miss E.M.R. Ditmas, that the Patent Office seemed determined to interpret literally the Patents Emergency Act's prohibition of the duplication of copyright materials except in cases of dire need. Apparently the Patent Office was too concerned with protecting business interests to recognize the urgencies of war. In the memorandum Miss Ditmas insisted that immediate action be taken to get around the Patent Office roadblock.[17]

In November 1941, the Department of Scientific and Industrial Research called a meeting of representives of governmental libraries, His Majesty's Stationery Office, and the Association of Special Libraries and Information Bureaux to consider the problem of reproduction. Somehow Miss Ditmas convinced those in authority of the dangers inherent in letting the breakdown in the supply of scientific information continue. The outcome of the meeting was the recommendation that microfilms be made of those scientific periodicals which were published in enemy countries and which the Aslib survey had found to be inadequately supplied to many English research libraries. Many such periodicals were available in Great Britain because, despite the inability of the book trade to obtain them from enemy countries, certain government departments were receiving them from their outposts in neutral countries.[18]

Thus, finally, the more than two years of bureaucratic infighting was over and the continued supply of vital foreign scientific publications was guaranteed. By November 1941, the British had set up the system that would, with American help after 1942, assure the flow of enemy scientific publications to the Allies for the remainder of the war.

UNITED STATES 1939-1945

German scientific research had made its imprint on American research libraries over the decades: Book trade channels for the importation of German scientific journals had existed since the nineteenth century, with certain subscription agencies, including G. E. Stechert in New York and F. W. Faxon in Boston, specializing in the import and distribution of these publications. *Chemical Abstracts* had indexed and abstracted German chemical information since its founding in 1907, and German reference books like Beilstein's *Handbuch der organischen Chemie* were staples of American scientific and technical collections. Of the $1.5 million that the United States was spending for foreign books and journals in 1939, most was spent for German publications.[19]

Upon the outbreak of the war in September 1939, American science librarians were fearful of the consequences of being deprived of German publications: Ralph Munn, president of the American Library Association, wrote to Secretary of State Cordell Hull: "Germany has made, and is making, many contributions to man's knowledge. The world of scholarship can not afford to be deprived of the German contribution to this knowledge."[20] To keep the German publications coming in to American libraries, the Joint Committee on Importation was organized by a consortium of American library associations in October 1939. The purpose of the committee was to coordinate purchases through the book trades of neutral countries such as the Netherlands or Switzerland. They were following a precedent set during World War I, when the American Library Association's importation service had operated under Department of State and War Trade Board licenses to secure scientific periodicals published in Germany and Austria (see Chapter 2).

The Joint Committee was based in New York and was initially chaired by Harry Lydenberg, director of the New York Public Library. In August 1941 Thomas Fleming of the Columbia Medical School Library assumed the chairmanship and the Committee's operations were shifted to Columbia University. The Joint Committee was at first successful in expediting the receipt of multiple copies of key foreign scientific journals and forwarding them to industries, research organizations and libraries. Since the United States was still neutral, it was not initially difficult to buy the belligerents' publications either from Germany or through agents in another neutral country such as Switzerland. Even the embargo on all German exports announced by the British on 26 November 1939 had little immediate effect. There was some outrage among American librarians about the British insistence on checking cargoes of German origin at control points like Gibraltar, Bermuda, or Trinidad. The British demanded that a list of German subscriptions be submitted to His Majesty's Government for approval.[21] Fury at British nitpicking colors the correspondance of Thomas Fleming, the chairman of the Joint Committee, but in actuality American supplies were not substantially hampered by British demands.   In the beginning of 1940, the bigger libraries were placing orders as they did before the war, and Fleming wrote in April of that year that "the British have been confiscating no publications sent to American libraries, and that is about all there is to the situation."[22]

The German invasion of the Low Countries and the fall of France in May and June 1940 ended this period of deceptive normalcy.   Not only was the number of neutral countries through which Americans could deal drastically reduced, but the submarine warfare in the North Atlantic increasingly endangered shippping of all kinds.   For a while the Committee advised its member libraries to have their orders stored on the Continent, but British area-bombing soon made this an unwise alternative.   Before the invasion of the Soviet Union in June 1941, German publications were successfully shipped to the United States via Siberia, but after this route also closed, the Committee despaired that access to the results of German science would close entirely.

Even if a safe passage had been found, importing German publications through the book trade would have, by that time, become impossible because of the question of payments.   By mid-1941 the State Department was forbidding Americans to transfer any money to Germany or to German-occupied territory. Since German publishers were prohibited from exporting materials for which payments had not already been received, the import of European materials by conventional means seemed to be coming to an end six months before the United States entered the war.

But the level of fear in the American scientific community about German science's potential for destruction lent a special urgency to finding a way to overcome these obstacles. The strategic potential of German science had already been brought to the attention of powerful Americaans with defense responsibilities. On August 2, 1939, Albert Einstein, after Otto Hahn's splitting of the uranium atom in Berlin in 1938, and the subsequent discoveries of Leitner, Frisch, Bohr and Wheelock, had written his famous letter to President Roosevelt warning of the possibility of German atomic weapons development. Fear of German science became a major dynamic in forging America's war strategy: In 1945, Under Secretary of War Robert Patterson revealed that the fundamental priority accorded German over Japanese defeat in the Anglo-American strategy was the fear of the new weapons that German science might develop in the course of the war.[23]

At any rate, in the United States the awareness of the dangers presented by German science led early on to governmental support for securing the flow of German publications.   The German government had not restricted publication of the Hahn papers and the Allies hoped that it might be equally lax in other cases, even after the war had broken out.   It was under these circumstances in December 1941 that William Langer, the Harvard historian, convinced the head of American intelligence operations, William J. Donovan, to organize a unit for the import of enemy printed information. This unit, the Interdepartmental Committee for the Acquisition of Foreign Publications (IDC), operating after June 1942 under the Office of Strategic Services (OSS), became the United States' central agency for enemy scientific information collection in World War II.

Many of the individuals involved in the work of the IDC were drawn from the relatively small group of Americans knowledgeable about the young technology of microfilm. In March 1942, Frederick Kilgour, a twenty-eight-year-old microfilm expert from the Harvard Library's newspaper microfilm project, took over supervision of the IDC as its executive secretary after Langer's resignation as chairman. Meanwhile, Eugene Power, the thirty-six-year-old founder of University Microfilm, Inc., was asked by the United States Office of the Coordinator of Information—the forerunner of the OSS, which was not founded till June 1942—to help film enemy documents obtained by the British so that they could be shipped to the United States. Power, an aggressive entrepreneur with a fine nose for profit, was interested in such a cooperative venture. His work for the American Council of Learned Societies project to microfilm war-threatened British manuscripts[24] brought him to England frequently, and he agreed.[25] This was the beginning of one of the war's most successful examples of joint Anglo-American intelligence work. As we will see, this success was the fruit of several years' clandestine cooperation before America's formal entrance into the war in December 1941.

ANGLO-AMERICAN COOPERATION 1939-1942

The Americans were aware at the outbreak of the war in 1939 that British military research was in many areas far more advanced than that of the United States—especially in airborne radar and in military applications of atomic energy— and they were interested in information the British might provide. In March 1940, Rudolph Peierls and Otto Frisch, refugee scientists working in Birmingham, had written a report to British defense chiefs asserting the feasibility of an atomic bomb. They described the critical mass of uranium necessary, the separation of enriched uranium, detonation, and the terrible effects of radiation.[26] This report led to the creation in Great Britain of an atomic bomb project, the Maud Committee, and by the summer of 1940 work was going on in London, Oxford, Cambridge, Birmingham, Liverpool and the Imperial Chemical Industries laboratories—all places vulnerable to German bombs and, possibly, occupation.

Against this background of danger of invasion and disparities in levels of achievement between British and American scientists, arrangements were made

to assure the exchange of scientific information between Great Britain and the
United States. The Americans hoped to benefit from British progress in certain
areas of military technology. Henry Tizard had first suggested a scientific
liaison with Washington in 1939 and in July 1940, President Roosevelt invited
a large-scale British scientific delegation to the United States. In September
1940 Tizard went to Washington as the head of a British scientific mission which
included representatives from both the British and Canadian armed forces and
the National Research Council of Canada. Not only did Tizard's group carry
with it a large amount of technical equipment,[27] but accompanying Tizard were
experts in a variety of fields who were responsible for the transfer of British
research results on a large scale to their oppposite numbers in the United States.
It is hard to assess cause and effect, but certainly Tizard's mission came at
something of a turning point for American war research: In nuclear research,
for example, the British physicist Cockcroft found at the time of the mission that
"nearly all the work in America seemed to be behind that carried out in Britain
and that it was not proceeding as fast as the British work."[28] Within a year
and a half, however, "it was clear that the Americans who had been well behind
the British in the race for the bomb had drawn level and were indeed passing
them by."[29]

Tizard's visit led directly to the establishment in early 1941 of a Washington
office for the British Central Science Office and a London office for the United
States National Defense Research Committee under Frederick L. Hovde, a
chemical engineeer from the University of Rochester. Once again business
interests threatened to slow down critically important scientific information
work: Both sides harbored individuals who feared that the exchange would lead
to patent infringements by the other country and would permit the businessmen
of the other country to gain a leading position in the market after the war.[30]
But ultimately these suspicions did not prevent the Washington and London
offices from functioning effectively. The British Central Science Office had a
staff of 17 scientists; it was intended among other things to obtain from the
United States government answers to questions posed by British officials and
scientists, to serve as a clearinghouse for the exchange of scientific and
technological reports, and to purchase books, journals, specifications and
scientific apparatus relevant to scientific projects in Great Britain.[31] But in the
early years of the war, more information flowed to the United States from Great
Britain than in the opposite direction.[32]

A precedent had thus been established before Pearl Harbor for the official
exchange of British and American scientific and technological documentation,
including books and journals, but no effort had been made to collaborate in the
solution of the problem of the acquisition of German scientific publications. For
the United States this did not represent a very urgent problem during the first
months of the war in Europe, as the library associations' Joint Committee on

Importation arranged for the purchase of multiple issues of German periodicals through subscription agents in neutral countries. But with the German occupation of the Netherlands, Belgium and France in the spring of 1940, and the intensification of submarine warfare in the North Atlantic in 1942, this system broke down almost completely. As we have seen, the United States government established the IDC early in 1942 to supervise the import of the foreign scientific and technological journals needed by federal agencies and the military. Under the broad organizational umbrella of the Office of Strategic Services, the IDC, chaired by Lieutenant Kilgour, eventually established outposts in countries on the periphery of enemy-occupied territories, acquired enemy periodicals by subscription— often under pseudonyms—or other means, microfilmed them on the spot, and sent the microfilms by air to Washington. Plans for European outposts in Sweden, Switzerland and Portugal were laid in the spring and summer of 1942, but the agents and their cameras were not in full operation until the autumn of that year.[33]

THE ASLIB MICROFILM SERVICE 1942-1945

Given the agreement of 1942 on Anglo-American cooperation in the exchange of scientific and technological information, and the difficulties confronting the Americans in the acquisition of publications from the enemy countries, it was logical that the United States should participate in the microfilm project planned in England by the Association of Special Libraries and Information Bureaux. By early 1942, this project, christened the "Aslib microfilm service," was beginning to be effective. The decision had been made by the Department of Scientific and Industrial Research and His Majesty's Stationery Office to let the association copy the foreign materials coming into the Stationery Office before they were distributed to the various agencies that had ordered them, and to make microfilm copies or enlarged prints on demand from the master negative. In January 1942, a standing advisory committee[34] was appointed to the microfilm service and efforts began to raise funds to buy cameras.[35]

It was at this point that American officials in Washington heard about the project and engaged the services of Eugene Power, who succeeded in coordinating British and American microfilming activities in the Aslib microfilm service and in centralizing several separate British governmental projects in the field. Power had developed his expertise in the photoreproduction of scholarly and scientific publications while working in Ann Arbor, Michigan, for Edwards Brothers, a scholarly reprint publisher using the new technology of photo-offset. He had then had gone on to found his own company, University Microfilms, Inc. In early 1942 Power was asked by William J. Donovan, the United States Coordinator of Information, to help film enemy documents obtained by the British, for shipment to the United States. University Microfilms was interested in establishing a retail trade in the sale of foreign scientific periodicals which were difficult to obtain, and Power agreed to assume the responsibilities proposed to him by Donovan. He arrived in London on 2 April 1942, as a special representative of the Library of Congress and an unofficial agent of the IDC.[36] It immediately became apparent to Power that it would be most efficient to combine American and English efforts and to have the Aslib microfilm service, strengthened by whatever technical resources the Americans could offer, satisfy both British and American demand, with Power the American agent for the product.

Power knew that the United States Coordinator of Information was also interested in enemy newspapers, an area in which he himself had no personal business interest. Donovan was planning to open offices in Lisbon and Berne to procure newspapers of enemy countries, but this had not yet been done and immediate needs were urgent. While Aslib did not microfilm newspapers, Power learned that the British Ministry of Information was beginning to act on a plan to collect, film, and distribute copies of issues of continental newspapers to interested governmental agencies. Power succeeded, before leaving London in May 1942, in bringing together all the bodies interested in importing enemy publications. In that month the interested parties established a new entity, called the executive committee of the Aslib microfilm service, to represent the interests of the American intelligence service, the British Ministry of Information, and the Association of Special Libraries and Information Bureaux.[37]

By December 1942, institutional arrangements of the Aslib microfilm service were complete and a staff was assembled. By that time the United States Office of Strategic Services had established a research and analysis branch in London, with Allan Evans in charge of the activities of the branch's IDC unit. Evans became the American representative to the Aslib microfilm service, while the representative for His Majesty's Government was H. Howard of the general overseas division of the Ministry of Information. As a result of their cooperation, the "Terms of Agreement between Participating Bodies" were drafted and officially approved by the microfilm service's executive committee in June 1943. The terms stipulated that the Aslib microfilm service was a permanent undertaking of the Association of Special Libraries and Information Bureaux, under whose association rules it would be conducted, but that "for the duration of the war emergency, Aslib joins with representatives of His Majesty's Government to be nominated jointly by the Ministry of Information and His Majesty's Stationery Office; and to members from the United States Government to be nominated by the director of the Office of Strategic Services, London.[38] This arrangement remained essentially unchanged even after the Association of Special Libraries became a grantee—and thus an affiliated research organization—of the Department of Scientific and Industrial Research in 1944.

The day-to-day operations of the microfilm service were the charge of the director, Lucia Moholy, who had been responsible for the microfilming at Cambridge University supported by the Rockefeller Foundation. Because the Science Museum Library subscribed to more foreign periodicals than any other British library, the Aslib microfilm service asked its librarian, J. Lancaster Jones, if its microfilming activities might be housed there. Lancaster Jones, who had been microfilming his holdings of periodicals from enemy countries even before the Aslib microfilm service came into being, readily agreed, and during the winter of 1942-43 the library of the Science Museum became the center of microfilming. In April 1943, with more microfilm cameras arriving from the United States and the Aslib microfilm service taking on additional work for the American intelligence services unrelated to its own work on periodicals, Mrs. Moholy and her staff moved to larger quarters in the nearby Victoria and Albert Museum.[39] Here were installed the five American Kodak Microfile cameras, the best then available—microphotography in the United States being at that time more advanced than elsewhere.[40] The new quarters also had a laboratory for developing film. The Aslib microfilm service remained at the Victoria and Albert Museum until the end of the war. Throughout its several years as a scientific intelligence agency, the service remained a British library service, charging its subscribers a penny a page for microfilm copies and a shilling for paper enlargments.

The sources of supply of the microfilm service included His Majesty's Stationery Office, which received all the periodicals to which it subscribed as the agent of about 50 governmental departments; the Foreign Office, through which it received large quantitites of newspapers and journals sent by British press attachés, particularly from Lisbon; the Air Ministry, which supplied the microfilm service with Soviet journals; and the Ministry of Economic Warfare, which sent over its German economic journals. One of the most important sources was the Ministry of Information, which received a vast amount of material from the combined Allied units copying Continental materials in Stockholm: The IDC agent in Stockholm, Dr. Adele Kibre, was responsible, with British aid, for shippping back to the Ministry of Information a total of 182 reels of microfilm.[41]

By the end of the war the IDC had agents operating in Stockholm, Lisbon, Istanbul, Cairo and Chungking, from where the IDC's agent, Harvard sinologist John Fairbanks, was able to send Washington Chinese and Japanese publications acquired along the borders. Rivaling Stockholm as the most productive source for German publications was Lisbon, where the IDC's agent Reuben Peiss, a philosopher from Harvard, was able to set up a network of subscriptions through Portuguese covers. Lisbon lost some of its usefulness after the Allied invasion in the summer of 1944 closed the land routes to Germany, but a daily Lufthansa flight from Germany to Spain, and a weekly flight from Germany to Portugal, kept German journals coming into the Iberian peninsula right into 1945.[42] The

British and American agents responsible for collecting the periodicals in the neutral countries and sending them back to England tried as far as possible to mask their identities through subscriptions in the names of cooperative—or fictitious—nationals of the countries from which the subscriptions were placed. The subscriptions were placed through firms or institutions in neutral countries with long histories of book trade with Germany.

Switzerland played a surprisingly small role in the supply network. In the early months of the war the Swiss book trade had maintained its position as an important channel of German and Austrian journals to Great Britain and the United States. The fall of France in 1940, enclosing Switzerland entirely by Axis territory, made Swiss authorities hypersensitive to any sign of Allied intelligence activity on their soil which might encourage German aggression. Moreover, an OSS unit under Allen Dulles, working in Switzerland on an operation of the highest priority, wanted no other OSS group operating which might endanger its relations with the Swiss government. Dulles' unit, deep in negotiations with members of the German high command who would participate in the assassination attempt against Hitler on 23 June 1944, managed to keep the IDC out of Switzerland.[43]

Especially in the first year of the IDC's collaboration with the Aslib project, before enough microfilm cameras had been installed at the outposts, much of the microfilming of the original issues had to be done in London. The actual physical collection and transfer of the individual issues of the periodicals to the Victoria and Albert Museum for copying, once they arrived at the various ministries from the collecting posts abroad, lay in the hands of the London branch of the Office of Strategic Services. Allan Evans drew on the services of several United States Marines whose days were spent picking up newly arrived publications at the ministries, delivering them to the microfilm service and then returning them to the lender within the agreed period: 48 hours for scientific and technological periodicals, 24 hours for newspapers. Within the allotted time, three negatives were made of the periodicals: one for the Association for Special Libraries and Information Bureaux's own retail service, one to send to Washington to the IDC, and one for Eugene Power's University Microfilms, Inc. Thus Power had a virtual monopoly within the United States of the commercial exploitation of the microfilm versions of the originals. Copyright problems were solved by the fact that the United States government had seized the copyrights of the enemy journals shortly after the outbreak of hostilities.

All in all, the Aslib microfilm service was enormously productive. By the end of 1943, it was regularly receiving about 280 periodicals and other serials from the British governmental posts and IDC agents in Lisbon, Stockholm and Istanbul (see Appendix A for the list of journals available to the public on Aslib microfilm). By late 1945, its total production of microfilms photographed, copied, recorded and indexed was five-and-a-half million pages.[44] Not all of this went on to Washington. As the war progressed, the IDC's outposts in neutral countries sent increasing amounts of microfilm directly to the United States. The Aslib microfilm service and the IDC were by this late stage acting to supplement each other's work, supplying what the other wanted and did not have. But in the early part of the program, the Aslib microfilm service was responsible for the largest part of the material reaching the IDC's offices in Washington. Years later, Frederick Kilgour credited the British institution as having gotten the IDC "off to a flying start."[45]

THE PERIODICAL REPUBLICATION PROGRAM IN THE UNITED STATES

The people intended to be the users of the microfilm were not as enthusiastic about the medium as were the documentation experts. There was, moreover, a shortage of microfilm reading machines due to wartime conditions. Lucia Moholy attributed to the physical format of the microfilm the failure of the retail trade in microfilm to live up to expectations,[46] but the paper shortage in Great Britain at that time left few alternatives. In the United States, however, the situation was different. There, by early 1943, the IDC began a journal reprint program in collaboration with the scholarly reprint firm of Edwards Brothers, in Ann Arbor.

Edwards Brothers, for which Eugene Power had worked before founding University Microfilms, pioneered in the use of the new photo-offset technology, whereby pages could be reprinted in facsimile from the negatives of photographs made of original pages. The negative was transferred to a rubber mat, and the mat was mounted on a cylinder press which transferred the image to paper. The process involved no cutting or setting of type; only the paper differed from the original version. Since 1942 Edwards Brothers had been using the process to reprint scholarly and scientific German books in collaboration with the United States Office of the Alien Property Custodian (APC). Originally set up in 1917 to seize and administer enemy properties in the United States, the APC operated as part of the Justice Department after 1934, but was recreated as an independent agency by President Roosevelt on 21 April 1942. Immediately thereafter the Custodian (first Leo T. Crowley, and after March 1944 James E. Markham) began seizing and licensing for American publication all enemy produced items that were normally copyrighted, including books, musical compositions and movies (the first copyright so seized was that of *Mein Kampf*). The sole criterion for licensing—under which arrangement the Custodian received the royalties normally accruing to the holder of the copyright—was that the republication be in the public interest. After October 1942 the APC was supported by the Advisory Committee on the Republication Program to help it choose titles for reprint. Of the eleven members of the advisory committee, eight were the leading librarians or specialists in documentation in the United States, including E. J. Crane, editor of *Chemical Abstracts*; Watson Davis, president of the American Documentation Institute; Sarah Jones, librarian of the United States Bureau of Standards; Keyes Metcalf, president of the American Library Association; Luther Evans, assistant librarian of Congress; and Paul North Rice, executive secretary of the Association of Research Libraries. The constitution of this group was intended to guarantee that the needs of the most important disciplines would be considered.

It was essentially the republication, under the APC's license, of the forty-nine-volume "Bible" of organic chemistry, Beilstein's *Handbuch der Organischen Chemie*, that inspired the idea of a republication program for periodicals. Published by Edwards Brothers at a list price of only $400 (compared to a prewar price of $2,000), the reprinted *Handbuch* struck readers with the quality of its reproduction and led to the question "If books, why not periodicals?" This thought was passed on to the Advisory Committee, which immediately urged the APC to undertake a periodical republication program. In its barest outline, the program called for the selection, with the help of the Advisory Committee, of a list of periodicals to be reprinted, and the acquisition abroad of a single copy of each desired issue by the IDC. Under the arrangements of the Periodical Republication Program, the Alien Property Custodian sent to libraries and laboratories mimeographed lists of the journal titles and numbers available from the Alien Property Custodian. The lists went out under the name of Howland H. Sargeant, Chief of the Department of Justice's Division of Patent Administration, and included the prices per volume offered (a volume of *Die Naturwissenschaften*, for example, cost the subscriber $132). A small number of journals were available by single issue (*Justus Liebig's Annalen der Chemie*, for example, and the *Berichte der Deutschen Chemischen Gesellschaft*). The announcements instructed subscribers to place their orders with any one of three established subscription agencies: F. W. Faxon Company of Boston; Moore-Cottrell Subscription Agencies of North Cohocton, New York; and G. E. Stechert and Company of New York City. Actual reprinting at Edwards Brothers was done on demand: reprinting proceeded only when a sufficient number of advance subscriptions had been received.

Not all the microfilm sent from the Aslib microfilm service and the IDC agents was considered suitable by the Advisory Committee for reprinting, and the list of reprinted journals fluctuated. Users were asked by the Alien Propery Custodian's Office in the list's cover letters to "send suggestions of additional war-urgent foreign scientific journals to be considered for reprinting and to send any other suggestions which will contribute to the operation of the Program generally." For some reprinted journals there was apparently not enough demand to justify their continuation in the program. The list circulated in November 1944 indicated that a number of journals, including *Angewandte Botanik* and even the classic *Botanische Zentralblatt*, would be withdrawn from the program unless additional orders were received.[47]

By the end of the war, the Alien Property Custodian had sent to a group of selected research libraries seven circulars announcing the availability of reprints of 116 separate Continental journals, principally German and Austrian. The reprinted titles also included 16 French, one Belgian, and three Dutch journals (see Appendix A for a list of the reprinted journals). These periodicals covered almost every phase of scientific and technological development of interest in wartime, including acoustics, aviation, biochemistry, electronics, engineering, enzymology, explosives, mathematics, medicine, pathology, petroleum, plastics, rubber and virus research.[48] An analysis done by the Alien Property Custodian at the end of the war showed that 94 percent of the over 900 subscribers to the reprints used them for war purposes and that 58 of the subscribers were in the British Empire.[49] The British Central Science Office in Washington subscribed to the reprints for His Majesty's Stationery Office, which then forwarded them to British governmental agencies. Other British libraries could subscribe through H. K. Lewis, a leading British bookseller specializing in scientific books and the agent of Edwards Brothers in Great Britain.

Both the Aslib microfilm service and the Alien Property Custodian's periodical reprint operation depended, of course, on the ability of the Continental publishers and booksellers to fill the orders placed by the British and IDC agents in neutral countries. Every effort was made by the British and Americans to keep the whole network secret, lest word of its importance to the Allied war effort endanger the suppliers and their intermediaries. Accompanying one of the first announcements of the Aslib microfilm service operations in 1942 was the request that "no communication be made of this information to the Press or to anyone outside your own institution."[50] The Americans were equally security-conscious. Printed on the cover of all seven of the circulars sent out by the Alien Property Custodian announcing available reprinted periodicals was the warning: "NOT FOR PUBLICATION! If any publicity is given, it will mean the cessation of the supply of copy and total failure of the enterprise."

Great efforts were also made overseas to protect the status of the journal subscriptions. The IDC agents scrupulously avoided any clandestine relations with publishers or booksellers in the enemy countries which might have jeopardized their subscriptions, and they did not respond to the personal messages that were sometimes slipped into German periodicals bound for Sweden.[51] Such was the secrecy surrounding the operation that the Alien Property Custodian only disclosed at the end of the war that it had obtained all its copy from the Office of Strategic Services, and only in 1985 did the declassification of the war diary of the London OSS unit make public the extent to which the OSS used British sources for its supply of enemy periodicals.

The subscriptions purchased by British and American agents in neutral countries were not actually in jeopardy until rather late in the war. It is clear that, even after 1939, the National Socialist regime continued its peacetime policy of encouraging research publications, both as a means of diffusing science within the Reich and the occupied territories and as a means of demonstrating German scientific superiority to the world. While articles on nuclear research disappeared from German journals after the spring of 1940, there was no move by the German government to restrict foreign circulation of the journals once their contents had been approved by their politically reliable editors. The suspicion that the knowledge thus made available might be of strategic value to their enemies seems to have dawned only in 1943, when Berlin issued a decree prohibiting the export of German printed matter potentially damaging to the Reich. High officials of the National Socialist Party found widespread disregard of the prohibition, and early in 1944 Martin Bormann wrote to the Ministry of Propaganda reminding its officials sternly of the earlier decree.[52]

In September 1944 a surprising breach of security on the Allied side led to the German discovery of the American program of reprinting German books. German agents in Sweden noticed an advertisement in the British trade publication *The Bookseller* for German books reprinted by Edwards Brothers. The advertisement listed H. K. Lewis as the distributor in the United Kingdom for the reprints. This occasioned yet another directive from the Reichskanzlei (Reich Chancellery) requiring the careful supervision of the export of German books and giving instructions to German agents in Sweden to obtain the catalog of the "jüdische Firma H. K. Lewis."[53] By November 1944, certain book dealers in Sweden had been identified as important suppliers of German publications to the Allies; these included the Gumpert firm in Göteborg and Fritzes Hovbokhandel in Stockholm.[54] While the advertisement in *The Bookseller* did not focus attention on the program of reprints of periodicals, by December 1944 suspicions in Berlin were awakened and produced a recommendation that periodicals be removed from the booktrade altogether.[55]

How Edwards Brothers or H. K. Lewis could be so careless as to place such an advertisement remains obscure. In any case, it does not seem to have had much effect on the flow of German materials. American records do refer to a temporary slowdown at an unspecified time in the deliveries of German periodicals to Lisbon as a presumed result of Nazi suspicion about the subscribers, all of whom were Portuguese nationals,[56] but it is not certain that the incident was connected with the advertisement in *The Bookseller*. The destruction of war by that time probably made an official restriction on the export of German publications superfluous: the German publication of books and periodicals had been severely reduced by the raid by the Royal Air Force of 3 December 1943 on Leipzig, which was the chief center of German publishing. By October 1944, German periodical publishing was reduced to 10 percent of its prewar production. So, even if the Germans had begun effective export restrictions after the autumn of 1944—and there is no evidence that they did—there were by that time relatively few important publications left for them to control.

How important was the acquisition program for the Allied war effort? Various scientists' recollections about the development of the atomic bomb, the main work on which had by 1943 shifted to the United States, provide the most compelling evidence that the program had been crucial indeed. Since Otto Hahn and his associates had first split the uranium atom in 1938, many Allied scientists, particularly the Americans,[57] feared that the Germans might be ahead of them in adapting nuclear energy to weapons. Niels Bohr was convinced that the Germans were working on a bomb at least during 1941. According to Bohr's physicist son, Aage, Werner Heisenberg brought up the subject of atomic weapons during a conversation he had with Bohr in occupied Copenhagen in the fall of 1941. Aage Bohr reported that his father "was very reticent and expressed his scepticism because of the great technical difficulties that had to be overcome, but he had the impression that Heisenberg thought that the new possibilities could decide the outcome of the war if the war dragged on."[58] Bohr's suspicions were communicated to British intelligence in the months leading up to his famous escape from Denmark in mid-1943.[59]

Meanwhile, back in England, close analysis of the German journals seemed to support the theory that the Germans were trying to find military uses for atomic energy, although it also indicated that the German effort was on a very small scale. Rudolph Peierls, one of the émigré physicists working on the Allied atomic project, recalls in his memoirs that in 1941 he was solicited by British intelligence for help in assessing the extent of German atomic energy research. His recollections give an interesting insight into the kind of information the scientific journals could give besides straightforward reports of research:

> I knew that each semester the *Physikalische Zeitschrift* published a list of the lecture courses in physics in all German universities. The lists showed that most physicists were in their normal places and teaching their normal subjects, which was completely different from the British or American situation. But there were a few exceptions. Heisenberg did not lecture, and a paper by a young man in Leipzig on a subject that would have interested Heisenberg acknowledged advice and help from others, but not from Heisenberg. This

suggested that Heisenberg either was not there, or he was busy with something else. Another suggestive fact was that in the abstracting journal *Physikalische Berichte* certain people regularly abstracted papers on nuclear physics and on isotope separation. The picture emerged that Germany had no crash programme, no large-scale project that required a major participation by scientists.[60]

Sometime in 1942, the German project was apparently abandoned as impractical, for a variety of reasons, one of which was that the Germans seem to have overestimated the amount of enriched uranium which would be necessary for the bomb's manufacture.[61] In any case, the German government's conclusion about the impracticability of atomic fission for use in the war resulted in the release and publication in 1942 and 1943 of the results of the research bearing on the German atomic bomb project that had been done over the preceding two years. Eight papers in issues of the *Zeitschrift für Physik* in 1942 and 1943 and three papers in issues of *Die Naturwissenschaften* in 1943, written by Otto Hahn, Fritz Strassmann, H. J. Born, W. Seelmann-Eggert and their associates at the Kaiser Wilhelm Gesellschaft's Institut für Chemie and the Radiologische Abteilung der Auergesellschaft, gave detailed descriptions of experiments on the fission of the uranium atom, the gaseous and other by-products obtained, and the energy released. These papers, all of which were microfilmed by the Aslib microfilm service and ultimately reprinted by the Americans, caused great excitement among the scientists at the Manhattan Project.[62] At the end of the war a United States government report stated that they had been critical to the Allies' ability to have their bomb operational by the summer of 1945.[63]

THE SOVIET ROLE

The German invasion of the Soviet Union in June 1941 forced the Soviets into the Allied camp and opened a new front for the exchange of strategic information. Because of the terrible destruction and dislocation of population suffered by the Soviets during the first three years of their involvement in the war, they contributed little to the Allies' access to German scientific literature and acted primarily as consumers of, rather than suppliers to, the Allied information network.[64] However, two aspects of the Soviets' involvement with Allied and German scientific information are relevant to our inquiry: One is the way the Americans reacted to their fear that the Soviet Union would act as a sieve through which strategic Allied information would leak; the other is the way in which the Soviets were able to use the Allies' published literature to determine the importance of atomic research to the Allied war effort.

American fear for the security of Allied information in Soviet hands was largely based on doubts before 1943 as to whether Soviet lines against the Germans would hold. The anxiety among American leaders was heightened in December 1942 when they learned of the Anglo-Soviet agreement that had been signed the previous fall. In September 1942, the British, eager to make amends for their failure to open a Western Front in Europe to take German military pressure off Stalin's lines, had signed an agreement promising Soviet access to British scientific and technical information of all kinds, and there were numerous visits by Soviet delegations to British factories and military installations during the following two years.[65]

At that time the Russians were facing three million German soldiers on a 1,600-mile-long front while the total number of all troops in North Africa (German, British and America) was only around 600,000. British sympathy for Russian suffering was great: R. V. Jones, the wartime head of British scientific intelligence for the air forces, remembered that during this period "it was an emotional thing to give everything to the Russians and there was enormous pressure from the air marshals to do so."[66] Although Jones himself resisted this pressure because of his distrust of Soviet war aims, a great deal of valuable information changed hands—much to the alarm of American scientific intelligence officers. Both President Roosevelt and Secretary of War Henry Stimson were shocked when they learned of the Anglo-Soviet information agreement in late December 1942, as the collapse of the eastern front would have put all this information in the hands of the Germans. In early 1943, therefore, the Americans embarked on a policy of limiting information exchange with the British because of their concern that atomic and other secrets might be passed to the Soviets.[67] But against the expectations of the other Allies, the Soviet Union's defensive lines held at Stalingrad in early 1943 and there is no evidence that any Allied information fell into German hands along the Eastern Front.

Behind Red Army lines some Soviet scientists were able to make good use of the libraries of foreign scientific literature which had been evacuated or maintained at enormous effort. To understand this use we must glance briefly at the state of Soviet nuclear physics on the eve of the German invasion in 1941. A national conference of Soviet nuclear physicists at Khar'kov in November 1939 had supplied the impetus for accelerated work on possible ways of achieving a chain reaction, and under pressure from I. V. Kurchatov, the Soviet Academy set up a uranium authority in June 1940. The authority was to oversee development of methods of uranium isotope separation and enrichment and to organize research into the control of a chain reaction. Despite most of his colleagues' conviction that the harnessing of atomic energy was not practicable, Kurchatov was able to convince senior physicist Nikolai Semenov to inform the government in early 1941 of the possibility of creating a bomb of enormous destructive power.

Publication of information about Soviet nuclear research was remarkably open right up till the German invasion. Arnold Kramish cites a number of popular articles appearing in the Soviet Union through mid-1941 in which the problems of atomic physics are discussed, and one in which Ioffe is quoted as saying that the atomic nucleus was the most important problem facing Soviet physics. Kurchatov was publicly identified as the chief of the Soviet atomic team, and in June 1940 a full description was given in *Izvestiia* of the new Leningrad cyclotron.[68] Efforts were also made to publish Soviet findings internationally: In July 1940 Kurchatov's team had published a note in the American *Physical Review* reporting the spontaneous fission of uranium. But in the wake of the invasion the atomic research project was suspended; Kurchatov was switched to practical defense work near the Black Sea and the younger members of his team drafted.

Careful reading of Western journals by a young nuclear physicist brought the Soviet atomic project back to life a year later. In February 1942 N. G. Flyorov, a member of Kurchatov's team serving in the Red Army, was posted to an airbase near Voronezh, where he paid a visit to the university's scientific library. Looking for reactions in the physics journals to the note he and his colleagues had published in mid-1940, he was surprised to find that reports of atomic research had disappeared from the Allied journals. Flyorov decided that nuclear science had become so important to weapons applications that it had been declared a state secret. He wrote accordingly to Stalin, who immediately reactivated Kurchatov's team.[69] (Flyorov's analysis was, of course, slightly inaccurate: American scientists themselves had, after intensive lobbying by Leo Szilard, decided to stop publishing the results of their atomic research lest it aid the Germans. In the spring of 1940 a reference committee, chaired by Gregory Breit of the University of Wisconsin and operating within the framework of the National Research Council, was founded to control journal publishing of research with possible military significance.)[70]

Thus the Soviets profited from the continued publication, circulation and availability of both Allied and German journals. It is ironic that an ally that was characterized by the English and Americans as unnecessarily secretive and unwilling to share information should have had such an open policy of publication of its atomic research. Undoubtedly the language barrier played a role in keeping the other Allies ignorant of how advanced was the state of Soviet atomic physics. There were, after all, no refugee Russian physicists in the West to keep Washington and London apprised of developments in Soviet laboratories. In fact, it is probable that by 1941 a regular lay reader of *Izvestiia* was more knowledgeable about Soviet atomic research than were members of the Manhattan Project. The Soviets were collecting and using the other belligerents' published scientific literature, but nobody else seemed to be doing the same for the Soviets.

THE INVASION OF GERMANY, 1945

The invasion and defeat of Germany did not bring an end to the Allied quest for German scientific and technical information—on the contrary, the efforts became more frantic as the dimensions of the prize grew apparent. This was, after all, the first time in history that the industrial secrets of one developed country were completely revealed to another. Moreover, England and the United States were still at war in the Pacific with a country that was expected to fight to the death. Given the wartime pace of technological innovation up till then—radar, jet aircraft, guided missiles and proximity fuses had all appeared during the fighting—it was hoped that secret weaponry still on German drawing boards might be applied in the war against Japan. On the heels of the invading American troops intelligence officers of the different services fanned out through Germany—the Navy Technical Mission, the Army's G-2 and "Operation Lusty" of the Air Force, the most aggressive of them all in its search for jet propulsion and rocketry secrets. Ultimately 200 tons of documents were shipped to the Air Documents Research Center in London and then in 1946 to the Air Document Division at Wright Field in Cleveland, Ohio, where they were translated, indexed and disseminated within the military. Partially as a result of this program a full complement of American-built V-2s were readied for use against the home islands of Japan, though they were never deployed. (It is worth mentioning here, if only in parentheses because of its low yield, the highly secret expedition of physicist Samuel Goudsmit into Germany after the Allied invasion. American assumptions about advanced atomic research in Germany proved to be unfounded).[71]

The purely economic potential of German technological advances was enormous, and as early as July 1944, Allied special troops were trained to capture and guard strategic scientific targets within Germany pinpointed by military intelligence. The booty of these "T-Forces" was then analyzed by men from the Allies' Combined Intelligence Objectives Subcommittee (CIOS), set up in August of 1944. The printed and mimeographed materials found—largely technical reports and memoranda—were microfilmed at sites at plants, universities and laboratories within Germany; by the end of 1945, 3,858,000 pages of material had been filmed. When the CIOS microfilm program ended in 1948, "the most minute aspects of science and technology, complete with drawings, flow sheets, minutes of the meetings of research groups and business firms, doctoral dissertations, and 186,000 applications to the German Patent Office were publicly available in the United States."[72]

For filling the gaps in holdings of Eureopean books and journals in American science libraries, the mission dispatched to Europe by the Library of Congress in the last months of the war was of great importance. In liberated Italy and France, and in Germany after the surrender, representatives of the library contacted booksellers with whom it had had relations before the war in order to purchase available stockpiles. Under the leadership of Reuben Peiss, formerly the IDC agent in Portugal, the Library of Congress Mission was able, just as the Russians were occupying Leipzig, to use army transport to secure truckloads of valuable books and journals stockpiled in that city by the bookdealer Harrassowitz.

Ultimately over one hundred American research libraries profited from the Library of Congress Mission. On 17 July 1945 Luther Evans, then Librarian of Congress, had requested permission from the State Department for his library's mission to use government facilities and services in order to buy multiple copies of books and journals to assist other American research libraries. Archibald MacLeish, Assistant Secretary of State for Public and Cultural Relations, granted Evans' request, but asked that a scheme be developed whereby the participating libraries agreed to collect in specific areas, rather than duplicate the holdings of others. Within a year the Association of Research Libraries had devised a plan assigning 254 subject fields to 115 libraries (it became known as the Farmington Plan, after the town in Connecticut where it was worked out). The books and journals gathered by the Library of Congress Mission were ultimately distributed to libraries designated by the Farmington Plan as collection centers for specific subject fields.[73]

The task of getting the technical reports and memoranda seized by the T-forces into public circulation was more complicated, as there were no long-established institutions with the necessary expertise to manage the job. Responsibility was given to the interdepartmental Publication Board, set up by the American government in June 1945 and in August of that year authorized to release captured German scientific and technical information with commercial potential. Examples of the information included an improved last system for shoes, a better way to waterproof textiles and, perhaps best known, the "sunshine ingredient" in a famous detergent.[74] With its greatest contribution in synthetics and optics, the Publication Board's program was later estimated to have advanced American research by several years and to have saved the United States billions of dollars.[75]

By the time these figures were known, the American and British governments were beginning to take legislative steps to ensure permanent institutionalization of the supply system that had brought them these riches. These steps will be discussed in our final chapter. For Great Britain the process was largely that of strengthening existing prewar government scientific information institutions. The United States government, however, based much of its postwar information infrastructure on models and techniques that had been forged as emergency measures between 1942 and 1945. And in the United States, two new additions to private sector publishing—micropublishing and scholarly reprinting—had made their entrance.

NOTES

1. E.S.B. Mackintosh, "War History of the Science Museum Library 1939-45," mimeograph, June 1945, file 201 in the archives of the Science Museum Library (hereafter SML).

2. P. R. Harris, "Microfilm Replacements in the British Library Reference Division," *Microfilm Review*, XV (Winter 1986), p. 16.

3. Library Association Committee for the Recovery of Books and Manuscripts, *The Restoration of Libraries: A Brief Account of the Inter-allied Book Centre* (London: Library Association, n.d.), p. 7.

4. Interview with Elizabeth Evans, librarian during the Second World War at the Cavendish Laboratory, later librarian at the Cambridge Philosophical Society, 3 July 1986.

5. Ibid.

6. Letter from Swets en Zeitlinger Boekhandel to the librarian, Cambridge Philosophical Society, 20 December 1939. Archives of the Scientific Periodicals Library, Cambridge University (formerly the Cambridge Philosophical Society Library).

7. Memorandum on "The Aslib Foreign Peridocials Survey and Other Bibliographical Projects Discussed with Dr. O'Brien on 12 December 1941," p. 3, mimeograph, SML, file 2109/2.

8. War Cabinet, Scientific Advisory Committee, "Supply and Availability of 'Enemy' Periodicals in This Country," 7 October 1941, mimeograph, marked "Secret," ibid.

9. Mackintosh, "War History of the Science Museum Library," p. 69.

10. J. D. Bernal, *The Social Function of Science* (London: Routledge and Kegan Paul, 1939), p. 212.

11. R. S. Hutton, "The Origin and History of Aslib," *Journal of Documentation* (1945/6), p. 14.

12. "Aslib Enemy Periodicals Project," June 1941, mimeographed circular to member libraries, file 2109/1, SML.

13. "Report on Work Done for Aslib Enemy Periodicals Project." 15 July 1941, mimeograph, file 2109/3, ibid.

14. War Cabinet, Scientific Advisory Committee, "Report to the Royal Society by the Association of Special Libraries and Information Bureaux on the

Survey of Scientific Periodicals from Enemy and Enemy-occupied Countries,"
15 August 1941, mimeograph, marked "Secret," ibid.

15. "Supply and Availability of 'Enemy' Periodicals in This Country,"
7 October 1941, mimeograph, marked "Secret," ibid.

16. "Report to the Royal Society," 15 August 1941, ibid.

17. "Supply and Availability," 7 October 1941, ibid.

18. Lucia Moholy, "The Aslib Microfilm Service: The Story of Its
Wartime Activities", *Journal of Documentation* 2 (December 1946), p. 147.

19. U.S. Office of Alien Property Custodian, "Report to the President
on the Periodical Republication Program," mimeograph, Washington DC, 1945.

20. Ralph Munn to Cordell Hull, 2 April 1940, Correspondence of the
Joint Committee on Importation, Special Collections, Columbia University.

21. See the correspondence between Fleming and the United States
Department of State among the papers of the Joint Committee on Importations
in Special Collections, Columbia University.

22. Thomas Fleming to Eileen Cunningham, 4 April 1940, ibid.

23. W. W. Rostow, *The United States in the World Arena* (New York:
Harper, 1960), p. 150.

24. The British Manuscripts Project, under way from 1941-1945, entailed
the microfilming of those Bitish archives identified as especially valuable by a
group of scholars. For details, see A. M. Meckler, *Micropublishing: A History
of Scholarly Micropublishing in America 1938-1940* (Westport CT: Greenwood
Press, 1982).

25. "War Diary of the Research and Analysis Branch, OSS, London."
Records Group 226, Military Records Division, United States National
Archives, Washington DC.

26. Margaret Gowing, *Britain and the Atomic Age* (London: St.
Martin's Press, 1964), p. 40. For a description of the background of the
"Frisch-Peierls Memorandum," see Rudolf Peierls, *Bird of Passage* (Princeton:
Princeton University Press, 1985), pp. 153-155.

27. Ronald Clark, *Tizard* (London: Methuen, 1965), p. 268.

28. Gowing, Britain and the Atomic Age, p. 39.

29. Ibid., p. 127.

30. Clark, *Tizard*, p. 281.

31. Alexander King, "International Relations in Science," *Empire
Scientific Conference 1946 (London: Royal Society, 1946)*, p. 121.

32. Gowing, *Britain and the Atomic Age*, p. 65.

33. See Pamela Spence Richards, "Gathering Enemy Scientific
Information in Wartime," *Journal of Library History* 117 (Summer 1981), pp.
253-264. See also Robin W. Winks, *Cloak and Gown* (New York: William
Morrow, 1987), pp. 101-106.

34. The committee was constituted as follows: the Royal Society, represented by Professor E. N. Da C. Andrade, Dr. E. F. Armstrong, Professor V. H. Blackman and Dr. C. H. Desch; the government libraries, represented by Sir David Chadwick (Agricultural Research Council), A. A. Gomme (Patent Office Library), Dr. F.H.K. Green (Medical Research Council), Mr. J. Lancaster Jones (the Science Museum Library), and C. S. Spencer (the Department of Scientific and Industrial Research); and the Association of Special Libraries and Information Bureaux, by E. J. Carter, E.M.R. Ditmas and Dr. R. S. Hutton. See Moholy, "The Aslib Microfilm Service," p. 147.

35. Ultimately the Rockefeller Foundation donated $10,000, British industrial firms more than 10,000 pounds, and the Royal Society 200 pounds. Ibid., p. 148.

36. "War Diary of the Research and Analysis Branch, OSS, London," Vol. I, p. 3, Records Group 226, Military Records Division, United States National Archives.

37. "War Diary of the Research and Analysis Branch, OSS, London," vol. 2, p. 43.

38. Moholy, "The Aslib Microfilm Service," p. 149.

39. Mackintosh, "War History of the Science Museum Library," p. 67.

40. Meckler, *Micropublishing*, p. 56.

41. "War Diary of the Research and Analysis Branch, OSS, London," vol. 1, p. 72.

42. File NS 6/440, Bundesarchiv, Coblenz.

43. Robin Wink, *Cloak and Gown: A History of the Scientific Intelligence Community* (New York: Macmillan, 1986), p. 178.

44. Journals available from the service are listed in Moholy, "The Aslib Microfilm Service," pp. 162-173.

45. Interview with Frederick Kilgour, Columbus, Ohio, 20 May 1987.

46. Moholy, "The Aslib Microfilm Service," p. 152.

47. Office of Alien Property Custodian, "Periodical Republication Program List VI and Statement Concerning Subscription to Reprints of Foreign Scientific Periodicals," Washington, D.C., November 1944, p. 1. See Appendix A for facsimile copy of the circular.

48. All titles offered for subscription up to November 1944 are listed in United States Alien Property Custodian, "Periodical Republication Program List VI," Washington, D.C., 1944, mimeograph, and are reprinted in the Appendix.

49. Alien Property Custodian, "Report to the President on the Periodical Republication Program," Washington D.C., 1945, mimeograph.

50. Aslib Microfilm Service, "Preliminary Note," 1942, file 2109/3 SML.

51. Interview with Frederick Kilgour, Columbus, Ohio, 20 May 1987.

52. A circular letter of Martin Bormann, dated 11 January 1944, refers to an earlier decree of Hitler— about which Bormann claims already to have written in April 1943— to stop the export of German printed matter which could be used against Germany. File NS 6/440, Bundesarchiv, Coblenz.

53. Krallert to Karasek, 26 September 1944, item 275, ibid. The advertisement noticed by the Germans may have been that in *The Bookseller* on 29 June 1944, under the heading "German Technical Books."

54. Reichskanzlei memorandum of 21 November 1944, ibid..

55. Reichskanzlei memorandum of 16 December 1944, item 571, ibid.

56. Edward Chapman, manuscript notes, in possession of the author. Chapman was wartime chief of the United States Alien Property Custodian's Copyright Administration.

57. Samuel Goudsmit, *ALSOS* (Los Angeles: Tomash, 1983), with an introduction by R. V. Jones). Jones expresses amazement at how little in comparison to the British the Americans knew about the Germans' nuclear activities, or indeed, lack of them, and how consequently the Americans were unnecessarily fearful of German competition (p. xi).

58. Stefan Rozenthal (ed.), *Niels Bohr* (Amsterdam: North Holland, 1976), p. 193.

59. Idem.

60. Rudolf Peierls, *Bird of Passage: Recollections of a Physicist* (Princeton: Princeton University Press, 1985), p. 168f.

61. R. V. Jones, *The Wizard War: British Scientific Intelligence, 1939-1945* (New York: Coward, McCann and Geoghegan, 1978), pp. 472 and 483. The role of Werner Heisenberg in the German decision not to pursue the bomb project is discussed in detail in Thomas Powers, *Heisenberg's War: The Secret History of the German Bomb* (New York: Knopf, 1993).

62. Interview with Frederick G. Kilgour, Columbus, Ohio, 20 May 1987.

63. United States Office of Alien Property Custodian, "Report to the President on the Periodical Republication Program," mimeograph, Washington, D.C., 1945, p. 6.

64. See John Deane, *The Strange Alliance: The Story of Our Efforts at Wartime Cooperation with Russia* (New York: Viking, 1947).

65. See E. M. Beardsley, "Secrets Between Friends: Applied Science Exchange Between the Western Allies and the Soviet Union during World War II," *Social Studies of Science* 7 (1977), p. 451.

66. R. V. Jones, interview with the author, Aberdeen, Scotland, 14 August 1990.

67. Richard G. Hewlett and Oscar E. Anderson, *The New World 1939/1946: A History of the United States Atomic Energy Commission*

(University Park PA: State University of Pennsylvania Press, 1962), p. 267. See also E.M. Beardsley, "Secrets Between Friends," p. 468.

68. Kramish, *Atomic Energy in the Soviet Union*, p. 58.

69. David Holloway, "Entering the Nuclear Arms Race: The Soviet Decision to Build the Atomic Bomb 1939-1945," *Social Studies of Science* 11 (1981), p. 174.

70. Hewlett and Anderson, *The New World*, p. 25.

71. See Goudsmit, *ALSOS*. Goudsmit's entire account reflects the surprise of his search team at not finding evidence of advanced research.

72. Clarence Lasby, *Project Paperclip: German Scientists and the Cold War* (New York: Atheneum, 1971), p. 26. For recent scholarshhip on this period, see John Gimbel, *Science, Technology and Reparations: Exploitation and Plunder in Postwar Germany* (Stanford CA: Stanford University Press, 1990).

73. See Julian P. Boyd, "A Landmark in the History of Library Cooperation in America," *College and Research Libraries* 8 (April 1947), pp. 101-109.

74. Mary Glen Chitty, *National Technical Information Service: The Concept of a Clearing House 1945-1979*, PB-300-947, p. 5.

75. Lasby, *Operation Paperclip*, p. 164.

5

Germany's Wartime Supply System for Enemy Scientific Information

In Chapter 3 we saw how the National Socialists supported the documentation of foreign science despite their racist ideology. As long as peace prevailed and normal channels abroad were open to the German book trade, the German government was able to brand foreign science as Jewish or hostile to the "Volk" while permitting certain libraries to collect foreign publications considered vital to Germany's power. After September 1939 and the breakdown of the book trade with Great Britain and the United States, the government knew it had to take emergency measures to acquire enemy publications for the technical colleges and the government's military research facilities. At German diplomatic missions in neutral countries such as Sweden, Portugal, Turkey and Mexico, scientific attachés arranged for the collection of foreign journals and their shipment to Germany in diplomatic pouches. These publications, as well as others acquired by the central acquisitions unit of the Notgemeinschaft der deutschen Wissenschaft at the Preussische Staatsbibliothek, and by private industry and other technical bodies, were forwarded to the Technische Hochschule in Berlin-Charlottenburg, where the photographic unit of the Reichszentrale für wissenschaftliche Berichterstattung reproduced them by photostat or microfilm. Copies of articles or whole issues of journals were then distributed to approved research institutions and to reviewing organs such as the *Chemisches Zentralblatt*, the *Physikalische Berichte*, and the medical reviews published by Springer. Further, an important role continued to be played by the foreign subsidiaries of the great German cartels, which had their own acquisitions networks and sometimes made their foreign journals available for photocopying at the Technische Hochschule at Berlin.

DEUTSCHE GESELLSCHAFT FUR DOKUMENTATION (GERMAN SOCIETY FOR DOCUMENTATION), 1941-1945 [1]

Germany had entered the war with a well-organized apparatus for the evaluation of technical literature and its dissemination to the technological universities and industry. However, the realities of a full-scale conflict, and in particular the British blockade of Germany after September 1939, soon made even the duplication work being done at Berlin-Charlottenburg inadequate, especially after the United States began to place restrictions on all American trade with Germany in early 1941. On 4 May 1941, the Committee on Professional Library Standards called a meeting in Berlin to address the situation. Present were, besides library leaders, publishers, and representatives of industry and professional associations, officials of the Ministry of Propaganda, the Ministry of Economics, the Foreign Office, and the Army High Command. The decision taken at this meeting to found a new organization, to be called the Deutsche Gesellschaft für Dokumentation (German Society for Documentation), marked the beginning of the National Socialist government's direct involvement with documentation matters. The society's governance placed it under firm Reich control: the chairman was to be appointed by the Minister of Education, and in turn appointed a board made up of representatives from science, technology, and industry, as well as agencies of the Reich; from this board the chairman named the society's vice-chairman, secretary, and treasurer.[2]

At the same meeting in May 1941 Fritz Prinzhorn (by then director of the Leipzig University Library)[3] was appointed chairman, and it was decided that the Documentation Society would assume the activities of the former Committee on Professional Library Standards, including continuing publication of its bulletin, *Dokumentation und Arbeitstechnik*. The task groups were taken over as a whole and three new ones formed: for terminology, journal clipping files and—significantly—the acquisition of foreign scientific literature.[4] The charge of this latter group was "to discuss, review and attempt all possible means of acquisition and to fill any gaps in the literature as they are discovered and to create an organization that establishes a central record of those information centers in Germany where each imported journal can be found."[5]

In December 1943 the new Documentaton Society published a classified 29-page union list (*Zentralnachweise für ausländischer Literatur*), which provided an inventory of all foreign publications imported into Germany since 1 September 1939. Published in Potsdam under the direction of Maximilian Pflücke (long-time editor of *Chemisches Zentralblatt*), the Documentation Society's union list issued three volumes by August 1944. Essentially a guide to the location of recent journals from the United States and the British

Commonwealth, the union list gave only titles, volumes available, and location. According to its introduction, it drew most heavily on the holdings of the Reich's five "official" acquisitions centers: the German Chemical Society, the Prussian State Library, the Hamburg World Economics Institute, and two commercial publishers: Lange und Springer in Berln, and Koehler and Volckmar in Leipzig. Fifteen locations were given, five of which were industrial libraries (four of these were I. G. Farben installations); curiously, Predeek's unit at Berlin Technolgical University is not on the list. Owners of the listed volumes were obliged to supply copies to querors.[6]

But the *Zentralnachweise* can only be considered an approximate reflection of the holdings of the Reich's publicly-funded libraries; despite an order from Deputy Reich Chancellor Martin Bormann stipulating that all current foreign holdings had to be reported to the Society for Documentation,[7] submission of titles by private firms, while extensive, was certainly not complete. The chief of the secret police (Sicherheitsdienst, or SD) complained to Goebbel's ministry in a letter of 10 February 10 1944, that he had proof that companies and research institutes were "selfishly" keeping their best new acquisitions to themselves, despite orders from the highest levels to inform the Documentation Society of their receipt.[8] Competition for patents was apparently still too intense among German firms to permit sharing everything with rivals. Just as in the Allied camp, business interests interfered with the circulaton of scientific information.

THE TECHNOLOGICAL UNIVERSITY AT
BERLIN-CHARLOTTENBURG

A number of German technological university libraries, especially those furthest west, managed to keep up limited foreign book trade relations: Aachen, for example, was still spending 20 percent of its budget on foreign materials in 1944, because of the close proximity of France and Belgium.[9] But as the war progressed, the decline in foreign scientific and technical journals entering the Reich made their duplication and dissemination an increasingly high priority. With the photographic units of the Reichszentrale on the premises, as well as Predeek's staff of abstracters and indexers, it was logical that most of the wartime dissemination activities came to be based in the library at Berlin-Charlottenburg.

Foreign publications were channeled to Predeek's unit from various sources: its own subscriptions, obtained through neutral countries such as Portugal; other technological institutions; private industrial research libraries; and Gisela von Busse's acquisitions unit of the Notgemeinschaft der deutschen Wissenschaft in the Prussian State Library in Berlin. Once reproduced by photostat or microfilm, copies of articles or whole issues were then distributed to the major libraries and to the established reviewing media. Copies were not automatically sent to industrial libraries, but orders for microfilm copies that came in from such libraries—in response to reviews seen in the professional journals—were duly processed.[10]

In 1942, the longstanding indexing and abstracting activities of the German learned societies and book trade were augmented by a monthly review (*Referatenblatt*), published by Predeek's Information Center in collaboration with the Information Center of the Technical and Economic World Press of the Hamburg World Economics Institute (Auswertungsstelle der technischen und wirtschaftlichen Weltfachpresse des Hamburger Weltwirtschaftsinstituts), run by Leo Hausleiter. Founded in 1908 as the Hamburg Colonial Institute (Hamburgische Kolonialinstitut), the unit became under the National Socialists an important collection center for foreign publications.[11] Hausleiter supervised thirty abstracters, who supplied the *Referatenblatt* with reviews of economic articles, while Predeek's unit supplied reviews of technical material. The *Referatenblatt* was comparable in size to the monthly *Chemical Abstracts* and provided quicker and more current coverage than the other reviewing media. Each issue contained approximately 3,000 reviews of current technical articles published in Europe, Britain and the United States (Russian, Asian, and Australian technical literature was not reviewed), with a detailed keyword index. Patent literature was also covered. Photostats of the originals could be ordered through the review service, which was only made available to subscribers approved for "membership" by a board under the minister of economics[12]; in practice, those approved seem mainly—if not exclusively—to have been industrial, governmental, and technological university libraries.[13] (See Appendix B for a copy of the *Referatenblatt*'s prefatory material.)

There is evidence that the German system kept an exclusive circle of privileged scientists quite up-to-date with foreign research, at least until 1943. After the war, Allied scientists were amazed by the extent to which their German counterparts had stayed current with British and American research: Maurice Wilkes, an American computer pioneer who was with the occupation forces in the summer of 1945, was surprised when his name was recognized by a captured German researcher, who was able to produce a photocopy of one of his 1940 articles.[14] Some of the most apparently innocuous material being published by the Allies contained information useful to the German war machine. In a typical case, Imperial Chemical Industries Ltd. (ICI), the British firm most deeply involved in advanced weaponry and atomic research in the first years of the war, regularly published results of the soccer matches played by its house teams. Each factory team played home and away matches with its counterparts in other factories, and using these ICI bulletins, German intelligence was able to target several ICI plants of whose existence it had not previously been aware.[15]   Of longer-term value was information in some of the articles appearing in American and British journals before publication restrictions were placed on nuclear research in the summer of 1940. In 1939, for example, *Reviews of Modern Physics* published a description of a gas centrifuge that scientists at Hamburg later attempted to adapt to work with uranium hexafluoride gas. Some important American findings in the area of atomic fission were released a few months later: Through notes in the March and April 1940 issues of *Physical Review*, experimental proof was given that slow neutrons had a greater probability of fissioning U-235; and in the 15 June 1940 number of the same journal, Edwin McMillan and Philip Abelson announced the discovery of new element, labeled element 94, which was probably fissionable (later christened plutonium, the element was a product of the bombardment of the common uranium-238 isotope with neutrons).[16] The significance of the discovery of element 94 was enormous. If it proved to be fissionable, as Abelson and McMillan suspected, it would provide an easily produced fissionable substance which could take the place of the rare isotope U-235 and save its producers the staggering cost of building isotope-separation plants. (In fact, the second atomic bomb used against Japan in August 1945—the destroyer of Nagasaki—would be a plutonium bomb.)

Thus, as some of the refugee scientists feared, German scientists were able to learn from American journals published *after* the outbreak of the war the results of physical investigations that they did not have the means to obtain themselves.[17]   Émigré physicist Leo Szilard, who had been responsible for Einstein's letter to Roosevelt in 1939, was obsessed by this danger and pressed throughout the first months of the war for a voluntary suspension of publication by atomic scientists outside Germany. His warnings bore fruit after the founding by Vannevar Bush of the Uranium Committee under the National Research Council. One of the Uranium Committee's members, University of Wisconsin physicist Gregory Breit, initiated a reference committee of physicists whose task it was to review for publication or restriction research articles on nuclear research with possible military significance.[18] The voluntary classification of nuclear science research by Allied scientists was ultimately effective: There is no evidence that the Germans were aware of the massive atomic bomb effort of the Allies. In fact, the surprise produced after German surrender by the attack on Hiroshima was evidence both of the embryonic state in which German atomic engineering had languished and of the effectiveness of the Allied publication blackout.

THE OCCUPIED TERRITORIES

For the Germans, all peoples and territories annexed or occupied by the Reich were viewed as resources to serve Germany's interests, but there were great differences both in the methods employed in the process of exploitation and in the degree of rapacity. Some of these differences stemmed from National Socialist racial policies, according to which the Scandinavian and Netherlandic peoples were regarded as Germanic "brothers" but the Slavic peoples as lower forms of humanity. Other differences stemmed from geopolitical considerations, from concern for world opinion and from the Germans' own cultural traditions—all of which were important, for example, in determining the treatment of the long-venerated (if not "racially pure") French. Because of these differences, we must examine German scientific information gathering in various parts of occupied Europe separately.

Scandinavia and the Low Countries

For Nazi ideologues the war opened the possibility of a new order of science in Northern and Western Europe, an Aryan community where Germans would share their world-view with other European scientists who would work collaboratively with the Germans for the ultimate good of the master race. The readiness of scientists of other nationalities to learn from the Germans was assumed on the basis of the belief that German science exhibited its superior qualities through German military victories. In the words of a Nazi lecturer at the Technological University of Berlin on the subject "Science in the Struggle for the Reich and Living Space" in 1941: "War is and always was the historical test of peoples. This is also true for science and scientists. Their value to their own people, and their ranking within their own people, is determined in an uncompromising way only by war. For them as well, war is the only judge."[19]

In the plans of the German occupational authorities the local educational institutions in the occupied countries of Western Europe were to play an important role. They were supposed to spread knowledge and appreciation of German science and encourage the collaboration of the best scientists in the occupied territories. Elaborate provisions were made to transform both the Universities of Strasbourg and Leiden into bulwarks of National Socialism in the west,[20] where they would train future generations of Germanic scholars and scientists. The University of Leiden in particular excited great hope among the Nazis because of its great international renown as a scientific center. Plans for its conversion to Nazi purposes remained alive for several years after the opposition of its teachers had become clear. The dismissal of Jewish professors at Dutch universities in November 1940 led to a series of strikes at the University of Leiden, and in April 1942 the entire teaching staff resigned rather than permit the university to be made into an instrument of National Socialists policies.[21] Undaunted, Bernard Rust, the German education minister, visited The Hague as late as fall 1943 to discuss with the Nazi official in charge of Dutch educational policy the transformation of Leiden into an all-male Germanic university for Dutch, Flemish, Norwegian and Danish students.[22]

Other universities in the Low Countries and Scandinavia were equally opposed to cooperating with the Germans. Attempts to appoint German Nazis to the staff of the University of Oslo met such vigorous protest from the Norwegian association of scientists and scholars in May 1941 that Norwegian higher education was ultimately suspended for the duration of the war. Similarly, the Université Libre of Brussels was closed after the refusal of its board of governors to appoint Nazi sympathizers as teachers in November 1941.[23]

Nazi plans for collaboration in technological research in the Western occupied countries also failed in the face of the resentment of the local population, including teachers and research workers. The Aerodynamische Versuchsanstalt (Aerodynamic Experimental Station) of the University of Göttingen, a favorite institution of Göring, commissioned experimental work in September 1940 to be done by the Nationale Laboratorium voor de Luchtvaart (National Aviation Laboratory) in Amsterdam, and German scientific and technical engineering teams were sent to supervise operations at existing research institutions such as the laboratory of the Philips industrial firm at Eindhoven. But no productive collaboration was ever forthcoming. According to Hendrik Casimir, the Dutch physicist in charge of the Philips laboratories, his Dutch scientists were never given any war-related work because the Germans realized that any such work would automatically be sabotaged; in fact, the German supervisor at Philips was so sensitive to Dutch resentment that he meticulously announced all his inspections in advance.[24]

The Philips supervisor was not unique: actually, a number of German scientists understood the depth of hatred of the occupation and were deeply embarrassed by it. The physicist Richard Becker of the Technische Hochschule of Berlin, for one, privately commiserated with Dutch colleagues about their conditions and commented to one that "the bill will soon have to be paid"; Hans Kopfermann, a physicist at the University of Berlin, was worried during his visits to the Netherlands that his Dutch friends might be compromised among their compatriots by receiving him in their homes.[25] Werner Heisenberg, however, in spite of his carefully cultivated image as the "good German," saw the refusal of cooperation by foreign scientists as a temporary phenomenon which would disappear with German victory. On a lecture tour of Holland in 1943, he remarked to Hendrik Casimir that he was certain that the persecutions which were causing so much anti-German sentiment would lessen once the war was over, and that, given the threat to European civilization from the east, "maybe a Europe under German leadership might be the lesser evil."[26] But few scientists in the occupied countries shared Heisenberg's feelings and virtually nothing grew out of the attempts of the National Socialists to create new centers of science in Scandinavia and the Low Countries. In fact, the brutality of the occupation destroyed the channels of informal personal communication that had long existed between Germany and Scandinavia and the Low Countries; and the formal collaboration agreements generated no research of any importance.

France

France had been for centuries the center of European learning and art, and—Nazi racial propaganda notwithstanding—its culture remained in 1940 too symbolic of high Western civilization for the Germans to try either to absorb it, like that of the Germanic peoples of Northern and Northwestern Europe, or to annihilate it, like that of the Slavs. France had many admirers in the still-neutral United States, and, indeed, within the Reich itself. But the most important reason of state behind the initially lenient treatment of France was Germany's focus in 1940 on its planned invasion of England: With a pacified France at its rear and the French Empire administered by a friendly client regime at Vichy, Germany would have to divert fewer of its troops from its main goal across the Channel.

The leaders of the occupying forces knew how crucial it was for victory not to drive a defeated and neutralized France back into the Allied camp,[27] and in two symbolically significant cultural arenas, universities and libraries, they tried to demonstrate their "sensitivity" to France's historically important position in Western civilization. As we will see, the German policy permitted the development of two rival branches of French scientific documentation: one sanctioned by the conqueror, the other illegal but destined to survive the occupation and flourish in the postwar period.

Except for the case of Strasbourg, which with all of Alsace-Lorraine the Nazis considered part of Germany, the universities were not as much interfered with as elsewhere—they were neither forced to introduce new Nazi-oriented scholars or disciplines, nor shut down as unnecessary, as in the Slavic countries. "In the future, France will naturally have a different relationship with the Reich than the Eastern Regions (Ostgebiete), and for that reasons it would seem to me appropriate not to restrict her institutions of higher education," commented the German chief of staff responsible for the administration of French culture in August 1940.[28]

There was only one major attempt to inject National Socialist propaganda into French university life; this occurred at Strasbourg, where elaborate provisions were made by the Germans to transform the university into a bulwark of National Socialism in the West after most of the faculty had fled south to

Clermont-Ferrand in 1940. German Nazis were appointed in their place to turn the university into a "battering ram of the party" which, after German victory, would "reduce to nothing the influence of French culture in Northern France," which was claimed as German cultural territory.[29] Such was the urgency of the party's desire to turn Strasbourg into a center of Nazi research that the university's library of one-and-a-half million volumes, which had been transported by the French to Clermont-Ferrand just before the invasion, was moved back north and made available to users early in 1942.[30]

But in the rest of France, where historical German cultural claims were not at issue, meddling with scholarly and scientific life was less extensive than in occupied Scandinavia and the Low Countries. Sometimes faculty "slow-downs"—such as in the preparation of new, approved textbooks—were responsible for keeping German incursions at bay, and sometimes the verbal pyrotechnics of the French professoriate were an effective defense; a case in point was the response of Gilbert Gidel, the rector of the Sorbonne, to a German official's suggestion in 1941 that classes be organized at the University of Paris by German academics in transit, and that the occasion be used for the exchange of views with French scholars. Gidel wrote to the German official: "It is not that the themes you suggest are not numerous and interesting for both parties, nor that I do not bow before the eminent scientific titles of the potential speakers. But the moment does not seem to me to have yet arrived when such an event could take place in the very heart of the university in a sufficiently disengaged atmosphere to be scientifically fruitful."[31] The Germans had evidently hoped that anti-German sentiment had died down after a huge student demonstration against the occupation in Paris in November 1940, which had closed the university for two months. The university was reopened in January 1941, purged of its Jewish faculty members (like all French schools by that time), but Gidel's response makes clear that collaboration was still out of the question. Interestingly, the Germans did not force the issue, and university life, including scientific research, continued in France until the liberation[32]—though marred hideously by deportations of Jews, resistance workers and forced laborers, and by the continued captivity in Germany of thousands of French prisoners of war, many of whom had been students and teachers.

The other culturally symbolic area in which the Germans treated France with special consideration was libraries, in which France was especially rich and which, as booty, could have substantially enriched the Reich's own collections. Certainly the Germans were eager to claim as theirs and remove to the Reich whatever they could historically justify as "German property"(as they did in the case of the library of the university of Strasbourg). To supervise German relations with French libraries, they established a special subgroup (Untergruppe Bibliothekschutz) of nine librarians under Dr. E. Wermke, director of the Breslau Municipal Library. The subgroup was located in the administrative division of the German military High Command of France. Its official purposes were to inventory book holdings in France and to encourage German-French publications exchange in general. Materials useful to German science were to be photocopied.[33]

With the encouragement of H. A. Krüss, director of the Prussian State Library, Wermke's subgroup devoted itself for three years to surveying French collections and to protecting them from the depredations and negligence of German army and party officialdom—particularly of the Einsatz Rosenberg. Party ideologue Alfred Rosenberg had been given a special mandate in 1942 by Adolf Hitler to confiscate property belonging to "Jews, Masons and their ideological allies," on whom Hitler blamed the war. Rosenberg's staff had a special subdivision for library research and for the construction of libraries out of confiscated collections (Sonderstab Bibliotheksforschung und Bibliotheksaufbau).[34] Wermke's subgroup was ineffective in preventing the looting by Rosenberg's men of valuable French collections of Hebraica, Masonic history and labor union history.[35]

The Subgroup for Library Protection also had an important public relations mission: Krüss had reminded Wermke of the importance of offsetting the "unsatisfactory impressions, especially in America," created by the German destruction—for the second time in twenty-five years—of the famous library of the University of Louvain in Belgium.[36] Wermke took the opportunity of a press conference called at the end of the committee's first year of work in 1941 to remind reporters that the committee "had not taken one single book or page from a French public library or transported it to Germany." He further explained that the real destruction of French libraries was caused not by the occupying forces but by British bombers.[37]

The committee's effectiveness did, at times, extend beyond pure window-dressing to some areas of practical assistance (following up French librarians' complaints about German soldiers with overdue books and maps, for example); but in achieving its important goal, facilitating the exchange of publications between France and Germany, it was less successful. In talks with the Bibliothèque Nationale concerning the reinstatement and widening of French-German exchange of journals and dissertations, the German committee was unable to get the French to accept the incorporation of Warsaw into the Reich and its inclusion in the French-German exchange agreement. France's cultural relations with Poland were traditionally strong, and validating Germany's aggression in Poland was apparently more than the French librarians were prepared to do. Ultimately, the whole exchange ageement broke down over the Warsaw question.[38]

The library protection subgroup certainly did not initiate criminal activities like those of Rosenberg's staff, but it equally did not serve, as Wermke repeatedly claimed, "to advance culture and science through comradely collaboration, counsel and assistance."[39]   Any   possibility of such cultural advance was more than stifled by the imposition by the Germans of library and book trade censorship in the guise of the notorious "Liste Bernhard" and "Liste Otto," whereby books by Jews or other "enemies of the Reich" were forcibly removed from circulation.[40] Much of the time of the library protection group was taken up with correspondence with French libraries concerning adherence to the censorship provisions, which French librarians applied very inconsistently throughout the occupation.[41]

The one reasonably successful area of German-French scientific collaboration, the exchange of scientific journals, was due not so much to the initiatives of the library protection group as to the energies of one Frenchman, Jean Gérard. Gérard had been the organizing spirit behind the World Documentation Congress in Paris in 1937 and was the secretary general of the Maison de la Chemie. As such, he was director of one of the best scientific periodical collections in the world. Moreover, the microfilming facilities of the Maison de Chemie were considered among the best in existence. Gérard sought desperately for a means to reactivate the Maison's subscriptions to German journals, which had been cut off by the terms of the Armistice following France's defeat in June 1940. In the fall of 1940 Gérard complained of the situation to Wermke, pointing out that the reopening of subscription channels would "put German and French chemists back in an atmosphere conducive to scientific collaboration." Gérard suggested that the same messenger service the Germans were now using to deliver German weeklies to Paris could be used for chemical journals.[42]   At Gérard's insistence a meeting was   called on this subject in October 1940 at the Bibliothèque Nationale, and its new, German-appointed director, L. R. Faij, reported to Wermke that the forty representatives of French scientific and scholarly libraries had asked (1) to be informed of what books and periodicals were appearing in Germany; (2) to receive those German journals to which they had subscribed; (3) to be allowed to receive those periodicals stockpiled for them in Switzerland which the Germans had not permitted into France; (4) to correspond with German subscription agents; and (5) to get the journals which were appearing in non-occupied France (Vichy).[43]

Gérard's zeal was not selfless: Besides running the Maison de la Chimie, he was   the   sole   proprietor   of   a   profitable   documentation   service   called SOPRODOC, a scientific indexing and abstracting service that enjoyed a monopoly in France during the occupation because of Gérard's access to German-controlled paper and printing licenses.[44]   His domination of official French documentation during the occupation[45] was based not only on his readiness to cooperate with the Germans and on his fluency in German, but also on the fact that he controlled microfilm facilities which the Germans wanted to use to photograph French rarities for Reich libraries, particularly the Leibnitz manuscripts in Paris.[46] His cooperation with German documentation activities continued throughout the occupation.[47] After the liberation, American troops found evidence in abandoned German archives that the Germans had considered Gérard almost as their own agent, going so far as to assign him a number. Subsequently Gérard was imprisoned for six months on charges of collaboration.[48]

Probably at least partially as a result of Gérard's influence, the exchange of journals between France and Germany improved rapidly after the meeting at the Bibliothèque Nationale in October 1940; by the next summer Gérard's complaint to the Germans was that he was *only* getting German, Belgian and Dutch journals, while his patrons (and customers) needed current information from Italy, Japan, Russia, Spain and the United States as well.[49] Gérard had heard about the Reichszentrale's microfilming center at Berlin-Charlottenburg and tried to get access to its copies of American journals,[50] but by early 1942 he was being informed by German documentalists of how inadequate and out-of-date their own supplies of Allied scientific literature were. While Gérard performed valuable services for the Germans by thoroughly indexing French scientific publishing during the occupation, and by making German research available for French scientists, there is no evidence that his library or documentation service provided any access to Allied science which the Germans did not already have.

French scientists had their own clandestine channels to Western science. An illegal indexing and abstracting service was operated throughout the occupation by the Centre Nationale de la Recherche Scientifique (CNRS), the French government agency set up in 1939 to centralize state funding for science. In 1940 the CNRS was a center of both French science and French scientific resistance to the Germans; in both cases the leading personality was Frédéric Joliot-Curie, winner with his wife, Irène Curie, of the Nobel Prize for chemistry in 1935 for their synthesis of new radioactive elements and in whose laboratories France's most important atomic research had been conducted before the war.

Joliot-Curie had spoken in his Nobel acceptance speech of the immense power that could be released by a chain reaction[51] and after the war the English physicist and Nobel Laureate P.S.M. Blackett commented that "towards the latter part of 1939, it is probably right that Joliot and his colleagues had carried realistic thinking about the practical possibilities of extracting useful power from uranium further than any other group in the world."[52] For all these reasons, the Germans kept this work under close scrutiny. (Unknown to them, Joliot-Curie's two closest coworkers, Lew Kowarski and Hans Halban, had escaped to England and were working on the Allied atomic bomb project; Joliot's poor knowledge of English, and the tuberculosis of his children and wife, kept him in France.)[53]

German hopes of Joliot-Curie's cooperation on atomic research were heightened by the fact that his laboratory contained the largest cyclotron operating in German-controlled territory. They permitted him to continue experiments with the cyclotron on the understanding that Walter Bothe of the Institut für Physik at Berlin—where plans for a cyclotron were stalled by lack of funds—could use the cyclotron regularly. Joliot-Curie, assuming that Bothe was doing uranium research with military applications potential, arranged with his French technician to have something go wrong with the cyclotron every time the unsuspecting Bothe tried to use it.[54]

At the beginning of 1941 Joliot-Curie asked a young crystallographer, Jean Wyart, to take over the embryonic documentation service started by the CNRS in 1939. Wyart recognized that the major problem confronting French scientific information was that France was divided in half by the "line of demarcation" separating occupied France from Vichy, a formally neutral state that maintained contact with the Allies. Using the contacts he had built up as a member of France's young scientific elite (a graduate of the Ecole Normale, he had studied with the great physicist Paul Langevin), Wyart began to lay the groundwork for a publication that would give French science access to research being done outside the Reich. Key to this process was the ability to pass back and forth over the line of demarcation into Vichy. This mobility was enjoyed by certain friends of Wyart's in the French telephone company, who helped procure English and American journals for him in the south. Soon Wyart himself was able to visit Vichy regularly: An officer in the science service of the Luftwaffe offered automatic passes to a French astronomer whom the German had known before the war—and who let Wyart use them.

Once able to travel freely to the south, Wyart made contact in Lyon with the science service of Pétain's "Army of the Armistice," which had just set up its own documentation center and received journals from Great Britain and the United States. (Technically neutral, Vichy had an American legation and some postal contact with the Allies.) The two intelligence officers in charge of the center were fiercely anti-German and helped Wyart procure much foreign material.[55] While unswervingly loyal to Marshall Pétain, a number of the officers in the army of Vichy were pro-Ally: In early 1941 the United States military attaché at Vichy, Robert Schow, was regularly supplied information about the Germans by the Vichy French military intelligence service; it is possible that in return Schow, and the OSS agent who became naval attaché to Vichy in January 1942,[56] helped the Vichy scientific service with its procurement of American journals.

Procurement was only the first problem that Wyart had to overcome: Jean Gérard had the authority to distribute paper for documentation purposes and he used that power to deny Wyart paper and thus secure SOPRODOC's monopoly. But by another fortunate coincidence, an old friend of Wyart's was director of the school of papermaking (Ecole de Papeterie) in Grenoble and was able to get Wyart all the paper he needed. Printing—only possible with German permission—was arranged through yet another acquaintance, the head of the prestigious Hermann scientific editions, who worked through a small local printer at Saint Amand Montrond in central France near the border with Vichy, where the local German authorities were cooperative. Official permission to publish from the Ministry of Education under the occupation was never forthcoming, making Wyart's publication illegal under occupation law, and its editors subject to arrest at any time.[57]

CNRS's *Bulletin Analytique* appeared monthly, offering three- to six-line summaries of French, British and American articles and the possibility of ordering the original on microfilm. German scientific literature was barely covered at all, as such coverage was available through SOPRODOC. In 1940 Wyart's center microfilmed 40,000 pages on order, and by 1944 this figure had risen to 800,000. Almost fifty years later, when the CNRS had grown to be one of the largest indexing centers in the world, Wyart still remembered the primitive conditions under which the three employees of the center worked during occupation years, with the single photographer hanging the microfilm on the elevator cage to dry.[58]

Curiously, the Germans made no effort to suppress the illegal index, despite the protestations of Gérard, with whose service it was competing successfully, because of its English and American content. This tolerance can hardly be explained by the Germans' need for the index themselves, since their own overseas contacts were sending American and British journals to the Reich's documentation services fairly efficiently, especially during the first years of the war. Possibly the specialized nature of Wyart's operation, and its limited audience, made it a low priority for the Germans, or it may have been protected by the confused chain of command characteristic of the French bureaucracy under the occupation. In any case, Wyart was never ordered to terminate his operation, which was well known both among the occupiers and even among scientists in England.[59] All of the literature processed by Wyart's group was put at the disposal of the Allies upon the liberation of Paris in June 1944 and, indeed, helped supply the Aslib Microfilm Service in London with microfilms of wartime publications hitherto unobtainable in Great Britain.

Eastern Europe

Hitler had made it clear from the beginning of his career that he regarded the Slavic races as born slaves whose historical mission was to provide labor and land for German expansion.[60] Education for Slavs was not only unnecessary but dangerous. As he put it: "At the most, one must let them learn not more than the meaning of road signs. Instruction in geography can be limited to one single sentence: the capital of the Reich is Berlin. Mathematics and the like are quite unnecessary."[61] Rather than collaborate with Slavic scientists, the Germans were simply to murder or enslave them. Although the history of

Czechoslovakia, Poland and the Soviet Union under the German occupation has local variations, there is a horrible sameness in the energy with which the Germans undertook to annihilate indigenous scientific activity and either to destroy the infrastructure of scientific life—books and equipment—or to sequester it for exclusive German use, usually by transport.

With the exception of the Baltic countries, a relatively privileged area where schools reopened soon after the German invasion, education and scientific research in the eastern occupied countries ceased almost completely after 1941. In Czechoslovakia, higher education was suspended and books in the Czech language removed from libraries as early as November 1939, following the killing of hundreds of students at the university and technological institute of Prague; German was made the official language.[62] After the invasion of Poland in September 1939 and the establishment of the Gouvernment-General in the part which was not annexed to Germany, Governor-General Frank declared that Poland was to be turned into an intellectual desert. The Universities of Warsaw, Poznan, Lvov and Cracow were closed (the entire staff of Cracow was jailed) in 1939 and early 1940, and the University of Lublin was destroyed by bombardment.[63] The University of Cracow was transformed into an institute for the collection of information about Germany's mission in Eastern Europe; the University of Poznan was reopened for German students in 1941 for "wide-ranging research on the eastern territories."[64] Important Polish scientific achievements of the past were transformed into German achievements: In May 1943, at a festive celebration at Königsberg of the four-hundredth anniversary of the death of Copernicus, where a Copernicus prize created by Göring was presented to Werner Heisenberg, it was announced that Polish claims to the astronomer were false, and that he was in fact German.[65]

In those parts of the Soviet Union that fell under German rule, schooling above the fourth grade was prohibited after 1941 except in the Ukraine, where the minister of the eastern territories, Alfred Rosenberg, allowed continued instruction in practical fields such as agriculture, forestry, medicine and veterinary medicine.[66] Universities and scientific institutes at Riga, Vilna, Minsk, Smolensk, Dorpat, Kiev and Khar'kov were stripped of their books and periodical collections, which were transported by Alfred Rosenberg's squads to a huge "library for the East" (Ostbücherei), first in Berlin, then in Ratibor.[67] The important laboratories of the Khar'kov Physico-Technical Institute were ransacked by a specially trained "econonomic commando," which dispatched much of its equipment and specialized literature to Germany. Millions of other volumes were simply destroyed, such as the books from the Korelenko Library in Khar'kov, which were laid out on muddy roads; the holdings of the University of Kiev and the Kiev Museum were burned in public.[68] At the end of the war, the Soviet delegation at Nuremberg formally declared that during the occupation the Germans had destroyed 334 institutions of higher learning and

605 scientific research institutes. Of its library holdings they estimated that over 100 million volumes had been destroyed.[69]

What is of interest to us here is the extent to which the acquisition of these eastern territories actually added to the fund of scientific knowledge available to the Germans. Certainly the hundreds of thousands of volumes accumulated by Rosenberg for his Ostbücherei represented a potentially impressive resource, but the collection was never cataloged or made accessible to scholars and scientists. The immense transport problems faced by the Germans on the Eastern Front meant that a large proportion of the confiscated scientific collections never got inside the Reich at all, but remained stockpiled at collection points in Belorussia and the Ukraine, where they could later be retrieved by advancing Soviet troops.

The Soviet Union's most important resources of scientific information never fell into enemy hands. They eluded the Germans either because they lay beyond German lines or because they had been transported there in the Soviet retreat behind Moscow in 1941 and 1942. Leningrad, with the Academy of Sciences Library and the Palace of Engineers, was besieged for three years but never taken, although these institutions as well as the university library were heavily damaged during the bombardment. An even greater scientific prize would have been Moscow, the site not only of the Lenin State Library and the Public Library for Science and Technology but also of numerous institutes of the Academy of Sciences.   But the most important scientific booty had been evacuated from both these cities by September 1941: Academy institutes in geography, mathematics, chemistry and physics were moved to Kazan' or to the industrial cities of the Urals. Here the scientific collections, often supplemented by materials donated by the Western Allies, were able to support the continuation of research as early as 1942 (see Chapter 4).

The ultimate failure of the Germans to profit from their occupation of a number of scientifically advanced countries was due to a number of factors. Probably the most important was the Germans' general disdain for the scientific accomplishments of the conquered peoples, which prevented any fruitful scientific communication. But there were important logistic obstacles as well: The difficulty of transporting library collections while carrying on a war constituted one; the lack of the manpower needed to catalog and make these collections available for use was another. The Soviets' decision to evacuate their whole scientific establishment to the Urals certainly diminished German profits further. The recalcitrance of captive populations was also important—as in the unwillingness of Dutch and French scientists to work collaboratively with the Germans, or in the refusal of French library administrators to accept the absorption of the national library of Poland into their exchange agreements with the Reich. With time, of course, many of these factors might have lost their significance, exactly as Werner Heisenberg calculated. But by 1943 the time that was needed for the absorption of the scientific resources of the occupied countries was running out.

THE DISINTEGRATION OF THE REICH

The Third Reich's supply of foreign technical information was brought to an end not by the lack of available foreign publications but rather by the destruction between 1943 and 1945 of the channels of collection and dissemination. The import of foreign periodicals, which depended most heaviy on Portugal and Sweden after America's entry into the war, continued through the regular Lufthansa flights to those countries right into 1945.[70] But inside the Reich itself, the information chain disintegrated under the carpet of British and American bombs.

In 1943, the entire technological university at Berlin-Charlottenburg, including its library of a quarter of a million volumes, was totally destroyed,[71] hardly anything remained of Predeek's Information Center—neither its clipping files, its photographic equipment, nor its massive collection of foreign technical and scientific journals. Predeek and the survivors on his staff took what was left of the materials with them to an evacuation site at Rossla in the Harz Mountains, where they kept working.[72]   Incredibly, the monthly issues of the *Referatenblatt* published collaboratively by the Information Centers at Hamburg and the Berlin Technological University continued to appear until 30 November 1944. (The review itself was printed in Hamburg, where, despite terrible destruction, the World Economics Institute survived the entire war relatively unscathed.)[73]

The traditional technical and scientific journals, some of them dating from the nineteenth century, were soon wiped out as well: *Chemisches Zentralblatt*, *Biologisches Zentralblatt*, and many other scientific and technical reviews were published in Leipzig, where, on the night of 3 December 1943, the Royal Air Force dropped 1,500 tons of bombs on the center of the city, destroying the plants of 90 percent of the "book city's" publishers, paper manufacturers, and type founders; subsequently shortages of paper, lead and electricity forced the merger or suspension of all journals not considered absolutely essential to Germany's daily information needs.[74] Busse's Acquisitions Bureau in the Prussian State Library was bombed repeatedly from 1941 on, and had to turn much of its foreign acquisitions work back to the individual research libraries.[75] In the last months of the war, when the Prussian State Library had been totally evacuated, the Bureau moved to Eberswalde, from which its workers finally fled before the advancing Russian army.[76]

The German wartime network was hampered by the information restrictions imposed by the National Socialists in the prewar years. Despite the apparent efficiency with which the network operated, it was saddled by the contradictions inherent in National Socialist policies. These are perhaps most clearly visible in the government decrees forbidding the import of foreign literature without Gestapo approval.[77]   Dismayed by the resulting scarcity of information, the National Socialists subsequently had to establish the German Society for Documentation to expedite the flow of scientific and technical information—foreign included—to designated libraries throughout the Reich. Totalitarian fear of public access to information led the government to isolate most academic librarians from the process and to foster the creation of a new profession—documentation—with a limited clientele.[78]

Reich policies were also inefficient. No mechanism was ever developed to exploit effectively the privately owned industrial research libraries, which only shared their holdings with other libraries or with the government when such action posed no threat to corporate profits.[79] Some government agencies were particularly favored with information from industrial libraries (the Army High Command, for example, was kept well supplied by I. G. Farben).[80] Others, such as several intelligence units, had to fend for themselves. An example of the extremes to which individual units went is furnished by the mission of the Sicherheitsdienst, the party's intelligence branch, to the United States in November 1944. Two German agents were actually dropped by submarine on the Maine coast with orders to proceed to New York's bookstores and public libraries, reduce essential information in technical books and journals to microform, and insert them in letters to the agency's men in Madrid. The Federal Bureau of Investigation picked up both men before any information was transmitted.[81]   The National Socialists' overt favoring of industrial libraries at the expense of general university collections is all the more interesting when compared to the American wartime organization of scientific information, in which university libraries occupied priority positions.[82] This difference surely had to do with where the most important research was taking place in either country.   Whether it was a fear of the liberal atmosphere of the great universities or the aggressiveness of the German cartels, the fact is that in Germany the most advanced work was being done in the laboratories and testing grounds of industry and government research institutes.   The United States government commissioned the theoretical work of the Manhattan Project to be done on the campuses of Berkeley, Columbia, and Chicago, whereas the center of atomic research in Germany was in the plants of I. G. Farben, which had a monopoly on heavy water production in the Reich.[83] Whatever the cause, the net effect of the Germans' wartime information policy reinforced the trend begun in 1933 whereby an increasing proportion of government-funded information bypassed publicly accessible libraries and was channeled to a preselected audience in industry and in restricted government institutes.

NOTES

1. An organization bearing the same name was founded in West Germany in 1946 with its headquarters in Frankfurt am Main.

2. *Dokumentation und Arbeitstechnik* (June 1941), pp. 2-3.

3. After the war, Prinzhorn was director of the West German Foreign Ministry Library from 1951 until his retirement in 1958.

4. Even in nomenclature this task group's similarity to its American counterpart is striking: compare the OSS's Interdepartment Committee for the Acquisition of Foreign Publications.

5. Marianne Buder, *Das Verhältnis von Dokumentation und Normung von 1927 bis 1945 in nationaler und internationaler Hinsicht* (Berlin: Deutsches Institut für Normung, 1976), pp. 70-72.

6. File NS 6/440, Bundesarchiv, Coblenz. Among the materials in this file is the introductory issue of the *Nachweise*.

7. Idem.

8. File R 55/919, Bundesarchiv, Coblenz.

9. Telephone conversation between Gisela von Busse and Gerhart Lohse, Bad Godesberg and Aachen, Germany, 23 August 1982. Lohse was director of the library of the Technical University of Aachen until 1979.

10. Letter of Gisela von Busse to the author, 17 January 1983.

11. Wolfgang Scherwath, "Die Bibliothek des HWWS-Institut für Wirtschaftsforschung-Hamburg," *Auskunft: Mitteilungsblatt Hamburger Bibliotheken* 3 (1983), pp. 191-194.

12. File R 7/2029 contains a copy of the initial issue of the *Referatenblatt* (February 1942), in which there is a statement of the reviewing service's purpose and restricted availability, as well as a warning that it may not be reproduced in any fashion or even quoted.

13. The author has been unable to locate a "membership" list. The British occupational authorities confiscated most of the files of the Hamburg Institute after the war, and very little was ever returned. See Scherwath, Die Bibliothek des HWWA," p. 194.

14. Maurice V. Wilkes, *Memoirs of a Computer Pioneer* (Cambridge MA: MIT Press, 1985), p. 99.

15. R. V. Jones, *Reflections on Intelligence* (London: Heinemann, 1989), p. 69.

16. The actual physical production of plutonium was demonstrated early in 1941 at Berkeley by Glenn T. Seaborg, who gave the new element its name. See Daniel J. Kevles, *The Physicists* (New York: Alfred J. Knopf, 1978), p. 325.

17. David Irving, *The German Atomic Bomb* (New York: Simon and Schuster, 1967), pp. 70-72.

18. Richard G. Hewlett and Oscar E. Anderson, *The New World 1939/1946: A History of the United States Atomic Energy Commission*, vol. 1 (University Park: Pennsylvania State University Press, 1962), p. 25.

19. Paul Ritterbusch, *Wissenschaft im Kampf um Reich und Lebensraum, Vortrag gehalten in der Technischen Hochscule Berlin am 7. Dezember 1941* (Stuttgart: Kohlhammer, 1942), p. 5.

20. Karl Julius Hartmann, "Die Universitäts- und Landesbibliothek Strassburg," *Zentralblatt für Bibliothekswesen* 59 (1942), pp. 441-452; and P. J. Idenburg, *De Leidse Universiteit 1928-1946: Vernieuwing en Verzet* (The Hague: Universitaire Pers Leiden, 1978), p. 222.

21. M. Dresden, *H. A. Kramers: Between Tradition and Revolution* (New York: Springer Verlag, 1987), p. 499.

22. J. Idenburg, *De Leidse Universiteit 1928-1946*, p. 222.

23. A. Wolf, *Higher Education in German-occupied Countries* (London: Methuen, 1945), pp. 14-83.

24. Hendrik Casimir, *Haphazard Reality: Half a Century of Science* (New York: Harper and Row, 1983), p.205.

25. Ibid., p. 206.

26. Ibid., p. 208. For more details on Heisenberg's attitude towards German victory, see Thomas Powers, *Heisenberg's War: The Secret History of the German Bomb* (New York; Alfred J. Knopf, 1993).

27. For a detailed treatment of Germany's attitude towards France between the Armistice of June 1940 and the German occupation of southern France in November 1942, see Robert Paxton, *Parades and Politics at Vichy* (Princeton: Princeton University Press, 1966).

28. Letter from the chief of Verwaltungsstab Gruppe 4427 to Ministerialdirektor Dr. Best, 25 August 1940. Paris, Archives Nationales (hereafter AN), file AJ 40, 566.

29. M. Schwabe, *Frankreich gegen die Zivilisation* (Berlin, 1940), p. 27. Quoted in Teresa Wroblewska, "Le rôle de l'Université nazie de Strasbourg," in Josef Buszko and Irena Paczynska (eds.), *Universities during World War II* (Cracow: Jagellonian University, 1979), p. 253.

30. Ludwig Klaibert, "Die wissenschaftlichen Bibliotheken des Elsass und Lothringens," *Zentralblatt für Bibliothekswesen* 58 (1941), pp. 1-10; and Karl-Julius Hartmann, "Die Universität- und Landesbibliothek Strassburg nach der Wiedervereinigung mit dem Reich," *Zentralblatt für Bibliothekswesen* 59 (1942), pp. 441-442.

31. Letter from Gilbert Gidel, rector of the Academy of Paris and president of the council of the University of Paris, to Dr. Klaehn, director of the German Institute of Paris, 23 December 1941. Paris, AN, file AJ 40, group 558.

32. The exceptions were at the universities of Aix-Marseille and Montpellier, which were closed in early 1944.

33. Memorandum from A. H. Krüss, director of the Prussian State Library, 1 September 1940, AN, file AJ 40, 569.

34. AN, file AJ 40, group 558. Rosenberg's mandate is included in a decree of Hitler's of 1 March 1942.

35. David Price-Jones, *Paris in the Third Reich* (New York: Holt, Reinhart and Winston, 1981), p. 89. See also Donald E. Collins and Herbert P. Rothfeder, "The Einsatzstab Reichsleiter Rosenberg and the Looting of Jewish and Masonic Libraries during World War II," *Journal of Library History* 18 (Winter 1983): 21-36.

36. Letter of A. H. Krüss to Wermke, 17 October 1940, AN, file AJ 40, 569.

37. "One Year of German Library Protection," speech given by E. Wermke, AN, file AJ 40569.

38. Report of a meeting between Dr. Jürgens (Administrative Division, German Military Command) and Messrs. Faij and Bonnerot of the Bibliothèque de la Sorbonne, 4 December 1940, Paris, AN, file AJ 40,569.

39. See E. Wermke, *Die öffentlichen wissenschaftlichen Bibliotheken Frankreichs mit besonderer Berücksichtigung des besetzten Gebieten* (Paris, May 1941), 30 pp., AN, file AJ 40, 569.

40. The regulations concerning the Liste Bernhard, as well as the August 1940 edition of that list, are contained in a circular from the propaganda division of the German military administration of 21 August 1940. (The Liste Otto is a later version of the List Bernhard). AN, file AJ 40, 569.

41. As late as 27 January 1942 the librarian at the Faculty of Law of the University of Paris still claimed in a letter to Wermke never to have heard of any such lists. AN, file AJ 40, 569.

42. Report from Gérard on the collaboration of French and German chemists (fall 1940), AN, file AJ 40, 569.

43. Letter from L. R. Faij to Wermke concerning the meeting at the Bibliothèque Nationale on 30 October 1940, AN, file AJ 40, 569.

44. Jean Wyart, "La fondation du CNRS et l'information scientifique," in *Cahiers pour l'histoire du CNRS 1939-1989*, 1989-2 (Paris: Editions du centre national de la recherche scientifique, 1989), p. 24.

45. Interview with Jean Wyart, Paris, 4 July 1990.

46. Letter from Krüss to Wermke, 17 October 1940, AN, file AJ 40, 569.

47. In 1942 Gérard's activities are mentioned with approval by the president of the German Chemical Society in a speech in Salzburg before the fledgling German Documentation Society. See Maximilian Pflücke, "Die

Dokumentation in der Chemie und der chemischen Technik," in *Die Dokumentation und ihre Probleme* (Leipzig: Harrassowitz, 1943), p. 51.

48. Jean Wyart, "La Fondation du CNRS et l'information scientifique", in *Cahiers pour l'histoire du CNRS 1989-2*, p. 28. After his release from prison, Gérard resurfaced briefly in documentation circles before his death in the late 1940s. J. Wyart, interview with the author, 4 July 1990.

49. Letter of Gérard to A. H. Krüss, 4 August 1941, AN, file AJ 40, 569.

50. Letter from Gérard to Krüss, 4 August 1941, AN, file AJ 40, 569.

51. Maurice Goldsmith, *Frédéric Joliot-Curie* (London: Lawrence and Wishart, 1976), p. 58.

52. Goldsmith, *Frédéric Joliot-Curie*, p. 75.

53. Goldsmith, *Frédéric Joliot-Curie*, p. 95.

54. Goldsmith, *Frédéric Joliot-Curie*, p. 99.

55. Wyart, "La fondation du CNRS et l'information scientifique," p. 24.

56. Fabrizio Calvi, *OSS: La guerre secrète en France* (Paris: Hachette, 1990), p. 112.

57. Wyart believes that the Ministry's failure to issue his bulletin a license to publish was due to the fact that the French Minister of Education was trying to sabotage all initiatives undertaken during the German occupation . See Wyart, "La fondation du CNRS et l'information scientifique," p. 24.

58. Interview with Jean Wyart, Paris, 4 July 1990.

59. Idem.

60. Alexander Dallin, *German Rule in Russia 1941-1945* (London: Macmillan, 1957), pp. 7-8.

61. *Hitler's Table Talk* (London: Weidenfield and Nicolson, 1953), pp. 424-425. Quoted in Dallin, *German Rule in Russia 1942-1945*, p. 459.

62. A. Wolf, *Higher Education*, p. 29. See also Karl Litsch, "Die Persekution der Hochschulen im sog. Protektorat Böhmen und Mähren," in Buszko and Paczynska, *Universities during World War II*, pp. 179-186.

63. Wolf, *Higher Education*, p. 94. See also Caeslaw Luczak,"Polnische Wissenschaft und polnische Hochschulwesen während der Hitlerokkupation," in and Paczynska, *Universities during World War II*, pp. 37-45.

64. Leo Stern, ed., *Die Berliner Akademie in der Zeit des Imperialismus* (Berlin: Akademie Verlag, 1979), p. 93. See also Michael Burleigh, *Germany Turns Eastward: A Study of Ostforschung in the Third Reich* (Cambridge: Cambridge University Press, 1988), p. 291.

65. Stern, *Die Berliner Akademie in der Zeit des Imperialismus*, p. 141.

66. Dallin, *German Rule in Russia l941-1945*, p. 463.

67. File NS 30/55, Bundesarchiv, Koblenz.

68. Wolf, *Higher Education*, p. 102.

69. Stern, *Die Berliner Akademie in der Zeit des Imperialismus*, p.95.

70. File NS 6/440, Bundesarchiv, Coblenz.

71. Paul Trommsdorff, "Die Bibliotheken der technischen Hochschulen," in Fritz Milkau, ed., *Handbuch der Bibliothekswissenschaft*, lst ed. (Leipzig: Harrassowitz, 1933), vol. 2, p. 601.

72. Hermann Neubert, "Dem Gedenken Albert Predeeks," *Zeitschrift für Bibliothekswesen und Bibliographie* 3 (1956), p. 227. After the war, Predeek was director of the library of the University of Jena from 1947 to 1951. In November 1951 he was made honorary professor of library science at the Free University of (West) Berlin. He died on 10 February 1956 at the age of seventy-three.

73. Closed for three years after the war, the institute and its enormous library and information center are now public scholarly facilities (Informationszentrum in HWWA-Institut für Wirtschaftsforchung-Hamburg) in new quarters on the outskirts of the city.

74. Exhibits A and B, U.S. Office of Alien Property Custodian, "Withdrawal of the Custodian from the Periodical Republication Program," 25 May 1945, typescript, copy in the library of the School of Library Service, Columbia University.

75. Gisela von Busse, letter to the author, 17 January 1983.

76. Gisela von Busse, letter to the author, 25 June 1982.

77. Most of the decrees were not published in official organs and can only be traced through surviving official correspondence. One such letter forbids public use of *Nature* because of the British journals's contemptuous remarks about German science. Ministry of Education, 12 November 1937. Staatsarchiv Hamburg, file "Hochschulwesen II Wd 36."

78. Not unexpectedly, many academic librarians looked with deep suspicion at the development of the favored new "rival" profession of documentation. For some idea of the resentment felt by librarians toward documentalists, see John Ansteinsson, "Wissenschaft und Forschung—Bibliothek und Dokumentation," *Zentralblatt für Bibliothekswesen* 56 (1939), pp. 37-59.

79. Joseph DuBois, *The Devil's Chemists* (Boston: Beacon Press, 1953), p. 58.

80. Ibid., p. 99.

81. See David Kahn, *Hitler's Spies* (New York: Macmillan, 1978), pp. 13-26.

82. Pamela Spence Richards, "Gathering Enemy Scientific Information in Wartime: The OSS and the Periodical Republication Program," *Journal of Library History* (1981), p. 262.

83. David Irving, *The German Atomic Bomb* (New York: Simon and Schuster, 1967), p. 194.

6

Postwar Consequences

In the previous chapter we have seen how World War II increased government interest in scientific documentation in the different countries involved in the conflict. It remains to be asked in this chapter to what extent these wartime documentation activities influenced postwar developments in the United States, Great Britain and Germany. We will see that of the institutions in the three countries being considered, those of the United States were most firmly rooted in the events of World War II.

THE UNITED STATES

In July 1945 Librarian of Congress Luther Evans was speaking for many in American government circles when he commented in a newscast: "I am allowing myself no poetic license whatsoever when I say that matters of large importance—battles won or lost, programs of action misdirected or well directed—are affected by the presence or the absence in the libraries of the nation of books, government documents, scientific periodicals and the other forms of publication."[1] Ultimately the federal government's recognition of the value of German information to both industry and the military during the war and occupation caused it to set up permanent agencies to guarantee a better foreign information supply than before the war. Thus, after the invasion and surrender of Germany, and the capture of hundreds of thousands of German research documents by scientific intelligence units, the need to process and disseminate their contents to American industry and research libraries led to the forming of new postwar agencies replacing the IDC, which had been disbanded with the whole OSS at the end of 1945. As we will see, these new agencies operated in a situation of entirely new challenges.

Technical reports seized from the Germans posed problems quite different from those of books and journals, for which there were established techniques and media for publicity, description and abstraction. Literally tons of unpublished reports were being imported from Germany by mid-1945. Late that spring, Vannevar Bush, head of the wartime Office of Scientific Research and Development, proposed to the President that measures be taken to expedite the flow of previously classified government-produced and owned information to industry to stimulate the peacetime economy. Consequently President Truman established the interdepartmental Publication Board by Executive Order 9569. In August 1945 the Publication Board was given the additional assignment to review and publish declassified captured enemy technical documents.[2] Operations of the Publication Board were located in the Commerce Department's newly established Office of Declassification and Technical Services (ODTS), to which captured foreign materials were forwarded from the War and Navy departments, the Office of Scientific Research and Development and British Intelligence. Working in coordination with the Field Information Agency—Technical (FIAT) in Germany, the Publication Board supervised microfilm teams all over Germany which forwarded seized materials to a central Frankfurt office where they were screened and edited before being sent to the United States.

In Washington, the Office of Declassification and Technical Services served as a clearing house where the documents could be duplicated on demand. In July 1946 the Office of Declassification and Technical Services was reorganized as the Office of Technical Services and put under an Assistant Secretary of Foreign and Domestic Commerce. Upon its establishment the Office of Technical Services had five divisions, two of which were directly charged with circulating scientific and technical reports. The Bibliographic and Reference Division (named at different times the Library Division or the Library and Reports Division) took over the activities of the Publication Board. The Technical Industrial Intelligence Division screened and processed captured German reports. By the end of 1947 the Office of Technical Services had received about five million documents from Germany alone.[3] The agency survived until 1965, when it was enlarged to become the Clearinghouse of Federal Scientific and Technical Information. In 1971 the Clearinghouse, still under the Department of Commerce, was reorganized into today's National Technical Information Service, part of whose responsibilities include supplying subscribers with summaries of foreign technical reports.

The military also needed new peacetime agencies to handle the foreign information it acquired overseas: The Air Force—interested in known German breakthroughs in jet propulsion and rocketry—had 1,500 technical personnel in Germany by late 1945 channeling documents first to Hanau and then to the Air Documents Research Center set up by Air Force Intelligence in London. By the end of December 1945 over 800,000 documents had been screened in Europe and sent to the Air Force Documentation Center at Wright Field in Dayton,

Ohio, where they were catalogued, translated and forwarded to researchers. These documentation centers set up by the Army Air Force in London in 1945 and at Wright Field in 1946 were part of the military's efforts, parallel to those of the Department of Commerce for commercial information, to keep its constituency supplied with the most advanced foreign technical information. In 1948 the Navy and Air Force joined forces to establish the Central Air Documents Office, which in 1951 became part of the Armed Services Technical Information Agency (ASTIA), expanded and rechristened as the Defense Documentation Center in 1965.

The high quality of the captured scientific information was one of the factors behind Vannevar Bush's plea in 1945 for a strong federal postwar science policy. As he watched plans develop for the dismantling of the wartime science agencies, he feared that the goverment would retreat after the war into its traditional peacetime mode of niggardly support for science and scientific information. By 1943-44 the university contracts awarded by Bush's United States Office of Scientific Research and Development were approximately triple the level of all prewar university scientific research.[4] Bush saw the threatening postwar cutbacks as particularly perilous because of the continuing reliance of the United States on foreign research: After all, the most important scientific advances of the war (jets, microwave radar, penicillin, DDT and the concept of the atomic bomb) all developed from work originally done by Europeans. Consequently, when Roosevelt asked Bush for a report on how the wartime government experience in sponsoring scientific research could be applied in peacetime, Bush seized the opportunity to lobby for a postwar government support system. In his report to the President in 1945, Bush recommended the creation of a national research foundation for strategic planning and funding of American research, with a scientific advisory board to coordinate the government's own programs.

What is often overlooked is that Bush saw his proposed national funding agency as providing a permanent mechanism for channeling foreign science to the United States. Bush maintained that "the Government should take an active role in promoting the international flow of scientific information,"[5] and he cited critical American inadequacies in reprint, abstracting and translation services. Bush's insistence on government involvement was the background for federal legislation in 1950 creating the National Science Foundation and mandating it "to foster the exchange of scientific information among scientists in the United States and other countries." One of the first units set up in the National Science Foundation in 1951 was the Office of Scientific Information, which during its first year of operation underwrote the translation of a Russian book on chemical thermodynamics and the proceedings of a symposium on Soviet science.[6] Activities of this office in the period before 1970 included the coordination of federally-financed technical translations (including those from the Japanese), the establishment of regional collections of technical translations, the development of new bibliographic systems, and the encouragement of American participation in international documentation organizations.

American federal government support for foreign information supply waxed and waned in subsequent decades—the waxing following threatening Soviet breakthroughs such as the hydrogen bomb in 1953 and Sputnik in 1957, and the waning a probably inevitable consequence of complacency as scientists from American laboratories captured almost 50 percent of the Nobel science awards between 1945 and 1975.[7] The Sputnik-inspired National Defense Education Act of 1958 made new funds available for scientific materials in all languages and supported the study of foreign languages, but by far the most innovative federal program for the massive import of foreign information of all kinds was Public Law 480, originally passed in 1954 but renewed in 1962 to allow the Library of Congress to pay for the acquisition (and redistribution to American research libraries) of foreign books, periodicals and related materials with surplus foreign currency reserves accumulated abroad through the sale of American agricultural products. Special information officers at foreign embassies were appointed by the Department of State to oversee the implementation of Public Law 480, which at the height of its operation was collecting publications in more than ten debtor countries.[8]

The fact that the United States federal government did not, under the pressures of the Cold War, underwrite a monolithic national scientific information agency was largely due to the presence in the United States of a strong information industry that defended the mixed public/private model as the most cost-effective for the country. There were a number of government initiatives in the wake of Sputnik to investigate whether a centralized government-supported organization could more aggressively disseminate scientific and technical literature than the existing decentralized, mixed model. In 1958 W. O. Baker, vice president for research at Bell Laboratories, chaired a President's Science Advisory Committee charged with determining whether the United States government should set up an agency along the lines of the highly centralized All-Union Institute of Scientific and Technical Information in Moscow. The Baker Panel decided against this and recommended instead that the National Science Foundation's role as coordinator of scientific information be strengthened. As a result the National Science Foundation's Office of Scientific Information was reorganized in 1958 as the Office of Scientific Information Services with an expanded charge of improving government information services.[9]

Among later groups assembled by the government to review the efficiency of American scientific information coordination were the President's Scientific Advisory Committee chaired by Alvin Weinberg in 1963 and the joint National Academy of Sciences and National Academy of Engineering Committee on Science and Technncal Communication (SATCOM), formed in 1966. The theme of the Weinberg Committee's report was that the scientific community should recognize scientific communication as an integral part of the scientific process and take more responsibility for communication.[10] The SATCOM report stressed the importance of information agencies' responsiveness and flexibility and called for a wide distribution of authority over them to maximize responsiveness.[11] None of the post-Sputnik government inquiries resulted in the federal government's taking significantly more responsibility for scientific and technical information dissemination.

Whether government supported or not, however, the knowledge of foreign science was now defended by all parties as vital to the nation's defense. However erratic United States government support for scientific information may have been, especially in the years after détente with the Soviet Union began in earnest, a precedent was set during World War II of including the acquisition of foreign information in *all* scientific and technical areas—not just in medicine and agriculture, as previously—among the nation's highest defense priorities. As the Cold War drew to a close, economic rather than military rivalries were invoked to defend the federal information agencies against budget cuts or liquidation. Reagan administration attempts from 1981 to 1988 to privatize the National Technical Information Service (NTIS) were defeated by a coalition of congressmen (in particular the House Subcommittee on Science, Research and Technology), representatives of scientific societies and library and information interest groups. Fearing that the NTIS's efficiency would be jeopardized by privatization, they cited the urgent need for global scientific and technical information coverage to maintain the United States' position as world economic leader.[12] Economic, not military, rivals were now the threat, and anxiety was now produced by the contrast of the United States' federal information agencies with the Japanese Institute for Science, Research and Technology (JICST) with its annual $100 million budget, over half provided by the Japanese government.[13] So a descendant of agencies created in the 1940s to monitor the scientific publications of Germany, and refined in the 1950s and '60s to help maintain American superiority over the Soviet Union, survives today with the help of arguments that it keeps the United States competitive with Japan.[14]

In the post-Cold War United States, the rhetoric of defense and the rhetoric of economics have become blurred, as they were in Great Britain almost eighty years ago.

GREAT BRITAIN

In Great Britain, the activities of the Aslib microflm service during the Second World War were a continuation of the quest, dating from the First World War, for information about foreign science. As Great Britain entered the Second

World War its government had already been supporting the import of foreign scientific information through the Department of Scientific and Industrial Research since 1916. The Second World War demonstrated the value of the department's activities but also the inadequacies of the services and holdings of the de facto national science library at the Science Museum. Much of the development in British libraries in the decades after World War II was a direct continuation of attempts ongoing since World War I to coordinate scientific and technical documentation through technology and administrative reorganization.

In the short term, the coordinating processes were handled as in the United States: At the end of World War II, circulation of enemy information was the responsibility of a department in the Board of Trade called the Technical Information and Documents Unit (TIDU). Operating originally under the Ministry of Economic Warfare, this unit was the receiving center and sorting house for economic and industrial information relating to enemy-controlled territories. At the TIDU library at Cadogan Square in London the original documents and their English summaries could be consulted, with some free distribution to scientific institutions, public libraries and trade bodies. Sale of copies was arranged through His Majesty's Stationary Office. TIDU had a representative attached to the British Commonwealth Scientific Office in Washington and worked closely with the United States Office of Technical Services.[15]

In the long term, the problems of coordinating scientific literature distribution were considered so complex and critical to national recovery that they became the focus of a two-week Scientific Information Conference in 1948 sponsored jointly by the government and the Royal Society (a 1946 Royal Society Empire Scientific Conference had concluded that the information problem was acute enough to warrant its own meeting).[16] The series of recommendations resulting from the 1948 conference included a challenge to the government to recognize the logic of central collections for science, including foreign literature. According to the drafters of the recommendations, the most important of the current problems were, first, that libraries with the right of legal copyright deposit (the British Museum Library, and the university libraries at Oxford and Cambridge) did not lend to other libraries and second, that access to foreign materials was in general inadequate.[17] A leader in the campaign for a central scientific library was D. J. Urquhart of the Science Library, a chemist turned librarian, who became involved in the documentation movement after the war.

Ultimately, the Department of Scientific and Industrial Research remained at the center of planning for national scientific information resources, with Urquhart prodding from the Science Library until moving to DSIR headquarters in 1948. The Department's Information Division absorbed the functions of the Board of Trade's TIDU in 1951, and in 1955 it was given the responsibility of planning a national lending library for science. Lack of access to Russian scientific literature was a major stimulus for the project's priority. It was initially suggested that the planned lending library focus on the acquisition of Russian material, since at that time only three hundred of the roughly one thousand Russian scientific and technical periodicals were available in the United Kingdom.[18] In 1962 the National Lending Library for Science and Technology was opened at Boston Spa, in Yorkshire, a location chosen both for its central postal connections with the rest of the British Isles and for its situation outside the range of a 1950s-vintage atomic bomb attack on London.[19] By 1970, lending almost entirely by mail, the National Lending Library was supplying over 55 percent of all interlibrary loan requests in Great Britain.[20] Upon the dissolution of DSIR in 1965, the management of the library became the responsibility of the Department of Science and Education. Now known as the British Library Document Supply Centre, it had in 1993 one of the largest collections of periodicals in the world.

The emergence of this library marked the culmination of a half-century of British governmental concern for economic and military competitiveness which, born of the First World War, was sustained through peacetime as a task of the first importance. Thus, while activities of documentation of the Aslib microfilm service during the Second World War represented an important chapter in the civil history of the war, they are equally interesting as evidence of the British government's relatively early recognition of the crucial place of scientific knowledge in practical affairs, and of its acceptance of the obligation to support and promote it—a decision in which Great Britain's increasingly insecure economic position as the twentieth century progressed played a major role.

GERMANY

The history of the rebuilding of Germany's scientific information system from the rubble of 1945 was complicated by the country's political division from 1945 until 1990. In the case of both German republics, political considerations led to the shaping of their postwar information policies, such as they were, along lines acceptable to their more powerful allies. In the Federal Republic, ideological opposition to cultural centralism—an opposition encouraged by the Western Allies in continued fear of Prussian and/or Nazi revanchism—permitted the retention and continuation of only a few of the projects launched before 1933 and further developed under National Socialism. These projects included programs for cooperative book and periodical acquisitions and a national interlibrary loan system. The Deutsche Forschungsgemeinschaft (German Research Association) was reconstituted in West Germany and during the late 1950s worked out a plan whereby existing libraries specializing in various fields assumed the functions and responsibilities of national collections. Under this plan a Technische Informationsbibliothek, or TIB (Technical Information Library), was established in Hannover in 1959 on the basis of the relatively large holdings of the Technische Hochschule Hannover. International in scope, The TIB had by the early 1970s 34,000 American scientific and technical dissertations on microfilm and 61,000 American reports. In collaboration with the European Translations Centre in Delft, the Netherlands, the TIB made translations of texts in less-well-known foreign languages. Translations from world languages could be commissioned on demand at the TIB.[21] By the mid-1980s, with 30 percent of its funding coming from the federal government and 70 percent from the West German states, the TIB had a collection of foreign scientific and technical periodicals comparable to that of the British at Boston Spa. It performed—with the advantages of modern electronic storage and photoduplication technology—most of the documentation services previously available at the old technical university at Berlin-Charlottenburg.[22]

In the German Democratic Republic central planning came naturally to the leaders of a socialist state tied to the Soviet Union by ideology and political interests. Here state agencies for the evaluation of foreign technical and scientific literature dated from the immediate postwar period and reflected the perception that in a centrally planned economy, the authorities needed a lot of information—including that from the capitalist world. Thus in 1950, the year after the republic's founding, a Zentrum für wissenschaftliche Information (Central Office for Scientific Literature) was established in Berlin and assigned tasks almost identical to those of the old Technological University at Berlin-Charlottenburg; naturally, these tasks included the supply of important foreign scientific literature.

The remarkable neglect of the national library system by the government of the German Democratic Republic has only been fully revealed since German unification in 1990. But already several years before, the Bonn government's official handbook of information about the German Democratic Republic noted that only one new research library—that of the Bergakademie in Freiburg—had been built in East Germany in over fifty years. There were, of course, scientific collections which had survived the war in Leipzig, Dresden, East Berlin and other cities, but even in these there was no development of the informational function of libraries. For example, the library of the technical university at Dresden was the nation's largest scientific collection, but it performed no national scientific documentation functions such as supplying copies or translations of articles to users elsewhere.[23] The agency entrusted with these functions, the Zentrum für wissenschaftliche Information in Berlin, was never able to fulfill the goals set for it by the central government, both because of the government's diversion of funds for equipment to matters of higher priority (such as the military), and because its services were crippled by the number of restrictions on who could read foreign publications.[24] Here again, as in Nazi

Germany, the totalitarian government's fear of unlimited public access to the scientific literature of the liberal West undermined the efficiency of its information system.

CONCLUSION

The postwar development of government agencies to monitor, import and circulate foreign scientific and technical information varied greatly in the different countries under consideration, but their founders all shared a common assumption, namely that published scientific information (i.e. non-secret, non-classified material) could be of strategic importance, if only the proper mechanisms were set up to gather and circulate it. But the establishment of similar kinds of collection agencies did not necessarily lead to the transformation of the same information into the same kinds of intelligence. In our own story of the wartime agencies, the gathering of the enemy's scientific information worked fairly efficiently for both sides for the course of the war, but we have seen the different conclusions that resulted from the analysis of the same material in a number of cases. The Germans, for example, had access to the same Allied physics journals as had the Russians, but there is no evidence that they concluded, as did Flyorov and then Stalin, that the cessation of Allied publication of articles about atomic research was an indication of heightened activity in Anglo-American nuclear physics. In retrospect, it is interesting to speculate about this failure of the Germans: Did it stem in some way from implicit arrogance about the quality of their science—a feeling that, if the Germans decided the bomb was impracticable, then certainly it was beyond the reach of others? Or was it the essentially irrationalist, antiscientific ideology of the political leaders that dulled the senses not of the scientists themselves, but of the organizers of the war effort?

Even within the Anglo-American alliance there were instances of different intelligence being drawn from the same raw information: Rudolf Peierls' reading of the German scientific press led him to conclude that the Germans were *not* seriously involved in an atomic bomb project, while the Americans, to whom the same journals were available, continued to be plagued by fears on this score until the invasion of Germany. Was this in some way due to traditional American beliefs in the superiority of German science? In any case, with both Flyorov and Peierls, the successful analysis of the information—the process by which the information was transformed into strategic intelligence—was dependent on the reader's evaluation of the context in which the information was generated.

There is a tragic postscript to the story of gathering and analyzing enemy scientific information during World War II. Our study has described the progress made on both sides during the war years in developing channels and technologies to import and circulate   foreign scientific information to the audience that could make best strategic use of it. But during the very period when the wartime system and its postwar legacy were consuming the attention of some of America's and Great Britain's most imaginative men of science and government, both Winston Churchill and Franklin Delano Roosevelt repeatedly refused to accept publicly available information and scientifically verified information.

Niels Bohr was the first to bring to Roosevelt's attention the advanced level of Soviet atomic research and to lobby for sharing atomic information with the Soviets in order to lay a basis for postwar nuclear arms control. He had been offered a position in the Soviet Union by Pyotr Kapitsa when he escaped from Denmark in 1943, and got some idea from Kapitsa's invitational letter of the type of questions being investigated by Soviet scientists.[25]   In a letter to the President in 1944 he wrote that, from what was known of the prewar work of the Soviet physicists, some of which had been published in Western journals, it was "natural to assume that nuclear problems will be in the center of [their] interest."[26]

Roosevelt and Churchill, who were convinced that the key to postwar global order lay in an Anglo-American atomic monopoly, discounted both Bohr's warning and that of the report initiated in 1944 by Zay Jefferies of General Electric. The Jefferies Report was drafted by a committee of the country's most eminent scientists, including Enrico Fermi. Submitted to Vannevar Bush in November 1944, it called—as Bohr had—for a postwar central authority for shared expertise and atomic energy control, since given the focus of their prewar research and publications, "it would be surprising if the Russians are not also diligently engaged in such work."[27] By the summer of 1945, both the presidents' top science advisors, Bush and Conant, favored sharing atomic information and establishing postwar international arms control. So did Army Chief of Staff George C. Marshall, who had suggested that Russian scientists be invited to witness the atomic test at Alamagordo, New Mexico, in July 1945.[28]

In his book on the origins of the arms race Martin Sherwin has summed up the birth of postwar Anglo-American nuclear policy in the hands of non-scientists as follows:

> The diplomacy of atomic energy came to rest during the war on a simple and dangerous assumption: that the Soviet government would surrender important geographical, political, and ideological objectives in exchange for the neutralization of the new weapon. Warnings from Bush and Conant that the Russians might be able to reach atomic parity within three to five years were ignored in favor of [Manhattan Project Director General] Groves's estimate

that it would take the Soviet Union twenty to fifty years to catch up. Although Groves and those who heeded his advice were aware that a similar kind of arrogance had led atomic scientists in Germany to underestimate American potential during the war, their low opinion of the Soviets blinded them to the validity of such an analogy.[29]

Thus the arms race, based on the determination of the Anglo-American alliance to maintain its monopoly of atomic knowledge, resulted from a fundamental misunderstanding among the Western leaders of the internationalism of science.

Obviously, then, the greatest challenge to the intelligence community in general lies not in the gathering of information, a process which has been facilitated by modern technology. Much more important is the next step, when specific pieces of raw information are identified as critical to decision-making and become intelligence. Analysis depends not only on a knowledge of the context in which the information is generated, but also on the imagination of the analysts, their ability to see what H. G. Wells called "the shape of things to come." Bohr, Bush, Conant, and the drafters of the Jefferies Report knew the context of scientific research and discovery well and had some idea of the future, but they failed to convey either convincingly to Churchill or Roosevelt. Their vision of an international agency for the sharing of atomic information only became acceptable to the Anglo-American political leadership decades after the end of World War II. By then the wealth of the United States and the Soviet Union had been almost exhausted by the arms race, and the global environment seriously threatened.

NOTES

1. Quoted in Theodore Besterman, "International Library Rehabilitation and Planning," *Journal of Documentation* 2 (1946/47), p. 174.

2. Ralph Shaw, "The Publication Board," *College and Research Libraries* 7 (April 1946), p. 106f.

3. Burton Adkinson, *Two Centuries of Federal Information* (Stroudsbourg PA: Dowden, Hutchinson and Ross, 1978), p. 33.

4. Roger Geiger, *To Advance Knowledge: The Growth of American Research Universities 1900-1940* (New York: Oxford University Press, 1986), pp. 258, 264.

5. Vannevar Bush, *Science: The Endless Frontier* (Washington: Government Printing Office, 1945), p. 19.

6. Adkinson, *Two Hundred Years of Federal Information*, p. 63.

7. Twelve of 36 awards in chemistry; 23 of 42 awards in physics; and 31 of 55 awards in physiology and medicine.

8. For a general overview of United States federal support for scientific information since 1945, see Adkinson, *Two Centuries of Federal Information*.

9. K. Subramanyan, "Scientific Literature," *Encyclopedia of Library and Information Science*, vol. 26 (New York: Dekker, 1979), p. 386.

10. Alvin M. Weinberg, *Science, Government and Information: The Responsibilities of the Technical Community and the Government in the Transfer of Information* (Washington DC: Government Printing Office, 1963), p. 14. (The Weinberg report)

11. *Scientific and Technical Communication: A Pressing National Problem and Recommendations for its Solution* (Washington DC: Government Printing Office,1969). (The SATCOM report)

12. See James Paul, "Scientific and Technical Information Policy and the Future of the NTIS: Hearings before the Subcommittee on Science, Research and Technology," *Government Information Quarterly* 5 (1988): 137-146.

13. Thomas Bold, "A Case Study of the Reagan Administration's Initiative to Privatize the National Technical Information Service" (unpublished report, American University, May 1990), p. 187.

14. During 1988 and 1989 the National Technical Information Service, part of the United States Department of Commerce, successfully warded off attempts by various Republican members of Congress to legislate its privatization. A number of supporters of the Service's continuation as a federal agency cited its Japanese translation services as particularly valuable.

15. L. R. Poole, "Processing and Dissemination of Technical Information," *Empire Scientific Conference* (London: Royal Society, 1946), p. 459.

16. Donald J. Urquhart, interview with the author, 4 July 1986, Leeds.

17. Bernard Houghton, *Out of the Dinosaurs: The Evolution of the National Lending Library for Science and Technology* (London: Clive Bingley, 1972), p. 16.

18. Houghton, *Out of the Dinosaurs*, p. 30.

19. Interview with Donald J. Urquhart, 4 July 1986, Leeds.

20. Peter G. Watson, "Great Britain's National Lending Library," unpublished master's essay, Graduate School of Library Service, University of California at Los Angeles, 1970, p. iv.

21. Gisela von Busse and Horst Ernestus, *Libraries in the Federal Republic of Germany* (Wiesbaden: Otto Harrassowitz, 1972), p. 78.

22. Helmut Drubba, "Interlending and Document Delivery in the Federal Republic of Germany," *IATUL Proceedings* 16 (1984), p. 24.

23. Bundesministerium für innerdeutsche Beziehungen, *DDR Handbuch* (Köln: Verlag Wissenschaft und Politik, 1985), vol. 1, p. 226.

24. For East German technical information systems in general, see Achim Bayer, "Information und Dokumentationswesen," in *Wissenschaft in der DDR* (Erlangen: Institut für Gesellschaft und Wissenschaft, 1973); and Pamela Spence Richards, "Government Information Policy in the German Democratic Republic," in Wesley Simonton, *Advances in Librarianship* (Orlando FLA: Academic Press, 1986), pp. 101-142.

25. Martin J. Sherwin, *A World Destroyed* (New York: Alfred J. Knopf, 1973), p. 106.

26. Quoted in Sherwin, *A World Destroyed*, p. 106.

27. Sherwin, *A World Destroyed*, p. 119.

28. Sherwin, *A World Destroyed*, p. 119.

29. Sherwin, *A World Destroyed*, p. 237f.

Appendix A

List of Journals Available in Reprint from the Office of Alien Property Custodian

LIST VI

Custodian's Number	Title	Volumes Offered 1943-1944	Price Per Volume
115.	Annales mycologici	v.41-42	$ 15.00
116.	Archiv fuer die gesamte virusforschung	v.3-4	16.00
117.	Archiv fuer hygiene	v.129-130	11.00
118.	Deutsche nationalbibliographie. Reihe A-B	1942-44	25.00
119.	Jahresbericht veterinar-medizin	v.71-72	27.00
120.	Journal de mathematiques pures et appliquees	v.22-23	12.00
*121.	Kautschuk	v.19 Jan-Mar 1943	1.50
122.	Phytopathologische zeitschrift	v.15-16	18.00
123.	Spectrochimica acta	v.1-2(1939-44)	25.00
124.	Technik in der landwirtschaft	v.24-25	8.50
125.	Tierernährung	v.15-16	28.00
126.	Vitamin und hormone	v.4-5	15.00
127.	Zeitschrift fuer angewandte mathematik	v.23-24	15.00
128.	Zeitschrift fuer hygiene	v.125-126	30.00
129.	Zeitschrift fuer infektionskrankheiten	v.60-61	13.00
130.	Zeitschrift fuer parasitenkunde	v.13-14	27.00
131.	Zeitschrift fuer tierzuchtung	v.54-55	13.00
132.	Zentralblatt fuer mechanik	v.13-14	20.00

* Kautschuk April-December, 1943 issued with Gummi-zeitung

ADDITIONAL BACK VOLUMES OFFERED

6.	Biochemische zeitschrift	v.307-309 (1940-42)	9.00
2.	Chemie (Issued as Angewandte chemie)	v.54 (1941)	23.00
31.	Hochfrequenztechnik und elektroakustik	v.59-60 (1942)	10.00
10.	Hoppe-Seyler's Zeitschrift	v.269-271 (1941-42)	6.00
77.	Ingenieur-archiv	v.13 (1942)	25.00
11.	Journal fuer praktische chemie	v.157-159 (1940-42)	6.00
61.	Kunststoffe	v.32 (1942)	15.00
14.	Mathematische annalen	v.117-118 (1939-42)	26.50
35.	Mikrochemie	v.30 (1942-43)	14.00
36.	Monatshefte fuer chemie	v.74 (1942)	12.00
16.	Naturwissenschaften	v.29-30 (1941-42)	19.00
64.	Recueil des travaux chimiques des. pays-bas	v.61 (1942)	22.00
106.	Societe de biologie	v.135-36 (1941-42)	15.00
20.	Verein deutscher ingenieure. Zeitschrift	v.86 (1942)	19.00
44.	Zeitschrift fuer instrumentenkunde	v.61 (1941)	20.00
45.	Zeitschrift fuer metallkunde	v.34 (1942)	12.00

CUMULATIVE LIST OF ALL TITLES OFFERED FOR SUBSCRIPTION

(November 1944)

NOTE: The titles for which no entries are found under the columns "completely reprinted" and "in process" are entirely new titles which are offered on List VI for the first time, or titles formerly offered but without sufficient subscriptions to permit reprinting to date.

Custodian's Number	Titles and Volumes Offered	Reprinting Completed	In Process	Cost per Volume
1.	Academie des sciences. Comptes rendus v.216-219 (1943-44)	216-217	218	$ 10.00
69.	Akustische zeitschrift. Leipzig v.8-9 (1943-44)		8	6.00
	Allgemeine oel-und fett-zeitung, see: Seifensieder-zeitung			
70.	Aluminium. Berlin v.25-26 (1943-44)	25	26	16.00
51.	Anatomischer anzeiger v.94-95 (1943-44)		94	15.00
87.	Angewandte botanik, v.25-26 (1943-44) (WITHDRAWAL CONTEMPLATED UNLESS ADDITIONAL ORDERS BY 1/1/45)			15.00
	Angewandte chemie, see: Chemie			
	Annalen der chemie, see: Justus Liebig's Annalen			
3.	Annalen der physik v.41-45 (1942-44)	41-42	43	15.50
4.	Annales de chimie v.17-19 (1942-44)	18	19	6.25
5.	Annales de physique v.18-19 (1943-44)	18	19	6.25
88.	Annales des fermentations, v.8-9 (1943-44) (WITHDRAWAL CONTEMPLATED UNLESS ADDITIONAL ORDERS BY 1/1/45)			7.00
115.	Annales mycologici v.41-42 (1943-44)			15.00
71.	Archiv der pharmazie und berichte der Deutschen pharmazeutischen gesellschaft v.281-282 (1943-44)	281	282	15.00
89.	Archiv fuer das eisenhuttenwesen v.17-18 (1943-44)	17	18	20.00
116.	Archiv fuer die gesamte virusforschung v.3-4 (1943-44)			16.00
52.	Archiv fuer elektrotechnik v.37-38 (1943-44)		37	25.00
90.	Archiv fuer experimentelle zellforschung v.25-26 (1943-44)	25	26	18.00
117.	Archiv fuer hygiene v.129-130 (1943-44)			11.00

Custodian's Number	Titles and Volumes Offered	Reprinting Completed	In Process	Cost per Volume
26.	Archiv fuer mikrobiologie			
	v.14-15 (1943-44)	14	15	$ 25.00
27.	Archiv fuer protistenkunde			
	v.97-99 (1943-44)	97	98	18.00
72.	Archives internationales de physiologie. Liege			
	v.53-54 (1943-44)		53	17.00
73.	Auszuege aus den patentschriften			
	(Reichspatentamt.) Berlin, v.64-65(1943-44)			39.00
	(WITHDRAWAL CONTEMPLATED UNLESS ADDITIONAL ORDERS BY 1/1/45)			
91.	Beitraege zur pathologischen anatomie und zur allgemeinen pathologie			
	v.108-109 (1943-44)			18.00
	(WITHDRAWAL CONTEMPLATED UNLESS ADDITIONAL ORDERS BY 1/1/45)			
	Bergbau, see: Glueckauf			
92.	Berichte ueber die gesamte physiologie und experimentelle pharmakologie			
	v.132-133 (1943-44)	132	133	25.00
	Beton und eisen, see: Beton und stahlbetonbau			
53.	Beton und stahlbetonbau (Formerly Beton und eisen)			
	v.42-43 (1943-44)	42	43	10.00
6.	Biochemische zeitschrift			
	v.307-319 (1941-44)	310-316	317	9.00
74.	Biologisches zentralblatt. Leipzig			
	v.63-64 (1943-44)	63	64	14.00
93.	Botanisches zentralblatt			
	v.37-38 (1943-44)			16.00
	(WITHDRAWAL CONTEMPLATED UNLESS ADDITIONAL ORDERS BY 1/1/45)			
28.	Brennstoff-chemie (After v.24 #6, March 15,1943, combined with Oel und kohle)			
	v.23-24 (1942-43)	23-24		18.00
94.	Bulletin des sciences mathematiques			
	v.67-68 (1943-44)			8.00
	(WITHDRAWAL CONTEMPLATED UNLESS ADDITIONAL ORDERS BY 1/1/45)			
95.	Cellulosechemie			
	v.20-23 (1943-44)		21-22	7.50
2.	Chemie (Formerly Angewandte chemie)			
	v.54-57 (1941-44)	55-56	57	23.00
7.	Chemiker-zeitung			
	v.67-68 (1943-44)	67	68	19.00
	Chemische fabrik, see: Chemische technik			
54.	Chemische industrie			
	v.66-67 (1943-44)	66	67	14.00

Custodian's Number	Titles and Volumes Offered	Reprinting Completed	In Process	Cost per Volume
29.	Chemische technik			
	v.15–17 (1942–44)	15	16–17	$ 11.00
8.	Chemisches zentralblatt			
	v.114–115 (1943–44)	114	115	91.00
30.	Chromosoma			
	v.3–4 (1943–44)	3	4	45.00
55.	Deutsche botanische gesellschaft. Berichte			
	v.61–62 (1943–44)	61	62	15.00
* 9.	Deutsche chemische gesellschaft. Berichte			
	v.72–77 (1939–44)	72–76	77	29.00
75.	Deutsche keramische gesellschaft. Berichte Berlin			
	v.24–25 (1943–44)	24	25	16.00
118.	Deutsche nationalbibliographie. Reihe A – B			
	1942–44			25.00
76.	Elektrische nachrichten-technik. Berlin			
	v.20–21 (1943–44)		20	20.00
56.	Elektrotechnik und maschinenbau			
	v.61–62 (1943–44)		61	15.00
57.	Elektrotechnische zeitschrift			
	v.64–65 (1943–44)		64–65	20.00
96.	Enzymologia			
	v.11–12 (1942–44)	11	12	10.00
97.	Fette und seifen			
	v.50–51 (1943–44)			18.00
	(WITHDRAWAL CONTEMPLATED UNLESS ADDITIONAL ORDERS BY 1/1/45)			
58.	Forschung auf dem gebiete des ingenieur-wesens. Ausgabe B with Beilage: VDI Forschungshefte 418–423			
	v.14–15 (1943–44)	14	15	20.00
	Gas-und wasserfach, see: GWF			
59.	Genie civil			
	v.120–121 (1943–44)		120–121	12.00
98.	Giesserei			
	v.30–31 (1943–44)	30	31	15.00
99.	Glueckauf. Berg- und huettenmaennische zeitschrift. Zeitweilig zugleich der Bergbau			
	v.79–80 (1943–44)			15.00
	(WITHDRAWAL CONTEMPLATED UNLESS ADDITIONAL ORDERS BY 1/1/45)			
60.	Gummi-zeitung und kautschuk			
	v.57–58 (1943–44)	57	58	12.00
	(Beginning with the April/May 1943 number issued in conjunction with Kautschuk)			

* Orders for single issues of v.73 and 74 may
be placed @ $3.00 per number, and $1.00 per
Registerheft. Other volumes are for sale
by volume only.

Custodian's Number	Titles and Volumes Offered	Reprinting Completed	In Process	Cost per Volume
100.	GWF; das Gas- und wasserfach v.86-87 (1943-44) (WITHDRAWAL CONTEMPLATED UNLESS ADDITIONAL ORDERS BY 1/1/45)			$ 15.00
31.	Hochfrequenztechnik und elektroakustik v.59-64 (1942-44)	61	62	10.00
10.	Hoppe-Seyler's Zeitschrift fuer physiologische chemie v.269-283 (1941-44)	272-279	280	6.00
77.	Ingenieur-archiv, Berlin v.13-15 (1942-44)		13-14	25.00
32.	Institut Pasteur. Annales v.69-70 (1943-44)	69	70	10.00
33.	Institut Pasteur. Bulletin v.41-42 (1943-44)	41	42	10.00
101.	Jahrbuecher fuer wissenschaftliche botanik v.91-92 (1943-44) (WITHDRAWAL CONTEMPLATED UNLESS ADDITIONAL ORDERS BY 1/1/45)			40.00
119.	Jahresbericht veterinar-medizin v.71-72 (1943-44)			27.00
	Jentgen's Kunstseide und zellwolle, see: Zellwolle und kunstseide			
102.	Journal de chimie physique v.40-41 (1943-44)	40	41	9.00
120.	Journal de mathematiques pures et appliquees v.22-23 (1943-44)			12.00
103.	Journal de physique et le radium v.4-5 (Ser.8) (1943-44)	4	5	15.00
34.	Journal fuer die reine und angewandte mathematik v.185-186 (1943-44)	185	186	11.00
11.	Journal fuer makromolekulare chemie (Formerly Journal fuer praktische chemie) v.1-3 (1943-44)	1	2	6.00
11.	Journal fuer praktische chemie (Becomes Journal fuer makromolekulare chemie after v.162) v.157-162 (1941-43)	160-162		6.00
** 12.	Justus Liebig's Annalen der chemie v.543-558 (1940-44)	543-544	555	6.00
121.	Kautschuk v.19 Jan.-Mar.,1943 (Issued with Gummi-zeitung beginning April/May,1943. Index to v.19 appears in Gummi-zeitung March/April,1944)			1.50

**Orders for single issues of v.543, 544, 547 may be placed @ $2.50 per number. Other volumes are for sale by volume only.

Custodian's Number	Titles and Volumes Offered	Reprinting completed	In Process	Cost per Volume
104.	Kolloid beihefte (After this volume merged with Kolloid zeitschrift) v.54 (1942/43) (WITHDRAWAL CONTEMPLATED UNLESS ADDITIONAL ORDERS BY 1/1/45)			$ 12.00
13.	Kolloid zeitschrift (Beginning with v.103 absorbs Kolloid beihefte) v.102-109 (1943-44)	102-104,106	105,107	8.00
	Kunststoff-berichte v.43 (1943) Appears in Gummi-zeitung, v.57			
61.	Kunststoffe v.32-34 (1942-44)	33	34	15.00
62.	Luftfahrtforschung v.20-21 (1943-44)	20	21	12.00
78.	Luftfahrtmedizin. Berlin v.8-9 (1943-44)		8	12.00
14.	Mathematische annalen v.117-120 (1939-44)		119	26.50
15.	Mathematische zeitschrift v.48-50 (1942-44)	48	49	26.50
79.	Melliand textilberichte. Heidelberg v.24-25 (1943-44)	24	25	25.00
80.	Metall und erz. Halle v.40-41 (1943-44)		40-41	16.00
81.	Metallwirtschaft, metallwissenschaft, metalltechnik. Berlin v.22-23 (1943-44)		22	25.00
35.	Mikrochemie v.30-32 (1942-44)		31	14.00
	Mikrochimica acta, now combined with Mikrochemie			
82.	Mineralogische und petrographische mitteilungen. Vienna v.55-56 (1943-44)	55	56	16.00
36.	Monatshefte fuer chemie v.74-76 (1942-44)	74	75	12.00
16.	Naturwissenschaften v.29-32 (1941-44)		31	19.00
37.	Naunyn-Schmiedeberg's Archiv fuer experimentelle pathologie und pharmakologie v.199-204 (1942-44)	199-201	202-203	20.00
63.	Oel und kohle in gemeinschaft mit Brennstoff-chemie, (Oel und kohle, formerly Petroleum, absorbs Brennstoff-chemie, beginning with v.39 #13/14, April 1, 1943) v.39-40 (1943-44)	39	40	30.00

Custodian's Number	Titles and Volumes Offered	Reprinting Completed	In Process	Cost per Volume
83.	Papierfabrikant. Wochenblatt fuer papierfabrikation. Berlin 1943-1944	1943	1944	$ 14.00
	Petroleum, see: Oel und kohle			
17.	Pflueger's Archiv fuer die gesamte physiologie des menschen und der tiere v.246 #4/6-249 (1943-44)	246 #4/6	247	22.00
84.	Physica. The Hague v.10-11 (1943-44)	10	11	18.00
18.	Physikalische zeitschrift v.43-45 (1942-44)	43	44	24.00
122.	Phytopathologische zeitschrift v.15-16 (1943-44)			18.00
38.	Planta v.34-35 (1943-44)	34	35	36.00
39.	Protoplasma v.37-39 (1942-44)		38	26.00
64.	Recueil des travaux chimiques des pays-bas v.61-63 (1942-44)		62-63	22.00
105.	Revue d'immunologie v.8-9 (1943-44)	8	9	10.00
65.	Revue de metallurgie v.40-41 (1943-44)	40	41	24.00
85.	Seifensieder-zeitung; in Krieggemeinschaft mit Allgemeine oel-und fett-zeitung. Leipzig. (Supplements Parfuemeur; Chemisch-technische fabrikant; und Mineraloele.)		1943-1944	15.00
66.	Societe chimique de France. Bulletin. Documentation and Memoires v.10-11 (Ser.5) (1943-44)	10	11	24.00
106.	Societe de biologie. Comptes rendus v.135-138 (1941-44)	137	138	15.00
67.	Societe de chimie biologique. Bulletin v.25-26 (1943-44)	25	26	12.00
123.	Spectrochimica acta v.1-2 (1939/41-1941/44)			25.00
19.	Stahl und eisen v.63-64 (1943-44)	63	64	19.50
124.	Technik in der landwirtschaft v.24-25 (1943-44)			8.50
125.	Tierernaehrung v.15-16 (1943-44)			28.00
	VDI Forschungsheft, see: Forschung auf dem gebiete des ingenieurwesens.			
20.	Verein deutscher ingenieur. Zeitschrift v.86-88 (1942-44)	87	88	19.00
40.	Virchows Archiv fuer pathologie und pharmakologie v.310-311 (1943-44)	310	311	30.00
126.	Vitamin und hormone v.4-5 (1943-44)			15.00

Custodian's Number	Titles and Volumes Offered	Reprinting Completed	In Process	Cost per Volume
41.	Wilhelm Roux' Archiv fuer entwicklungsmechanik v.142-143 (1943-44)		142	$ 35.00
	Wochenblatt fuer papierfabrikation, see: Papierfabrikant			
21.	Zeitschrift fuer analytische chemie v.123-128 (1942-44)	123-126	127	10.00
	Namen-und sach-verzeichnis	N.u.S.		
	v.101-120	v.101-120		12.00
127.	Zeitschrift fuer angewandte mathematik v.23-24 (1943-44)			15.00
22.	Zeitschrift fuer anorganische und allgemeine chemie v.249-254 (1942-44)	249-251	252	8.00
42.	Zeitschrift fuer biologie v.101-103 (1942-44)		102	20.00
23.	Zeitschrift fuer elektrochemie und angewandte physikalische chemie v.48-50 (1942-44)	48-49	50	18.00
128.	Zeitschrift fuer hygiene v.125-126 (1943-44)			30.00
43.	Zeitschrift fuer immunitaetsforschung und experimentelle therapie v.103-106 (1943-44)		103	13.00
129.	Zeitschrift fuer infektionskrankheiten v.60-61 (1943-44)			13.00
44.	Zeitschrift fuer instrumentenkunde v.61-64 (1941-44)	62	63	20.00
107.	Zeitschrift fuer klinische medizin v.142-143 (1943-44) (WITHDRAWAL CONTEMPLATED UNLESS ADDITIONAL ORDERS BY 1/1/45)			32.00
68.	Zeitschrift fuer kristallographie, mineralogie und petrographie. Abt. A Zeitschrift fuer kristallographie v.105-106 (1943-44)		105	14.00
	Zeitschrift fuer kristallographie, mineralogie und petrographie. Abt. B see: Mineralogie und petrographische mitteilungen			
45.	Zeitschrift fuer metallkunde v.34-36 (1942-44)	35	36	12.00
130.	Zeitschrift fuer parasitenkunde v.13-14 (1943-44)			27.00
108.	Zeitschrift fuer pflanzenkrankheiten und pflanzenschutz v.53-54 (1943-44) (WITHDRAWAL CONTEMPLATED UNLESS ADDITIONAL ORDERS BY 1/1/45			20.00

Custodian's Number	Titles and Volumes Offered	Reprinting Completed	In Process	Cost per Volume
24.	Zeitschrift fuer physik			
	v.118-125 (1941-44)	118-121	122	$ 16.00
25.	Zeitschrift fuer physikalische chemie			
	(Combines A and B beginning v.192)			
	v.192-196 (1943-44)	192	193	7.00
25A.	Zeitschrift fuer physikalische chemie			
	Abt. A (Merges with B beginning v.192)			
	v.190-191 (1941-43)	190-191		7.00
25B.	Zeitschrift fuer physikalische chemie			
	Abt. B (Merges with A after v.53)			
	v.51-53 (1941-43)	51-53		7.00
46.	Zeitschrift fuer technische physik			
	v.23-25 (1942-44)	23	24	18.00
131.	Zeitschrift fuer tierzuchtung			
	v.54-55 (1943-44)			13.00
109.	Zeitschrift fuer untersuchung der			
	lebensmittel			
	v.85-88 (1943-44)			18.00
	(WITHDRAWAL CONTEMPLATED UNLESS			
	ADDITIONAL ORDERS BY 1/1/45)			
110.	Zeitschrift fuer wissenschaftliche			
	mikroskopie und fuer mikroskopische			
	technik			
	v.58-59 (1943-44)	58	59	15.00
	Zeitschrift fuer zellforschung. Abt. B			
	see: Chromosoma			
86.	Zellwolle und kunstseide. Berlin			
	Gemeinschaftsausgabe der zeitschriften			
	"Jentgen's Kunstseide und zellwolle",			
	und "Zellwolle, kunstseide, seide".			
	v.1-2 (1943-44)	1	2	10.00
111.	Zentralblatt fuer allgemeine pathologie			
	und pathologische anatomie			
	v.81-82 (1943-44)			16.00
	(WITHDRAWAL CONTEMPLATED UNLESS			
	ADDITIONAL ORDERS BY 1/1/45)			
47.	Zentralblatt fuer bakteriologie, parasitenkunde			
	und infektionskrankheiten. Abt. I, Originale			
	v.148-153 (1942-44)	150	151	10.00
48.	Zentralblatt fuer bakteriologie, parasitenkunde			
	und infektionskrankheiten. Abt. I, Referate			
	v.141-148 (1942-44)	143	144-145	12.00
49.	Zentralblatt fuer bakteriologie, parasitenkunde			
	und infektionskrankheiten, Abt. II			
	v.105-108 (1942-44)		106	12.00
112.	Zentralblatt fuer die gesamte hygiene mit			
	einschluss der bakteriologie und			
	immunitaetslehre			
	v.51-52 (1943-44)			28.00
	(WITHDRAWAL CONTEMPLATED UNLESS			
	ADDITIONAL ORDERS BY 1/1/45)			

Custodian's Number	Titles and Volumes Offered	Reprinting Completed	In Process	Cost per Volume
113.	Zentralblatt fuer mathematik und ihre grenzgebiete			
	v.27-28 (1943-44)	27	28	$ 20.00
132.	Zentralblatt fuer mechanik			
	v.13-14 (1943-44)			20.00
50.	Zoologischer anzeiger			
	v.137-147 (1942-44)	137-143	144	10.00
114.	Zuechter			
	v.15-16 (1943-44) (WITHDRAWAL CONTEMPLATED UNLESS ADDITIONAL ORDERS BY 1/1/45)			12.00

U. S. GOVERNMENT PRINTING OFFICE: 1944 O - 617900

Appendix B

**Title Page, Prefatory Material and First Contents Page
of the First Issue of the *Referatenblatt*, Issued
Collaboratively by the Information Centers of the
Welt-Wirtschafts Institut in Hamburg and the
Technische Hochschule in Berlin, 1942.**

Jahrgang 1942   Erstes Heft

REFERATENBLATT

der
Auswertungsstelle
der technischen und wirtschaftlichen
Weltfachpresse

Herausgegeben
unter Mitwirkung

der Technischen Hochschule Berlin / Informationsstelle
und des Hamburgischen Welt-Wirtschafts-Instituts e.V.

REFERATENBLATT

DER AUSWERTUNGSSTELLE DER TECHNISCHEN UND WIRTSCHAFTLICHEN WELTFACHPRESSE E.V.

HERAUSGEGEBEN
UNTER MITWIRKUNG DER
TECHNISCHEN HOCHSCHULE BERLIN / INFORMATIONSSTELLE
UND DES HAMBURGISCHEN WELT-WIRTSCHAFTS-INSTITUTS E.V.

Verlag des Referatenblattes:
Auswertungsstelle der technischen und
wirtschaftlichen Weltfachpresse e.V.
Hamburg 36, Poststraße 13-19, Ruf: 346336

Verlagsleiter: Hans-Hermann Hoffmann
Hamburg 36, Poststr. 17, Fernruf: 345951

Hauptschriftleiter: Johannes-Renatus Renner
Hamburg 36, Poststr. 13, Fernruf: 346337

Bearbeitung des technischen Inhaltes:
Technische Hochschule Berlin-Charlottenburg, Informationsstelle, Fernruf: 310011
Leitung: Dr. Albert Predeek, Direktor
der Bibliothek der Technischen Hochschule

Bearbeitung des wirtschaftlichen Inhaltes:
Hamburgisches Welt-Wirtschafts-Institut
Hamburg 36, Poststr. 13-19, Fernruf: 345952

Geschäftsführung: Hamburg 36, Poststraße 13
Banken: Commerzbank Aktiengesellschaft Hamburg
Hamburgische Landesbank · Girozentrale, Hamburg
Postscheckkonto: Hamburg 922 99
Berliner Geschäftsstelle: Berlin NW 7-
Friedrichstraße 105 B, Fernruf: 41 55 85

Mit diesem Einführungsheft beginnt das Referatenblatt der Auswertungsstelle der technischen und wirtschaftlichen Weltfachpresse e.V. Die ersten Seiten geben einen Bericht über die außerordentlichen Umstände seiner Begründung, über seine Aufgabe und seinen Aufbau. Diesen Erläuterungen folgen einige Probeseiten, zusammengestellt aus Referaten des ersten Heftes. Den Probeseiten schließen sich an ein umfassendes Schlagwörterverzeichnis und die Sachgliederung.

Der zweite Weltkrieg und die Informationsbeschaffung!

Das Referatenblatt beginnt inmitten eines neuen Weltkrieges. Die politische Gestalt der Erde wandelt sich. Die drei gegenwärtig im Kampfe stehenden Großräume: Europa, Anglo-Amerika und Ostasien werden in Zukunft die Technik und Wirtschaft der Welt nach ihren Bedürfnissen bestimmen. Damit ändern sich auch die Publizistik, das Informationswesen und die Nachrichtenbeschaffung grundlegend. Sie sind gegenwärtig auch noch einschneidenden Einschränkungen unterworfen. Dennoch und gerade deshalb ist für die deutsche Technik und Wirtschaft die Beschaffung und Auswertung des fachlichen Informationsstoffes des gesamten Auslandes eine Aufgabe von außerordentlicher Bedeutung.

Die ausländischen Fachzeitschriften . . .

Mit dem Ausbruch dieses Krieges stiegen sofort die Bezugspreise der ausländischen Fachzeitschriften an. Sie hatten infolge der Zuschläge, Zwischenspesen und Risikoprämien bereits eine durchschnittliche Höhe von 500 v. H., seit dem Eintritt der USA. in den Krieg in einigen Fällen eine Höhe von 1000, ja von 2000 v. H. erreicht.

Diese Gründe, aber auch devisenwirtschaftliche Überlegungen deutscher Reichsstellen machen es unmöglich, daß den deutschen Unternehmungen der Strom der ausländischen Literatur und Fachzeitschriften so wie früher zufließt.

. . . und ihre Beschaffung

Die europäischen und die künftigen weltwirtschaftlichen Aufgaben des deutschen Unternehmers erfordern aber erst recht genaueste Unterrichtung über die technische Entwicklung und deren wirtschaftliche Voraussetzungen und Auswirkungen in der ganzen Welt. Große und dauernde Lücken in dieser Unterrichtung müßten die Führerstellung des deutschen Unternehmers auf das schwerste beeinträchtigen. Bei der Schwierigkeit, wenn nicht Unmöglichkeit des privaten Einzelbezuges ist eine zentrale Besorgung zweckmäßig geworden. Denn nur eine zentral arbeitende Institution, die von den zuständigen Stellen wirksam unterstützt wird und entsprechende Mittel einsetzen kann, ist noch in der Lage, zusammenhängendes Informationsmaterial des Auslandes zu beschaffen.

Eine Auswertungsstelle – beweglich und straff

Aus diesen Ursachen hat der Herr Reichswirtschaftsminister im Benehmen mit anderen Reichsstellen angeordnet, daß eine derartige Einrichtung geschaffen wird. welche die technische und wirtschaftliche Weltfachpresse besorgt und den deutschen Unternehmungen Mitteilungen und Kurzreferate über deren Inhalt zur Verfügung stellt. Für diese „Auswertungsstelle der technischen und wirtschaftlichen Weltfachpresse e. V." wurde die Form eines Vereins gewählt, weil damit die schnellstmögliche Anpassung an die jeweiligen Verhältnisse gegeben ist und weil ferner das von diesem Verein herauszugebende Referatenblatt keine unkontrollierbaren Wege nehmen darf, sondern sich nur an Mitglieder dieses Vereins wendet. Diese Auswertungsstelle lehnt sich an die Organisation der gewerblichen Wirtschaft an.

Dem Vorstand gehören an: die Reichswirtschaftskammer, die Reichsgruppe Industrie, die Reichsgruppe Handel, der Technisch-wirtschaftliche Beratungsdienst im Reichskuratorium für Wirtschaftlichkeit, die Technische Hochschule Berlin / Informationsstelle, das Hamburgische Welt-Wirtschafts-Institut e. V., das Institut für Weltwirtschaft an der Universität Kiel.

Die Aufgaben des Referatenblattes

Diese Auswertungsstelle bezieht die technischen und wirtschaftlichen Fachzeitschriften des Auslandes. Aus naheliegenden Gründen fallen bis auf weiteres einige Gebiete aus, wie Australien, Ostasien und Sowjetrußland. Dagegen ist es gelungen, in einem außergewöhnlichen Umfange die britische und nordamerikanische Fachpresse zu beschaffen; die europäische Fachpresse ist selbstverständlich vollständig vertreten.

Der Inhalt dieser Weltfachpresse wird der deutschen Wirtschaft in der bestmöglichen Form zugänglich gemacht werden. Hierzu gibt die Auswertungsstelle ein Referatenblatt heraus. Dieses Referatenblatt enthält auszugsweise Inhaltsangaben (Kurzreferate) der wichtigen Artikel, darunter auch Patente. Diese Auswertung erfolgt möglichst vollständig, denn die Wirtschaft soll die Gewißheit haben, daß nichts übersehen, sondern alles Wichtige erfaßt wird. Der gebotene Stoff wird sich nicht nur auf die laufende Zeit und auf das Jahr 1941, sondern auch, um die Kriegslücken möglichst zu schließen, auf das Jahr 1939/40 erstrecken. Die sachlich richtige Aufschließung des Stoffes geschieht durch hierfür besonders qualifizierte Institute, zu denen eine große Zahl weiterer Mitarbeiter kommt; die Auswerter sind akademische Fachleute. Hierzu tritt noch die Mitwirkung der Wirtschaftsgruppen für einzelne Gebiete.

Es unterscheidet sich von anderen ...

Der im Referatenblatt gebotene Stoff ist systematisch geordnet. Das Referatenblatt unterscheidet sich in seiner Berichterstattung und Sachgliederung grundsätzlich von jenen Referatorganen, die sich mit Einzel- oder Sondergebieten befassen. Denn jene wenden sich an einen meist engumgrenzten Leserkreis und treffen unter Sondergesichtspunkten ihre Stoffauswahl. Ein Referatorgan über Werkstoffe z. B. wird seine Referate aus chemischen, physikalischen, mineralogischen, keramischen, metallurgischen, elektrotechnischen und anderen Quellen entnehmen. Aber die gleichen Aufsätze können auch für Referatorgane der Chemie, Physik, Mineralogie, Keramik, Metallurgie, Elektrotechnik und andere wichtig sein. Einzelorgane werden also immer einseitig referieren müssen.

... durch sein Prinzip!

Das Referatenblatt der Auswertungsstelle über das Gesamtgebiet der technischen und wirtschaftlichen Weltfachpresse muß nach anderen Gesichtspunkten verfahren. Hier muß auf allen Gebieten gleichmäßig referiert werden und der Stoff so angeordnet sein, daß der einzelne Gegenstand nur einmal an seiner zuständigen Stelle eingegliedert wird. Diese Auswertung des Stoffes strebt an, die gesamte Technik und ihre wirtschaftlichen Voraussetzungen und Auswirkungen zu erfassen. Die Kreise der produzierenden und verteilenden Wirtschaft sowie der Forschung werden dadurch über das ganze sie interessierende auf ihren Arbeitsgebieten erschei-

nende Material unterrichtet; gleichzeitig werden sie auf Neuerungen in Nebengebieten hingewie-
sen. Diese Aufgabe kann nur durch eine einheitliche, nach großen Gesichtspunkten angelegte
Sachgliederung gelöst werden.

Die Menge des Stoffes macht eine möglichst einfache, jedoch präzise Ordnung erforderlich,
um sowohl eine rasche Ermittlung des gewünschten Stoffes zu ermöglichen als auch Überschneidungen
auszuschließen. So finden die metallbearbeitenden Industrien in der Sachgliederung ihren Stoff
hauptsächlich unter „Maschinenwesen" und „Hüttenwesen"; das die Spezialindustrien, die Gewerbe und das Handwerk interessierende Material dagegen ist unter „Industrien, Gewerbe,
Handwerke" zusammengefaßt. Wenn jeder Industriezweig in der Sachgliederung gesondert
berücksichtigt werden sollte, würde die Sachgliederung in eine lange Reihe von Einzelbiblio-
graphien mit häufigen Überschneidungen zerfallen und dadurch zu einem nicht mehr übereh-
baren Umfang anwachsen, wobei überdies Nebengebiete des einzelnen Faches unberücksichtigt
bleiben müßten.

Die Sachgliederung des Referatenblattes

Die unter diesen Gesichtspunkten aufgestellte Sachgliederung unterteilt den Gesamtstoff in die
sechs Fachgebiete: Technik und Wirtschaft (TW); Bauwesen (B); Maschinenwesen (M); Energie-
wesen (E); Berg- und Hüttenwesen (BH); Industrien, Gewerbe, Handwerke (IG). Die Fachgebiete werden unterteilt in Hauptabteilungen, Abteilungen, Hauptgruppen und Gruppen; ihre
Kennzeichnung erfolgt durch Signaturen aus Großbuchstaben und Zahlen.

Die zu Grunde gelegte Aufteilung der Fachgebiete bringt es mit sich, daß gewisse Sachgruppen
an mehreren Stellen auftreten. So erscheint z. B. die Werkstoffkunde im Bauwesen, im Maschinenwesen, im Schiffbau, in der Elektrotechnik, im Hüttenwesen. Die jeweiligen Arbeitsmaschinen erscheinen sowohl im Maschinenbau als auch bei den Baumaschinen, Eisenbahn-
maschinen, Bergbau- und Hüttenmaschinen und in fast allen Gruppen des Fachgebietes Industrien, Gewerbe, Handwerke. An sich wäre es wohl möglich, zusammenhängende Gruppen zu
bilden wie „Werkstoffkunde", „Arbeitsmaschinen", oder etwa „Regelung", „Motoren". Aber
es entspricht der Natur der zu referierenden Schrifttumsquellen besser, auch in der Stoffordnung
den technologischen Begriff nicht vom Orte seiner praktischen Verwendung zu trennen. Deshalb
werden die Maschinen, Geräte, Vorrichtungen, Verfahren zusammengehalten, die begrifflich oder
systematisch den verschiedenen Hauptgebieten angehören können.

Keine Referate zu den Grundwissenschaften . .

Die sogenannten Grundwissenschaften der Technik treten nicht selbständig auf. Denn Mathematik, Physik, Chemie, Geologie usw. als solche sind nicht Gegenstand des Referatenblattes.
Dagegen werden theoretische Abhandlungen über technische Gegenstände bei diesen selbst eingeordnet. Daher sind auch bei den einzelnen Fachgebieten und Fachabteilungen meistens theoretische oder grundlegende Gruppen vorgeschaltet wie z. B. Mechanik, Statik, Dynamik. Ver-
messungswesen, technische Geologie (in der Baukunde), angewandte Geologie, Geophysik (in der
Markscheidekunde), Aerodynamik (bei Luftfahrzeugen). Auch kann, wenn der Stoff es erfordert,
die theoretische Behandlung des Gegenstandes in die jeweilige Fachgruppe selbst eingeordnet
werden.

. . . und zur Chemie?

Was die Chemie betrifft, so wird sich die Berichterstattung in diesem Referatenblatt auf die
technische und wirtschaftliche Seite beschränken. Auch bei Material über technische und wirt-

schaftliche Vorgänge, an denen chemische Prozesse beteiligt sind, wird auf eine Berichterstattung vom Standpunkt der chemischen Fachwissenschaft aus verzichtet und die Berichterstattung auf die technische und wirtschaftliche Seite beschränkt.

Technik und Wirtschaft

Für den in der Praxis stehenden Wirtschaftsführer bilden Technik und Wirtschaft eine unlösbare Einheit. So ist bei der Wahl des technischen Verfahrens oft die Frage der Wirtschaftlichkeit von ausschlaggebender Bedeutung. Auf der anderen Seite ist das von der Wirtschaft erwartete Produktionsergebnis nicht zu beurteilen ohne die genaue Kenntnis der technischen Möglichkeiten. Es ist also zum Zwecke einer erschöpfenden Berichterstattung über das Gebiet der Technik unabweisbar, daß die wirtschaftlichen Voraussetzungen, die einem technischen Prozeß zu Grunde liegen, und die wirtschaftlichen Auswirkungen, die die technische Dynamik im Gefolge hat, in die Berichterstattung einbezogen werden, ohne daß dadurch der Charakter eines vorwiegend technischen Referatenblattes in Frage gestellt wird. Die Berichterstattung über rein wirtschaftliche Theorien und wirtschafts- und handelspolitische Themen liegen jenseits des Aufgabenbereiches dieses Referatenblattes. Die Einordnung der wirtschaftlichen Referate in die Sachgliederung erfolgt — soweit es sich um allgemeingültige Themen handelt — bei dem Fachgebiet TW oder — soweit es sich um spezielle wirtschaftliche Fragen handelt — sinngemäß bei den einzelnen Spezialgruppen.

Das Schlagwörterverzeichnis

Das Schlagwörterverzeichnis im Einführungsheft ergänzt die Sachgliederung. Dieses Verzeichnis gibt mit seinen mehr als 4000 Begriffen eine Vorstellung von der Fülle der in den Einzelheften des Referatenblattes behandelten Gegenstände und erleichtert gleichzeitig die rasche Auffindung des Standortes der interessierenden Referate über ein bestimmtes Thema. Dem Schlagwörterverzeichnis wurde die Aufteilung der Organisation der gewerblichen Wirtschaft, insbesondere der Reichsgruppe Industrie, einschließlich ihrer Wirtschafts-, Fach- und Fachuntergruppen, sowie das Stichwörterverzeichnis des Reichspatentamtes zu Grunde gelegt.

Das mit diesem Einführungsheft herausgegebene Schlagwörterverzeichnis trägt hinter jedem Begriff die Signatur der Sachgliederung. In dieser Form erscheint das Schlagwörterverzeichnis nur in diesem Heft. Jedes künftig zur Ausgabe gelangende Einzelheft des Referatenblattes enthält ein Schlagwörterverzeichnis über die in dem jeweiligen Heft gebrachten Referate. Bei diesen künftigen Schlagwörterverzeichnissen der Einzelhefte stehen hinter jedem Begriff die durch den Jahrgang fortlaufenden Nummern der Referate.

Während also im Schlagwörterverzeichnis die Einzelbegriffe erscheinen, zeigt die Sachgliederung die systematische Ordnung. Diese Sachgliederung wird nur einmal mit diesem Einführungsheft ausgegeben. Eine zweite Ausgabe erfolgt erst dann, wenn der zunehmende Umfang des Referatenblattes eine weitere Aufgliederung des Stoffes notwendig macht.

Wie wird referiert?

Das Referatenblatt berücksichtigt nur Originalartikel, nicht aber Wiederholungen, Auszüge, Übersetzungen, die irgendeiner anderen Quelle als der Originalquelle entstammen.

Maßgebend ist ferner nicht der Umfang oder die Aufmachung einer Originalquelle, sondern die Frage, ob sie wertvoll oder beachtlich zu sein scheint.

Die Berichterstatter geben nur den Standpunkt des Verfassers der Originalquelle, nicht aber ihre eigene Meinung wieder.

Die drucktechnische Anordnung der Referate umfaßt den Verfassernamen, den sinngemäß verdeutschten Titel des Originals (dazu Originaltitel in Klammern), den in Anlehnung an gebräuchliche Methoden gekürzten Namen der Zeitschrift oder der Schrifttumsquelle (mit Angaben über Erscheinungsort, Band, Druckjahr, Heft), sowie den Inhalt des Referates.

Jedes Referat wird nur an einer einzigen Stelle des Referatenblattes aufgenommen. An anderen etwa in Betracht kommenden Stellen werden Hinweise auf den Standort dieses Referates gemacht. Das Referatenblatt will nicht in erster Linie das Lesen des Originals ersetzen, sondern über den Inhalt des Originals unterrichten und auf die Quelle hinweisen. Infolgedessen ist Vorsorge getroffen, daß eine Fotokopie des Originals dem Interessenten zugänglich gemacht werden kann. Hierzu ergeht eine besondere Mitteilung.

Darüber hinaus kann das Referatenblatt Auskünfte wissenschaftlicher Art (Recherchen) durch die an seiner Herausgabe mitwirkenden Institute vermitteln.

Es sind zu richten Fragen technischen Inhalts an die Informationsstelle der Technischen Hochschule Berlin, Berlin-Charlottenburg, Berliner Str. 171, Fragen wirtschaftlichen Inhalts an das Hamburgische Welt-Wirtschafts-Institut e. V. Hamburg 36, Poststr. 19.

So viel Papier ...

Aus einem Monatsheft des Referatenblattes mit etwa 3000 Referaten kommt zwar nur ein Teil für den jeweiligen Interessenten in Betracht. Aber ganz abgesehen davon, daß eine auszugsweise Zusammenstellung des Inhalts nach Wirtschaftsgruppen ein erhebliches Mehr an Arbeit — und zwar Menschen- und nicht Maschinenarbeit! — und damit eine wesentliche Erhöhung des Preises verursachen würde, ginge mit einer solchen Zerlegung gerade der Wert einer universellen Berichterstattung verloren. Der Vorteil der universellen Berichterstattung liegt darin, daß jeder Interessent in die Lage versetzt wird, Anregungen aus verwandten oder parallelen Vorgängen auf benachbarten oder fremden Arbeitsgebieten zu erhalten.

... und die deutschen Fachblätter?

Das Referatenblatt der Auswertungsstelle wird deutsche Fachblätter nicht überflüssig machen: im Gegenteil! Denn auch die deutsche Fachpresse erhält durch das Referatenblatt der Auswertungsstelle wieder Überblick über die Auslandsliteratur, vielleicht vollständiger als bisher. Da das Referatenblatt nur Kurzreferate gibt, bleibt es Aufgabe der deutschen Fachpresse, den Inhalt wichtiger Artikel für ihren Leserkreis zu entfächern. Sie kann dadurch eine wertvolle Ergänzung der Arbeit des Referatenblattes der Auswertungsstelle bewirken.

Aus einem solchen Zusammenwirken des Referatenblattes der Auswertungsstelle mit der deutschen Fachpresse und der Organisation der gewerblichen Wirtschaft kann das entstehen, was heute der deutschen Technik und Wirtschaft noch fehlt:

eine umfassende, erschöpfende, zuverlässige Berichterstattung über die technische und wirtschaftliche Weltfachpresse und deren schnelle und wirkungsvolle Auswertung.

Die Aufgliederung des Kurzreferates

| Beispiel eines Referates | Erläuterungen zum Referat |

1941 — 3413

① Die Numerierung der Referate beginnt mit 1 und wird durch den ganzen Jahrgang laufend fortgeführt. Die jeweilige Nummer eines Referates dient zugleich als Bestellnummer bei der Anforderung einer Fotokopie. Bei der Bestellung sind außerdem der Jahrgang und sonstige Kennzeichen zwischen der Jahrgangsziffer und der laufenden Nummer anzugeben; z. B. 1941 — F — 3469.

Bonnet, L. J. Lamoen

② Die Verfassernamen. Wenn der oder die Verfasser im Originalbeitrag nicht genannt sind, wird der Name durch sechs in runde Klammern gesetzte Punkte ersetzt (......). In manchen Fällen ist der Originalbeitrag nur mit den Anfangsbuchstaben des Verfassers gezeichnet.

Modellversuche über die Möglichkeiten zur Verbesserung der Schiffahrtsbedingungen an der Jambes-Brücke über die Maas bei Namur

③ Der Übersetzungstitel braucht nicht wörtlich den Originaltitel wiederzugeben. In vielen Fällen wird zur genaueren Kennzeichnung des technischen oder wirtschaftlichen Vorganges eine sinngetreue Übersetzung vorgezogen.

(Essais sur modèle réduit en vue de déterminer les moyens d'améliorer les conditions de navigation au pont de Jambes sur la Meuse près de Namur)

④ Der Originaltitel. Bei den russischen, ukrainischen, bulgarischen und serbischen Zeitschriften ist der Titel nach den Instruktionen für die alphabetischen Kataloge der preußischen Bibliotheken transkribiert.

Rev. univ. Mines, Lüttich, 84 (1941) 10, 273—97 (3 Abb 6 Sk 11 D)

⑤ Die Quellenangabe zitiert die Zeitschriftentitel, die einheitlich nach den Regeln des Normblattes DIN 1502 des Fachnormenausschusses für Bibliotheks-, Buch- und Zeitschriftenwesen gekürzt werden. Dies gilt auch für die transkribierten Titel. Der Erscheinungsort ist genannt, damit der Benutzer in Zweifelsfällen die Sprache des Originalbeitrages bestimmen kann. Anschließend folgen die Nummer des Jahrganges oder des Bandes. Erscheinungsjahr in Klammern, Heftnummer und Seitenzahlen. In Klammern sind angegeben: Abb = Abbildung, Sk = Skizze, Sch = Schaltskizze, D = Diagramm und Nomogramm, M = Mikrophotographie, R = Röntgenbild, Sp = Spektrogramm, Oz = Oszillogramm, K = Kurvendiagramm, Ke = Karte.

Der belgische Conseil des Ponts et Chaussées beauftragte das Laboratorium für hydraulische Untersuchungen in Antwerpen, an Hand eines Modells die Möglichkeiten zur Beseitigung oder Milderung der Hindernisse zu untersuchen, die sich für die Schiffahrt besonders bei Hochwasser an der im Mittelalter erbauten Jambes-Brücke ergaben, unter Berücksichtigung dieses historischen Bauwerkes und seiner landschaftlich schönen Umgebung. Zahlreiche Versuche, werden an Hand eingehender hydrodynamischer Berechnungen und Abhandlungen genau beschrieben. Es zeigte sich, daß dem Schiff entgegengesetzter Widerstand sowie die Strömungen, verursacht durch Brückenpfeiler, eine Energieverschwendung verursachen, so daß wirksame Abhilfe nur durch Beseitigung eines Pfeilers möglich ist. (vCo)

⑥ Der Text des Kurzreferates vermittelt dem Leser in gedrängter Form eine möglichst vollständige Vorstellung vom Inhalt des Originalbeitrages. Eine eigene Stellungnahme des Referenten erfolgt nicht, sondern das Referat gibt nur den Standpunkt des Verfassers des Originals wieder.

⑦ Die Chiffre des Referenten steht in runden Klammern am Ende des Referates; sie ist aus organisatorischen Gründen hinzugefügt und für den Leser ohne Belang.

B 301

⑧ Die Signatur der Sachgliederung steht am Schluß rechts ausgerückt. Hinweis-Signaturen werden in eckigen Klammern in der systematischen Reihenfolge vorangestellt; z. B. [B 393, M 132.7] B 342.

References

BOOKS

Adkinson, Burton W. *Two Centuries of Federal Information*. Stroudsbourg PA: Dowden, Hutchinson and Ross, 1978.

Alter, Peter. *The Reluctant Patron: Science and the State in Britain 1850-1920*. Trans. Angela Davies. Oxford: Berg, 1987.

Ambruster, Howard Watson. *Treason's Peace: German Dyes and American Dupes*. New York: Beechhurst, 1947.

Auswärtiges Amt. *Die Stellung der deutschen Sprache in der Welt*. Bericht der Bundesregierung. Reihe Bericht und Dokumentationen. Bonn: Auswärtiges Amt, 1986.

Badash, Lawrence. *Kapitsa, Rutherford and the Kremlin*. New Haven: Yale University Press, 1985.

Barry, Joseph A. *Libraries in Need*. Paris: UNESCO, 1949.

Becker, Heinrich, Dahms, Hans-Joachim, and Wegeler, Cornelia. *Die Universität Göttingen unter dem Nationalsozialismus: Das verdrängte Kapitel ihrer 250-jähriger Geschichte*. München: K. G.Saur, 1987.

Ben-David, Joseph. *Centers of Learning: Britain, Germany and the United States*. New York: McGraw-Hill, 1976.

Ben-Zohar, Michel. *The Hunt for German Scientists*. Trans. Len Ortzen. New York: Hawthorne, 1967.

Bernal, J. D. *The Social Function of Science*. London: Routledge and Kegan Paul, 1939.

Borkin, Joseph. *The Crime and Punishment of I. G. Farben*. New York: Macmillan, 1978.

Born, Max. *My Life: Recollections of a Nobel Laureate*. New York: Charles Scribners, 1978.

Bower, Tom. *Maxwell, The Outsider*. London: Aurum Press, 1988.

Bradford, S. C. *Documentation*. London: Crosby Lockwood, 1948.

Buder, Marianne. *Das Verhältnis von Dokumentation und Normung von 1927 bis 1945 in nationaler und internationaler Hinsicht*. Berlin: DIN

Deutsches Institut für Normung, 1976.

Bush, Vannevar. *Science: The Endless Frontier. A Report to the President.* Washington: Government Printing Office, 1945.

———. *Modern Arms and Free Men.* New York: Simon and Schuster, 1949.

Busse, Gisela von, and Ernestus, Horst. *Das Bibliothekswesen der Bundesrepublik Deutschland.* Wiesbaden: Harrassowitz, 1968.

Buszko, Joseph and Irena Paczynska, eds., *Universities during World War II.* Cracow: Jagellonian University, 1979.

Buzas, Ladislaus. *Geschichte der Universitätsbibliothek München.* Wiesbaden: Dr. Ludwig Reichert Verlag, 1972.

Casimir, Hendrik. *Haphazard Reality: Half a Century of Science.* New York: Harper and Row, 1983.

Clark, Ronald W. *The Rise of the Boffins.* London: Phoenix House, 1962.

———. *Tizard.* London: Methuen, 1965.

Clarke, I. F. *Voices Prophesying War 1763-1984.* London: Oxford University Press, 1966.

Coates, W. P. and Coates, Zelda. *A History of Anglo-Soviet Relations.* London: Lawrence and Wishart and the Pilot Press, 1945.

Dallin, Alexander. *German Rule in Russia 1941-1945.* London: Macmillan, 1957.

Deane, John R. *The Strange Alliance: The Story of Our Efforts at Wartime Cooperation with Russia.* New York: Viking, 1947.

De Jong, L. *Het Koninkrijk der Nederlanden in de Tweede Wereldorloog.* 'sGravenhagen: Nijhoff, 1978.

Die Deutsche Universität im Dritten Reich: Acht Beiträge. München: R. Piper Verlag, 1966.

Dosa, Marta. *Libraries in the Political Scene.* Westport CT: Greenwood Press, 1974.

Dresden, M. *H. A. Kramers: Between Tradition and Revolution.* New York: Springer, 1987.

DuBois, Josiah. *The Devil's Chemists.* Boston: Beacon Press, 1952.

Dupree, A. Hunter. *Science in the Federal Government: A History of Policies and Activities to 1940.* Cambridge MA: Harvard University Press, 1957.

Farkas-Conn, Irene. *From Documentation to Information Science.* New York: Greenwood Press, 1990.

Flexner, Abraham. *I Remember.* New York: Simon and Schuster, 1940.

French, A. P. and Kennedy, P. J. *Niels Bohr: A Centenary Volume.* Cambridge MA: Harvard University Press, 1985.

Gehlen, Reinhard. *The Service.* Trans. David Irving. New York: World Publishing, 1972.

Geiger, Roger L. *To Advance Knowledge: The Growth of American Research*

Universities 1900-1940. New York: Oxford University Press, 1986.

[Die] Gesellschaft für Dokumentation. *Die Dokumente und ihre Probleme.* Leipzig: Harrassowitz, 1943.

Goldsmith, Maurice. *Frédéric Joliot-Curie.* London: Lawrence and Wishart, 1976.

Goudsmit, Samuel A. *ALSOS.* Los Angeles: Tomash Publishers, 1983. Reprint of 1947 edition.

Gowing, Margaret. *Britain and the Atomic Age.* London: St.Martin's Press, 1964.

Groueff, Stephane. *Manhattan Project.* London: Collins, 1967.

Hahn, Otto. *My Life: The Autobiography of a Scientist.* Trans. Ernst Kaiser and Eithne Wilkins. New York: Herder and Herder, 1970.

Hartshorne, Edward Y. *The German Universities and National Socialism.* London: Allen and Unwin, 1937.

Heisenberg, Elisabeth. *Inner Exile.* Trans. S. Cappellari and C. Morris. Boston: Birkhaüser, 1980.

Heisenberg, Werner. *Physics and Beyond: Encounters and Conversations.* Trans. Arnold J. Pomerans. New York: Harper and Row, 1971.

Hewlett, Richard G. and Anderson, Oscar E. *The New World 1939/1946: A History of the United States Atomic Energy Commission.* Vol. I. University Park PA: Pennsylvania State University Press, 1962.

Houghton, Bernard. *Out of the Dinosaurs: The Evolution of the National Lending Library for Science and Technology.* London: Clive Bingley, 1972.

Irving, David. *The German Atomic Bomb.* New York: Simon and Schuster, 1967.

Jeffreys-Jones, Rhodrick. *American Espionage: From Secret Service to CIA.* New York: Free Press, 1977.

Jones, R. V. *The Wizard War: British Scientific Intelligence 1939-1945.* New York: Coward, McCann and Geoghegan, 1978.

————. *Reflections on Intelligence.* London: Heinemann, 1989.

Kahn, David. *Hitler's Spies: German Military Intelligence in World War II.* New York: Macmillan, 1978.

Kent, Sherman. *Strategic Intelligence for American World Policy.* Princeton NJ: Princeton University Press, 1951.

Kevles, Daniel J. *The Physicists.* New York: Alfred J. Knopf, 1978.

King, Alexander. *Science and Policy: The International Stimulus.* London: Oxford University Press, 1974.

Knightly, Phillip. *The Second Oldest Profession: Spies and Spying in the Twentieth Century.* London: Penguin, 1988.

Kramish, Arnold. *Atomic Energy in the Soviet Union.* Stanford CA: Stanford University Press, 1959.

Laqueur, Walter. *Russia and German: A Century of Conflict.* Boston: Little, Brown, 1965.

Leyh, Georg. *Die deutschen wissenschaftlichen Bibliotheken nach dem Kriege.* Tübingen, 1947.

————, ed. *Handbuch der Bibliothekswissenschaft* 2nd edition. Wiesbaden: Harrassowitz, 1952-1965.

Leverkuehn, Paul. *German Military Intelligence.* New York: Praeger, 1954.

Ludwig, Karl-Heinz. *Technik und Ingenieure im Dritten Reich.* Düsseldorf: Droste Verlag, 1974.

McConnell, Frank. *The Science Fiction of H. G. Wells.* London: Oxford University Press, 1981.

Manchester, William. *The Arms of Krupp 1587-1968.* Boston: Little, Brown, 1964.

Medvedev, Zhores A. *Soviet Science.* London: Oxford University Press, 1979.

Mehl, Ernest, and Hannermann, Kurt. *Deutsche Bibliotheksgeschichte.* Berlin: Eric Schmidt Verlag, 1951.

Melville, Sir Harry. *The Department of Scientific and Industrial Research.* London: George Allen and Unwin, 1962.

Meyer, Fritz. *Die technisch-wissenschaftlichen Bibliotheken.* Braunschweig: Georg Westerman, 1949.

Miles, Wyndham Davis. *A History of the National Library of Medicine.* Bethesda MD: U.S. Department of Health and Human Services, 1982.

Milkau, Franz, ed. *Handbuch der Bibliothekswissenschaft.* Leipzig: Harrassowitz, 1933.

Milward, Alan S. *The German Economy at War.* London: Athlone Press, 1965.

Moss, George L. *The Crisis of German Ideology: Intellectual Origins of the Third Reich.* New York: Grosset and Dunlap, 1964.

————, ed. *Nazi Culture: Intellectual, Cultural and Social Life in the Third Reich.* Trans. Salvator Attanasio et al. New York: Grosset and Dunlap, 1966.

Nemeyer, Carol A. *Scholarly Reprint Publishing in the United States.* New York: Bowker, 1972.

Peierls, Rudolf. *Bird of Passage: Recollections of a Physicist.* Princeton: Princeton University Press, 1985.

Poste, Leslie I. *The Development of U.S. Protection of Libraries and Archives in Europe during World War II.* Fort Gordon GA: U.S. Army Civil Affairs School, 1958.

Powers, Thomas. *Heisenberg's War: The Secret History of the German Bomb.* New York: Knopf, 1993.

Pryce-Jones, David. *Paris in the Third Reich.* New York: Holt Rinehart and Winston, 1981.

Reid, Constance. *Hilbert-Courant.* New York: Springer, 1986.

Ringer, Fritz. *The Decline of the German Mandarins: The German Academic Community 1890-1933*. Cambridge MA: Harvard University Press 1969.

Roosevelt, Kermit. *War Report of the OSS*. New York: Walker and Company, 1975.

Rostow, W. W. *The United States in the World Arena*. New York: Harper, 1960.

Royal Society. *Empire Science Conference 1946*. London: Royal Society, 1946.

Rozenthal, Stefan, ed. *Niels Bohr*. Amsterdam: North Holland, 1967.

Sasuly, Richard. *I. G. Farben*. New York: Boni and Gaer, 1947.

Sherwin, Martin J. *A World Destroyed*. New York: Knopf, 1973.

Scheibert, Peter. *Lage und Erfordernisse der westdeutschen wissenschaftlichen Bibliotheken*. Bad Godesberg: Notgemeinschaft der deutschen Wissenschaft, 1951.

Schroeder-Gudehus, Brigitte. *Les Scientifiques et la Paix*. Montréal: Presses de l'Université de Montréal, 1978.

Simon, Col. Leslie E. *German Scientific Establishments*. PB Report 19849. Washington: U.S.Department of Commerce, Office of Technical Services, 1945. Reprint: Brooklyn NY: Mapleton House, 1947.

Smith, R. Harris. *OSS: The Secret History of America's First Intelligence Agency*. Berkeley: University of California Press, 1972.

Snow, C. P. *The Physicists*. Boston: Little, Brown, 1981.

Stern, Leo, ed. *Die Berliner Akademie in der Zeit der Imperialismus*. Teil III: Die Jahre der faschistischen Diktatur 1933 bis 1945. Berlin: Akademie-Verlag, 1979.

Stevens, Robert D. *The Role of the Library of Congress in the International Exchange of Official Publications: A Brief History*. Washington DC: Library of Congress, 1953.

Stevenson, William. *A Man Called Intrepid*. New York: Harcourt Brace Jovanovitch, 1976.

Turner, Henry A., ed. *Nazism and the Third Reich*. New York: Quadrangle, 1972.

Vorstius, Joris. *Grundzüge der Bibliotheksgeschichte*. Wiesbaden: Harrassowitz, 1969.

Vucinich, Alexander. *The Empire of Knowledge: The Academy of Sciences of the USSR 1917-1970*. Berkeley: University of California Press, 1984.

Wall, Joseph. *Andrew Carnegie*. London: Oxford University Press, 1980.

Weinberg, Alvin M. *Science, Government and Information: The Responsibilities of the Technical Community and the Government in the Transfer of Information. A Report of the President's Science Advisory Committee*. Washington DC: Government Printing Office, 1963.

Werth, Alexander. *Russia at War 1941-1945*. New York: E.P. Dutton, 1964.

Wilkes, Maurice V. *Memoirs of a Computer Pioneer.* Cambridge MA: Massachusetts Institute of Technology Press, 1985.

Williams, Robert Chadwell Williams. *Klaus Fuchs, Atom Spy.* Cambridge MA: Harvard University Press,   1987.

Winks, Robin W. *Cloak and Gown: Scholars in the Secret War 1939-1961.* New York: William Morrow, 1987.

Wright, Peter. *Spycatcher.* New York: Viking, 1987.

JOURNAL ARTICLES

Abb, Gustav. "Ein Jahr Staatsbibliothek Krakau." *Zentralblatt für Bibliothekswesen* 60 (1943): 59-62.

Beardsley, E. H. "Secrets Between Friends." *Social Studies of Science* 77 (1977):447-73.

Collins, Donald E., and Rothfeder, Herbert P. "The Einsatzstab Reichsleiter Rosenberg and the Looting of Jewish and Masonic Libraries during World War II." *Journal of Library History* 18 (Winter 1983): 21-36.

Des Coudres, H. P. "Das verbotene Schrifttum und die wissenschaftlichen Bibliotheken." *Zentralblatt für Bibliothekswesen* 52 (1935): 459-471.

Ditmas, E. M. R. "Dr. S. C. Bradford." *Journal of Documentation* 4 (December 1948): 169-174.

Gomoll, Heinz. "Die Werkbücherei der Friedrich Krupp AG in Essen." *Zentralblatt für Bibliothekswesen* 54 (1937):191-95.

Harris, P. R. "Microfilm Replacements in the British Library Reference Division." *Microform Review* 15 (Winter 1968):15-18.

Holloway, David. "Entering the Nuclear Arms Race: The Soviet Decision to Build the Atomic Bomb 1949-1945." *Social Studies of Science* 11 (1981):159-97.

Hövel, Paul. "Die Wirtschaftstelle des deutschen Buchhandels. "*Buchhandelsgeschichte* 1 (1984):B1-B16.

Hutton, R. S. "The Origin and History of Aslib." *Journal of Documentation* 1 (1945/6): 6-20.

Jacob, William F. "When Books Are Boomerangs." *Library Journal* 71 (1 February 1946): 169.

Macrakis, Kristie. "Wissenschaftsförderung durch die Rockefeller-Stiftung im Dritten Reich." *Geschichte und Gesellschaft* 12 (1986): 348-79.

Müller, Hans. "Aus bolschewistischen Bibliotheken." *Zentralblatt für Bibliothekswesen* 60 (1943): 266-72.

Northedge, F. S. "The Work of the League of Nations for Documentation." *Journal of Documentation* 13 (September 1957): 117-31.

Peiss, Reuben. "Report from Leipzig." *Library Journal* (15 October 1946):

1444-51.

———. "Problems in the Acquisition of Foreign Scientific Publications." *Department of State Bulletin* 22 (30 January 1950): 151-55.

Predeek, Albert. "Die Dokumentationsstelle für das technisch-wissenschaftliche Schrifttum in der Bibliothek der Technischen Hochschule zu Berlin." *Zentralblatt für Bibliothekswesen* 52 (1935): 607-627.

———. "Noch Einmal die Dokumentation." *Zentralblatt für Bibliothekswesen* 53 (1936): 502-519.

Rayward, Boyd. "The International Exposition and the World Documentation Congress, Paris 1937." *Library Quarterly* 53 (1982): 254-68.

Richards, Pamela Spence. "Gathering Enemy Scientific Information in Wartime: The OSS and the Periodical Republication Program," *Journal of Library History* (1981): 243-64.

———. "Aryan Librarnianship: Academic and Research Libraries under Hitler." *Journal of Library History* (1984): 231-58.

———. "German Libraries and Scientific and Technical Information in Nazi Germany." *Library Quarterly* (1985):151-73.

———. "Great Britain and Allied Scientific Information." *Minerva* (1988):177-98.

———. "Information Science at War: Pioneer Documentation Activities during World War II." Journal of the American Society for Information Science (1988): 301-9.

———. "The Movement of Scientific Knowledge to and from Germany under National Socialism." *Minerva* (1990):401-25.

"Reichszentrale für wissenschaftliche Berichterstattung 1929-1939." *Forschungen und Fortschritte* 15 (December 1939): 436-438.

Schultz, Claire K., and Garwig, Paul L. "History of the American Documentation Institute—A Sketch." *American Documentation* (1969): 152-160.

Shaw, Ralph L. "International Activities of the American Library Association." *ALA Bulletin* 41 (June 1947): 199-232.

Siegmund-Schultze, Reinhard. "Bieberbachs'Jahrbuch'." *Spectrum* 19 (1988): 30-31.

———. "Kerkhofs Reichszentral." *Spectrum* 11 (1988): 30-31.

Starke, F. J. "Zur Wiedereröffnung ukrainischer Bibliotheken." *Zentralblatt für Bibliothekswesen* 60 (1943): 229-31.

UNPUBLISHED MATERIALS

Mackintosh, E.S.B. "War History of the Science Museum Library."June 1945
    (mimeographed).
U.S. Alien Property Custodian. "Report to the President on the Periodical
    Republication Program." 1945 (mimeographed).
Watson, Peter G. "Great Britain's National Lending Library." School of Library
    Service, University of California at Los Angeles, 1970.   Master's
    essay.

INTERVIEWS

Busse, Gisela von. 23 August 1982. Bad Godesberg, Germany.
Fleming, Thomas. 18 April 1979. Leonia, New Jersey.
Jones, R.V. 14 August 1990. Aberdeen, Scotland.
Kilgour, Frederick. 31 May 1979; 15 October 1987. Columbus, Ohio.
Perry, Brian. 2 July 1986. London, England.
Swets, W.A. 13 August 1979. Hilversum, The Netherlands.
Tamme, Herbert. 31 December 1982. Fort Lauderdale. Florida.
Urquhart, Donald. 4 July 1986. Leeds, England.
Wyart, Jean. 4 July 1990. Paris. France.

ARCHIVES

Archives Nationales. Paris.
Bundesarchiv. Koblenz.
Library Association. British Library. London.
Martinus Nijhoff. The Hague.
Public Records Office. London.
Science Museum Library. London.
Scientific Periodicals Library. Cambridge.
Springer Verlag. Heidelberg.
U.S. National Archives. Military Records Division. Washington DC.

Index

About the Author

PAMELA SPENCE RICHARDS is Professor of Library and Information Studies at Rutgers University. The author of four books, she has had many articles published in German and English journals and has lectured widely in both countries.